The Christian
Educator's Handbook
on Spiritual Formation

The Christian Educator's Handbook Series

The Christian Educator's Handbook on Spiritual Formation

**Edited by
Kenneth O. Gangel
and James C. Wilhoit**

Baker Books

A Division of Baker Book House Co.
Grand Rapids, Michigan 49516

1994 by Kenneth O. Gangel and James C. Wilhoit

Published by Baker Books
a division of Baker Book House Company
P.O. Box 6287, Grand Rapids, MI 49516-6287

Paperback edition published 1997

First published 1994 by Victor Books, a division of Scripture Press Publications Inc., Wheaton, Illinois

Printed in the United States of America

Library of Congress Cataloging-in-Publication Data

The Christian educator's handbook on spiritual formation / edited by James C. Wilhoit
& Kenneth O. Gangel.
    p.   cm.
Includes bibliographical references.
1. Spiritual formation. 2. Christian education. 3. Evangelicalism. I. Wilhoit, Jim.
II. Gangel, Kenneth O.
ISBN 0-8010-2167-7
BV4511.C48   1994
268—dc20   94-16443

For information about academic books, resources for Christian leaders, and all new releases available from Baker Book House, visit our web site:
http://www.bakerbooks.com

CONTENTS

INTRODUCTION

Ninety years ago with the founding of the Religious Education Association (REA), a clear call was issued for a new approach to religious education. Many people followed that call and sought to correct some of the perceived abuses in the Sunday School model of Christian education. Some of these correctives, like the criticism of rote memorization without understanding and a naive connection between nationalism and Christianity, were on target. However, the modern religious education movement brought in its train a whole host of presuppositions and problems. Among them was the humanizing of the field of Christian/religious education. Much damage has come to the teaching ministry of the church through the liberal assumption that learning of religious subjects was entirely analogous to the learning of similar content in everyday life and that religious learning was largely a cognitive and mildly affective affair.

The naturalistic assumptions set forth by the REA (which became part of the very fabric of our culture) have certainly influenced many religious educators. The implicit goal for many Christian educators was the efficient transmission of religious information. The main variables the educator sought to alter were: (1) the efficiency of this information transmission, and (2) the learner's positive affect toward the material.

The writers in this volume are diverse in their church affiliations and intellectual training, but they share a commitment to nurturing Christians in a holistic way. To see the contrast between those who might view Christian education as a sophisticated form of religious information management and transmission, these writers speak about education as a means of receiving God's transforming grace. They see nurture as a way to establish the Christian symbolic system in a learner. They believe learning should imitate the devotional lifestyle of Christ as a means of transformation. Consider a few important commonalities amid the diversity.

1. The authors acknowledge the inability of a teacher to ultimately change a learner. They view learning as an invitation to a lifestyle and to a way of living, but acknowledge that ultimately the responsibility of learning lies with the student. This stands in contrast to the "social engineering," confidence in the teacher's knowledge, and personal efficacy that so often accompanied the old paradigm of teaching.

2. The authors see the direct connection between the person of the teacher and the outcome of the teaching. The words of Jesus, "A student is not above his teacher, but everyone who is fully trained will be like his teacher" (Luke 6:40), seems to overshadow every chapter. Religious instruction is not viewed here as a subject that could be carried out irrespective of one's faith commitment, but rather essentially linked to the individual person.

3. The authors who wrote these chapters see the need for learning to take place in a multiplicity of contexts, involving all avenues of learning. Without any denigration of the human intellect and analytic facilities, they celebrate what symbol, ritual, and community can teach.

4. The authors implicitly talk about a sacrament of learning. That learning becomes a way to receive God's transforming power—called grace—that can strengthen and renew believers. Through teaching, students are encouraged to open themselves to God's grace and thereby be changed. The time-honored analogy of teacher-as-midwife speaks to the humble and necessary role of those entrusted with spiritual formation.

This book represents a beginning. Evangelicals have not written as extensively on spiritual formation as they did in an earlier age. Other traditions have recently explored this area more exhaustively, and there is much wisdom to be found in their writings. We offer this volume as an alternative to a humanistic education which has robbed some churches of the ability to transform believers. We want to assist congregations in producing the kind of people who can witness to the world through both their words *and* the depth of their being. Our hope is that it will be used to educate and nurture believers in the process of spiritual formation.

James C. Wilhoit, Wheaton, Illinois
Kenneth O. Gangel, Dallas, Texas

WHAT IS SPIRITUAL FORMATION?
John M. Dettoni

Spiritual formation (of which nurture and discipleship are integral parts) is not just a new piece of cloth placed on old and worn-out garments of Christian education. Spiritual formation represents a radical paradigm shift, a new way of looking at the church's ministry. Of course, this new paradigm can also be seen as a return to the original model—to the nurturing patterns of the early church. Three elements mark the approach to Christian nurture and discipleship called spiritual formation: (1) it involves the whole church's ministry; (2) knowledge is viewed as a means to Christian growth and never as an end in itself; and (3) there is a distinct accent on the work of God's grace in the process of formation.

THE NEED FOR A UNIFIED MINISTRY
OF SPIRITUAL FORMATION

Peter Benson directed a large research project, funded by the Lilly Endowment, which examined the effectiveness of Christian education at the congregational level. In the report of their findings he and Carolyn Eklin express a concern over the way Christian education is often seen as a separate entity of the church; their report asserts that it must be linked to other aspects of congregational life (Benson and Eklin, 1990, p. 67). In a summary of this report, Benson's call for integrating Christian education into the life of the whole church was under-

Traditional Church's Ministries

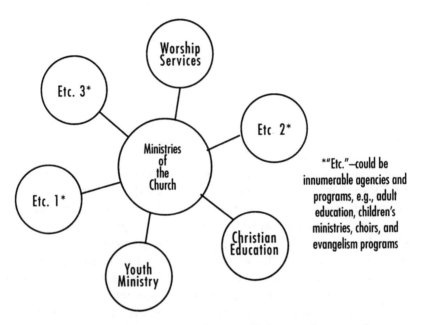

*"Etc."—could be innumerable agencies and programs, e.g., adult education, children's ministries, choirs, and evangelism programs

Theoretical literature and program literature (books, curriculum materials, other helps) emphasize and assume that Christian education is quite distinct from the rest of the church's ministries

Figure 1

scored: "Christian education cannot be set apart as a separate entity. . . . We cannot afford to merely tinker with Christian education; we must thoroughly restructure it . . . " (Youth Resources, 1990, p. 3).

The Lilly report provides a telling critique of the state of Christian education in mainline churches and, for those of us in evangelical churches, a word of warning. In the Benson and Eklin study 64 percent of the youth surveyed have an underdeveloped faith (underdeveloped faith was defined as being low on the vertical dimension of a "deep, personal relationship with a loving God"). Most discouraging, the largest percentage of adults in four of the five denominations studied had a poorly integrated faith (an integrated faith includes high levels of both vertical faith and horizontal faith—actions of love, mercy, and justice) (Benson and Eklin, 1990, pp. 13–16).

Spiritual formation works with the whole person, not only with a soul to be saved or a mind to be taught. The implications and programming of spiritual formation, nurture, and discipleship in the church should concern us all. Often traditional church ministry looks like figure 1. The church is divided into distinct agencies or organizations that have been given their own roles—often overlapping roles—to fulfill the church's overall ministry. Christian education often is seen as quite separate from the rest of the church's ministry. Not every aspect of the church is Christian education proper, but all aspects of the church have an educational dimension. A presentation of the church budget implicitly teaches the priorities of the congregation; a pastor's sermons subtly educate about the value of Scripture.

A spiritual formation approach to the ministry of the church is represented better by figure 2. This diagram shows that the nurturing process of transformation lies at the very heart of the church's ministry. The programs of the church are outgrowths of this singular ministry, rooted and grounded in what the church is called to be: a nurturing, discipling, equipping, renewing, and compassionate ministry of Christ in this world.

In figure 2, each of the smaller circles represents a sub-ministry and usually a program of the church. Each sub-ministry and its program are logically and essentially related to Christian nurture and discipleship. Sub-ministries of the church, rooted, grounded, and emanating from spiritual formation are both logically necessary and of the essence of the church in its cultural context.

Not all the circles are distinct from each other. Lay enablement, for example, occurs throughout all ministries. Yet it, along with others, is included here to show its vitality in the church's nurturing and discipling. The church's program flows from its ministry. The programs take many different forms and serve different functions, depending on the particular church and its given socio-cultural milieu. Various agencies and depart-

Christian Formation and Discipleship and the Church's Ministry

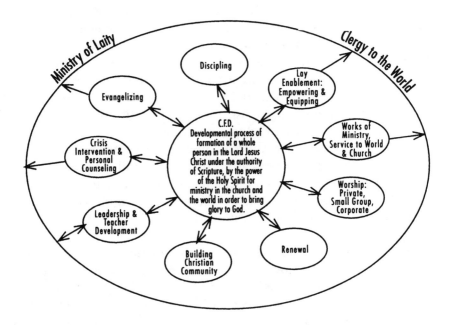

Figure 2

ments can be organized to fulfill the church's mission once it has consciously affirmed its reason for being. The critical factor in the design and development of the church's program is that it be faithful to the understanding of its central mission of spiritual formation.

BEYOND KNOWLEDGE TO TRANSFORMATION

The foundation for spiritual formation is found in several Scripture passages: "be transformed by the renewing of your mind"

(Rom. 12:2); "My dear children, for whom I am again in the pains of childbirth until Christ be formed in you" (Gal. 4:19); "Go and make disciples of all nations" (Matt. 28:19); "We proclaim him, admonishing and teaching everyone with all wisdom, so that we may present everyone perfect in Christ. To this end I labor, struggling with all his energy, which so powerfully works in me" (Col. 1:28-29); and, "until we all reach unity in the faith and in the knowledge of the Son of God and become mature, attaining to the whole measure of the fullness of Christ" (Eph. 4:13).

These five passages lay the foundation for spiritual formation and discipleship. They contain three key words: (1) formation, (2) disciple, and (3) maturity.

Formation is the first key word in spiritual formation (Gal. 4:19). This word is the root word *morphe,* found in Romans 12:2 and 2 Corinthians 3:18. It suggests that the inner being of the person is radically altered so that he or she is no longer the same. Information alone will not make the difference. The person who has taken in the information has been reshaped, remolded, and significantly altered by the active transformation of the data into meaning for oneself. God is remaking Christians; our very central core of being is transformed into something quite different. It is not just an outward change but a metamorphosis from one form to another new and better one. We are being changed from the "old" to the new who is "in Christ," being conformed to His image.

Formation is not concerned merely with passively receiving the information, even true information. Formation requires knowledge of specific data as well as integrating those data within the larger whole of one's life. It requires prizing that information for one's own value system. Formation also requires that there be a change in behavior based on the knowledge acquired and willingly valued. Ultimately, knowledge, valuing, and behavior lead to a change in one's inner being, the existential core of personhood. Thus, continual transformation occurs (2 Cor. 3:18).

The second word, discipleship (Matt. 28:19), suggests an active following of Jesus. Christ's disciples do not just have a mass of information about Him in their heads. Disciples have forsaken all others and followed Jesus (Luke 9:23-24, 57-62; 14:25-

35). One of the most concrete ways of following Jesus involves patterning our life after His. This patterning means that we seek to do what He did; in other words, live a life filled with prayer, quiet service, Scripture reading, meditation, worship, and fasting, to name a few.

Too often we are urged to copy His tremendous public acts, such as forgiving His enemies from the cross, before we have followed Him in His quiet acts of piety. Jesus did His great public acts because of a life formed through the spiritual disciplines. To give up all that one has in order to attain the kingdom (e.g., Matt. 13:44-46 regarding the treasure in a field or the pearl of great price) is equivalent to giving up one's self, in Pauline terms to "die daily" or "to be a living sacrifice" (1 Cor. 15:31; Rom. 12:1; Gal. 2:20), and to follow Jesus (Luke 18:18-30).

Discipleship is not achieved just by memorizing Scripture verses. Nor is discipleship merely going to church. A transformation must take place within the person in order to become a disciple and to continue becoming a follower of Christ. This transformation comes through regeneration and grows as one learns about the character of the Lord we follow.

The third word is maturity. The goal of transformation is to become a disciple and, even more importantly, to become mature, complete, and perfect like Jesus Christ. The only standard or norm by which disciples measure their spiritual development is the standard of Jesus Christ. The Apostle Paul says that he labors with all the energy God gives him in order to present everyone perfect or mature or complete in Christ (Col. 1:28-29). There can be no other goal, no other end *(telos)* toward which we move, and no other purpose for communicating the Gospel to others than to help each person to become mature like Christ.

 In summary, from a biblical foundation, spiritual formation is an intentional, multifaceted process which promotes the transformation by which Christ is formed in us so that we can become His continually maturing disciples.

Teachers As Nurturers

The means to do Christian formation and discipleship is found in Scripture, which clearly shows that teachers are nurturers.

The role of home and church is to facilitate, aid, help, teach — in a word, *nurture!* A short list of what parents and teachers do is found in 1 Thessalonians 2:11-12: "For you know that we dealt with each of you as a father deals with his own children, encouraging, comforting and urging you to live lives worthy of God, who calls you into his kingdom and glory." Paul states that wise parents and effective teachers do at least three things: they help provide nurture for their learners; they encourage, comfort, and urge learners to maturity in Christ, or in his words, they "live lives worthy of God, who calls you into his kingdom and glory." Encouraging, comforting, and urging are all nurturing actions.

Encourage. The root idea of the word "to encourage" means to come alongside of. Jesus uses this same word to describe the Holy Spirit as the Paraclete, the "Comforter" (KJV) and the "Counselor" (NIV) (see John 15:26; 16:7-15). Teachers stand in relationship to their learners just as the Holy Spirit does to us: we comfort, encourage, counsel, and assist learners in their growth and development. The major role of teachers is to encourage learners to learn not only spiritual things, but all things that the teachers can teach the learners for holistic development.

Comfort. This second word Paul uses in 1 Thessalonians has a meaning similar to the idea of encourage. In fact, both words could legitimately be translated comfort or encourage. It seems that Paul sees that teachers, as well as parents, have a major role in encouraging and comforting their learners. Why? Because learning is not always easy. We usually learn best when things do not make sense to us, and we are struggling for new ideas and new ways of doing something.

Remember when you learned a foreign language, some new mathematics, or a physics formula? It took a lot of work to actually learn and not just memorize data. You were probably uncomfortable as you struggled with the new ideas and expressions. The teacher must help the uncomfortable learner to become comfortable learning new material and making sense out of new ideas. Teachers do this by comforting the uncomfortable, all the time encouraging them to keep pressing on in their integration of spiritual knowledge for transformative living.

Urge. The third word is to urge — to bear witness, to testify.

The English word "martyr" as one who testifies to his or her faith even through death comes from this Greek word. The Thessalonians passage carries the idea of an emphatic demand or an urgent action. And so it is that teachers must urge their learners to learn. Paul states that teachers, as well as parents, should not only encourage, comfort, and urge children to learn in general, but also to learn in the specific area of growing up in Christ, that is, "to live lives worthy of God."

Every wise and effective teacher echoes Paul's comments in 1 Thessalonians 2:19-20: "For what is our hope, our joy, or the crown in which we will glory in the presence of our Lord Jesus when he comes? Is it not you? Indeed, you are our glory and joy." When people whom we teach grow up to be more mature in Christ and in other areas of their development as whole people, they become our glory and joy.

Wise and effective teachers, viewing their learners, must feel like Paul in 1 Thessalonians 3:8-9: "For now we really live, since you are standing firm in the Lord. How can we thank God enough for you in return for all the joy we have in the presence of our God because of you?" If we have truly been encouragers, comforters, and urgent teachers of our learners, then we can really live when we realize that our learners continue to walk in Christ and stand firm in Him.

The teacher's prayer for his or her learners follows Paul's for the Thessalonians: "May the Lord make your love increase and overflow for each other and for everyone else, just as ours does for you. May he strengthen your hearts so that you will be blameless and holy in the presence of our God and Father when our Lord Jesus comes with all his holy ones" (1 Thes. 3:12-13).

AN ACCENT ON GOD'S GRACE

Spiritual maturity is a gift of God to us. While we cannot earn this gift, we exert effort to receive it. Those involved in true spiritual formation are keenly aware that the disciplines are the catalyst for, but not the cause of, spiritual transformation. Spiritual change comes from God alone, who is pleased to work through the nurturing structures He designed for His church.

This emphasis on God's grace calls the teacher to pray more, point the students more clearly to Jesus, focus on the essentials of the Gospel, and frees the teacher from manipulative short-cuts like behavior modification.

In spiritual formation teaching takes on a deeply spiritual meaning so that one can almost speak of the "sacrament of learning." Learning becomes a means to receiving God's trans-forming grace.

CONCLUSION

Jesus taught faith, not just facts; a way to live, not just words; understanding and wisdom, not just knowledge; divine love, not just divine law. Jesus taught for whole-person learning, growth, and development. He nurtured His disciples, encour-aging, comforting, and urging them to learn through His self-less ministry to them and to the world. Through His relation-ship with them, Jesus helped His disciples to grow and develop toward more consistently doing what He did.

Learning cannot be done for us; no one can "learn us." We alone can learn for ourselves. Yet, we can create an environ-ment that promotes learning. We make meaning out of our own experiences. Skilled and dedicated teachers can assist learners to see the whole from God's perspective and thereby discover a personal meaning rooted in God's providential care for them.

Spiritual formation represents a pattern of nurture found in the early church, which stressed discipleship, nurture, and an awareness that is the only source of true growth and maturity.

For Further Reading

Bloesch, D. (1988). *The crisis of piety: Essays toward a theology of the Christian life* (2nd ed.). Colorado Springs: Helmers & Howard. A helpful collection of essays on aspects of the Christian life. Particularly relevant to those interested in the role of asceticism, liturgy, and mysticism. Reflects a strong concern for spiritual renewal leading to a prophetic witness.

Downs, P. (1994). *Teaching for spiritual growth: An introduction to Christian education.* Grand Rapids: Zondervan. This volume begins with theology and addresses the question of "What is the nature of spiritual growth?" and then suggests how the church can teach so that spiritual growth takes place.

Fowler, J. (1984). *Becoming adult, becoming Christian.* San Francisco: Harper and Row. Application of Fowler's seminal faith development research to the question of spiritual formation in adulthood.

Richards, L. (1987). *A practical theology of spirituality.* Grand Rapids: Zondervan. A very readable and practical introduction into the whole area of developing a deeper spiritual life. Many suggestions on what to try.

Steele, L. (1990). *On the way: A practical theology of Christian formation.* Grand Rapids: Baker. A clear statement of a program of spiritual formation grounded in theological reflection and informed by various developmental theorists.

Wilhoit, J. (1991). *Christian education and the search for meaning* (2nd ed.). Grand Rapids: Baker. Intended as an introduction to Christian education, this volume places a heavy emphasis on spiritual formation.

SPIRITUAL FORMATION IN THE EARLY CHURCH
Craig A. Blaising

In the New Testament, conversion to Christ took place in the context of Jewish religion. Jesus, of course, was a Jew; the apostles were Jews; and the initial converts both in Jerusalem and in various cities across the Roman world were Jews. Even those Gentiles who came to faith in Christ at that time were most often "God fearers," a term which indicated a relationship to Jewish religion, including faith in the God of Abraham and respect for the law of Moses (Acts 10:2).

The apostles assumed on the part of their hearers a knowledge of the Old Testament Scriptures. They proclaimed Jesus Christ as the one prophesied by those Scriptures. He was their fulfillment in form and content. Most importantly, He was to be seen as the author and initiator of a new covenant (predicted by the prophetic Scriptures) by which God would form His people through the indwelling Holy Spirit. By His Spirit, God would now write His law directly into the hearts of His people. In fact, He would recreate their hearts; He would make them a new people, a holy people.

But the apostles also had to teach that Christians received only a down payment on these blessings. Although this ministry of spiritual formation had begun in them, it would not be completed until Christ returned.

In the meantime, Christians met regularly for prayer and instruction in the Scriptures, and lived by the Spirit, growing in faith and love, with their hope fixed on the coming of the Lord.

Even with their background knowledge of the Old Testament

Scriptures, the nurture and formation of new Christians was not easy. Paul wrote some of the churches that he was experiencing "the pains of childbirth until Christ is formed in you" (Gal. 4:19), that he felt as though he were being "poured out like a drink offering" (Phil. 2:17) in the process of their sanctification in Christ. He spoke of "the pressure of my concern for all the churches" which he faced "daily" (2 Cor. 11:28).

By the time a century had passed, the task of ministry became even more difficult. Most of the inquirers about Christianity were Gentile pagans. They knew practically nothing about the Old Testament Scriptures (Irenaeus, *Adversus Haereses*, 4.23.2–4.24.2 [Irenaeus, 1985, pp. 494–495]). Their background for understanding the message about Jesus Christ varied, depending on their social status and geographical location. But generally it was some form of pagan religion, whether a local cult, a particular mystery religion, imperial religious rites, popular hellenistic polytheism, magic, astrology, or most likely some combination of these.

Gnostic cults flourished in the second century, many claiming to present the truth about Jesus Christ. Actually, they syncretized elements from various religions resulting in a complete distortion of the Christian message.[1] But many followers of these cults thought they were true Christians, and that the knowledge *(gnosis)* which they received prepared their souls for eternal salvation.

A Christian minister in the late second century needed to closely question a pagan who wanted to become a Christian, professed to believe in God or in Christ, or wanted to be baptized, because for many a professed faith in Christ was just an element added to their syncretistic faith. Conversion involved a total transformation of worldview, of self-understanding, and a complete new set of social relationships.

To assist in this process, the church developed new forms (or new expansions of old forms) of ministry, worship, and instruction. The goal was a massive reeducation in religion resulting in a pure faith and a godly life of faith in Jesus Christ. Everything had to be taught: the nature and identity of the true God; the history of His relationships with the human race (covering the narratives of the Old Testament); the person of Christ and the nature of salvation; the contrast of sin and godliness; the reality

SPIRITUAL FORMATION IN THE EARLY CHURCH

of the resurrection; the nature of the judgment to come; and the hope of eternal life.

The forms of instruction, worship, and ministry developed in the second century and refined, modified, and reformulated as the years went on, show us how spiritual formation took place in the early church. They began with a period of instruction leading up to baptism. The ceremonies of baptism and the Lord's Supper (the Eucharist) were greatly elaborated with teachings, prayers, and symbolic acts to communicate the great truths of Christian faith. Liturgy provided repetitive expression of faith in the content of Christian truth and even for the re-structuring of time as a life of faith grounded in the knowledge of the Scriptures.

In this chapter, we will look at some of these structures of spiritual formation in four contexts: initiation into the church; worship in the assembly of the church; life in the non-Christian world; and the spiritual disciplines of solitude.

SPIRITUAL FORMATION IN CHRISTIAN INITIATION

Preparation for Baptism

Spiritual formation began with enrollment into the catechu-menate, the ranks of those preparing for baptism. Their desire for salvation certainly evidenced faith. But the church needed to hear that faith professed with knowledge and accompanied with the fruits of a converted life before it would admit that person to baptism, the Eucharist, and the status of full membership in the church.

In the second and third centuries, the length of catechesis, the instruction preparatory for baptism, varied from region to region. It could be a matter of a few weeks or as long as three years (Hippolytus, *Apostolic Tradition*, 17 [Hippolutus, 1992, p. 28]). During this time, the initiates were admitted to sessions in which the Scriptures were read and interpreted. These sessions were held daily in some places and sought to familiarize the hearer with both Old and New Testament writings. Toward the end of the period, closer to the time of baptism, churches offered theological instruction from the rule of faith expressed perhaps as a baptismal creed (after the fourth century, the Nicene creed would be used; Finn, 1992, pp. 4–5).

The goal of catechesis was not simply a cognitive understanding of Christianity. As Thomas Finn puts it, "Formation rather than information was [the] thrust" (Finn, 1992, p. 5). The catechumens were instructed in Christian character and all aspects of their lives examined with respect to the faith. Many churches maintained exorcists on their ministerial roles, and their function primarily related to the preparation of catechumens, exorcising demons in the process of redirecting the initiates to a Christian lifestyle (Finn, 1992, pp. 5–6).

At the end of the time of preparation, the candidates not only gave a profession of their faith before the church, but also withstood a public "scrutiny" of their character and conduct. They took part in ceremonies in which they formally renounced the devil and their pagan past. A final and formal exorcism was typically performed in conjunction with this renunciation. Following this they publicly swore their allegiance to Jesus Christ (Finn, 1992, p. 7).

Catechesis (the preparatory instruction and training leading to baptism) was, for the early church, the initial stage of discipleship. From one standpoint, it might be called "conversion therapy" (Kavanagh, 1990, p. 39). It helped pagan inquirers make the transition into Christianity, by leading them to a knowledgeable faith united to the practice of Christian conduct. It helped them adjust to a new community with new values (and it also helped the community adjust to them).

By the fourth century, however, two tendencies threatened the preparatory role of catechesis. On the one hand, the fear of denying Christ during persecution caused many to delay baptism until they were close to death. In this case, one's whole lifetime would be spent as a catechumen. Since a catechumen was not fully recognized as a Christian, this practice created a large subclass in the church, reserving the full notion of Christian for a ministerial elite (Meyendorff, 1986, p. 357).

On the other hand, the practice of infant baptism was on the rise, overtaking the practice of adult baptism completely by the sixth century. As a consequence, catechesis disappeared from the churches. The concern was not so much the formation of faith, but its preservation or restoration through penance (Meyendorff, 1986, p. 355).

Baptism

At the end of the period of preparation, candidates were admitted to baptism. By the end of the second century, baptism had become quite an elaborate ceremony, involving anointings, immersion, a profession of faith, prayer, the exchange of garments, benedictions, and admission to the Eucharist. The order of the profession, anointing, and immersion varied in different locations. Some churches practiced triple immersion, and the form of the prayers also varied somewhat. But baptism was consistently administered in the name of the Father, the Son, and the Holy Spirit, and was seen as the admission of the candidate into full membership with the church (Finn, 1992, pp. 8, 18–21; White, 1993, pp. 44–52).

The rites and prayers associated with baptism reflected the rich diversity of biblical typology which the church saw as fulfilled in Christ. This included the great events of redemptive history: "creation, the fall, the flood, the promise to the ancestors, the exodus, the covenant, the exile, and the return" (Schneiders, 1986, p. 5). As Finn writes, "Everything converges: Creation, the Exodus from Egypt, crossing the Jordan, Christ's baptism, and the Christian's baptism" (Finn, 1992, pp. 10, 22–27).

And the symbolic proclamation of typological fulfillment would not be lost on those who had been prepared (through catechesis) with a knowledge of the Scriptures. The symbols, allusions, and citations were meant to resonate with the profession and enactment of the faith of the one being baptized. For as he or she was being united with Christ, all the benefits and blessings of Christ, the fullness of the whole pattern of redemption focused in Him, was passing to the believer.

The earliest dominating motif was Christ's own baptism in the Jordan River.[2] As Christ received the Holy Spirit, designating Him the Son of God, so Christians were believed to receive the Holy Spirit as they were baptized, professing their faith in Him. Among the many levels of symbolism was the view of the baptistery as a womb; the candidate having put off the clothes of the old life, emerged naked from the waters as a newborn child of God, to be wrapped in a new robe for a new life.

Although the motif of Christ's baptism continued in the East, the Western churches, beginning in the fourth century, centralized the motif of Christ's death and resurrection. The "womb" was first the "tomb," the believer entering into the waters in union with the Lord's death and emerging newborn in the triumph of His resurrection (Finn, 1992, pp. 8–9; Meyendorff, 1986, pp. 352– 353). These themes were reinforced by the inculcation, at this time, of catechesis into the preparations of Lent and baptism into the celebration of Easter.

The believer who underwent baptism was to understand himself or herself as a new person in a new family. All the preparation, symbolism, profession of faith, and dramatic entrustment of one's self into Christ was to effect a total reconception of one's life. A clear boundary had been crossed, both inwardly in spiritual birth and outwardly in new relationships with others (Norris, 1990, pp. 28–29). As newly baptized believers were brought directly into the fellowship of the church to partake, for the first time, in the Eucharist, they came to realize that they were now members of a new community, with new privileges and new responsibilities.

Baptism contributed to spiritual formation by bringing the instructed faith of catechumens to a specific act of entrustment into Christ with spiritual rebirth and incorporation into the church. From this point on, new Christians were to live out the life of the Spirit in communion with Christ and His church.

As the practice of infant baptism increased, becoming universal in Christendom by the sixth century, baptism became a profession of the church's faith rather than the faith of the individual receiving baptism. Consequently, baptism was no longer seen as the culmination of conversion, the spiritual birth and resocialization of a believer. The rich symbolism, although retained in the rites, was not comprehended by the one being baptized so as to be drawn into his or her profession of faith.

Nevertheless, the church believed that the gift of the Holy Spirit was imparted to baptized children. The little ones would grow up as members of the church, coming to understand more and more by faith, a set of spiritual relationships God had already given them through the church at infancy. In this case, baptism was to begin the process of spiritual formation by imparting the Holy Spirit to a person prior to any, much less religious, intellectual development. The hope was that the Spirit would guide that intellectual development in the context of the life of the church to the mature manifestations of faith, hope, and love in Christ.

WORSHIP IN THE ASSEMBLY OF THE CHURCH

Despite the careful attention given to preparing believers for baptism and the dramatic and climactic event of the baptism itself, spiritual formation did not come to an end when Christians were finally admitted to the church.

The baptized are "children of God. Nevertheless they are children, and the living out of the new life is therefore . . . an affair of continuous learning and growing. To put the matter briskly [sic.], what Baptism creates is a collection of disciples, apprentices of the divine Word, whose common life is, in every sense of the term, a practice" (Norris, 1990, pp. 28–29).

Although specifically referring to the views of Clement of Alexandria, these comments by Richard Norris apply to the early church in general. Baptized Christians had entered into a life of discipleship. But how and in what manner was that discipleship to take place?

Purpose of Liturgy

For the most part, it took place in the liturgical worship of the assembled church. Here, Christians listened to readings of the Scriptures, to homilies applying Scripture to their daily lives, and to prayers offered by the officers of the church in praise and petition. But their experience was not merely passive. Together, the worshipers responded in corporate prayers, acclamations of praise, recitations of psalms, and the singing of hymns. They took the Eucharist together and presented offerings for the church collection.

By regular participation in the liturgy, Christians were to form habits of worship which would characterize their Christian experience. It was, in fact, ongoing practice (to use Norris' term) in the Christian experience. The praise and petitions of the psalms and hymns became the faith and expression of the assembly and of its individual constituents. Together, the believers experienced boldness and joy in their faith, which hopefully would be reinforced in repeated gatherings.

These gatherings were held daily in many places, except when hindered by persecution. Evidence suggests that morning and evening prayers were held at most churches (some held services three or more times a day), until the sixth century when the prayer times were regulated by monastic discipline, eliminating common people from the observances (White, 1993, pp. 52–55). Special weekly observances were held on Sunday with other observances on other days, usually Wednesday and Friday. In this way, the liturgy completely structured time for the Christian church: the beginning and end of each day and the division of days in the week. Add to this the special liturgical celebrations of Advent and Easter which helped give structure to each year. *Thus the whole cycle of life constituted for the church an uninterrupted process of spiritual formation.*

The focal point of liturgical worship was the celebration of the Eucharist. Early interpretations of this common meal centered on the lordship of Christ and the unity of the church *(Didache* 9, [Anonymous, 1953, p. 175]). However, identification with Christ in His death soon became the central motif. Whereas baptism was not a repeatable act, the Eucharist became the structure by which the spiritual realities of baptism would be a repetitive experience. By the fourth century, the communal aspect of the Eucharist meal practically disappeared when so many postponed baptism until they were close to death. The Eucharist became more "an act of personal devotion" in which corporate "participation was not so essential" (Meyendorff, 1986, p. 357).

Liturgical Drama
Dramatic elements in liturgy helped reinforce the Christian's union with Christ, both with Christ in His sufferings and resurrection and with Christ in His eschatological glory. By the middle of the fourth century, Cyril, bishop of Jerusalem, developed a processional liturgy for holy week (the week leading up to Easter Sunday). Earlier in the century, Constantine, having established peace for the churches in the empire and having declared his own allegiance to Christ, funded the construction of numerous memorials to the ministry of Christ in Jerusalem and throughout Palestine. This led to large numbers of pilgrims

visiting these sites, especially during Lent. Cyril developed and led liturgical services at the various sites which commemorated the events leading up to and constituting the death and resurrection of the Lord. This had a profound effect in strengthening the faith of the participants, as they sensed (through their own dramatic involvement) the historical reality of the Gospel.

Impressed with the value of this form of worship, churches across the empire adopted a stational liturgy for their own holy week services. In their case, their own church buildings would become the stage for representing the passion of Christ.

Meyendorff (1986, p. 359) describes another form of liturgical drama, this time a representation of the eschatological hope of the church developed by Maximus the Confessor in the seventh century.

> He adopted the Dionysian spiritualizing approach but added his own interpretation, which saw the liturgy as the memorial of the divine economy in Christ and the anticipation of the parousia and the eschaton. Thus, the liturgy represents all salvation history: the church building is the type and image of the whole universe; the Gospel reading is the consummation of the world; the bishop's descent from the throne, the expulsion of the catechumens, and the closing of the doors represent the descent of Christ in parousia, the expulsion of the wicked, and the entrance into the mystical chamber of the bridegroom (Mystagogy 14–16 [Maximus the Confessor, 1985, pp. 200–202]).

The function of liturgy as drama was assisted by highly developed forms of Christian art. Separated from the motifs of pagan idolatry and sensuality, art forms were refined to express the themes of Christian revelation, both of creation and redemption. The locus of beauty was the incarnation and the eschatological redemption of humanity and the created world in Christ. Paintings and frescoes adorned the walls of the churches, expressing Old and New Testament themes. The apses boldly portrayed the figure of the glorified Christ, typically surrounded by angels and saints (Ouspensky, 1986, pp. 382–386; also see Weitzmann, 1980).

Drama and art contributed to the liturgy of the church to

shape and form a Christian view of reality. Time and history became biblical time and biblical history. And through the ecclesiastical drama, Christians practiced roles and parts which both actualized the spiritual realities of their lives and prepared them for their eternal entry into these realities in the eschatological age.

SPIRITUAL FORMATION IN THE CONTEXT OF PAGAN SOCIETY

Prior to the remarkable events of the fourth century, during which Christianity was first officially tolerated and then officially established, life as a Christian in Roman society was somewhat precarious. While many religions managed to coexist in the Roman world, acknowledging and even affirming the religious pluralism of the empire, Christianity, like Judaism, rejected that pluralism. But unlike Judaism, it did not have the respectability of antiquity to lend it a privileged status. Given the fact that pagan piety, with its various levels of deities (from the imperial court to family gods), was seen as a form of social stability, Christian rejection of all such religion was deemed by some not only as offensive but as a danger to society itself.

Yet even if Christians had the good will of their neighbors, it was not easy to maintain a Christian lifestyle in a pagan society. Pagan religion permeated the entire culture — the schools, the markets, the military, and all social events and festivals. In any of these situations Christians found themselves expected to honor various idols. Prostitution, adultery, pornography, and sadism challenged Christian values of a holy life.

From out of the support and nurture of church assemblies (often secret meetings in houses), Christians went about the task of living in the pagan world, practicing the denial of ungodly and idolatrous behavior. And this activity of living out Christian standards and values in the pagan culture was just as much a part of spiritual formation as participation in the liturgical worship of the church.

The testimony of Cyprian in his letter to Donatus reveals a Christian consciousness of liberating power from the evils that pervaded his culture. This sense, not only of detachment, but of freedom and of power, was nurtured in the prayers and readings of the assembly. It was called forth in the constant need to reaffirm a Christian lifestyle in the daily context of the world in which he lived.[3]

The hostility of the pagan world broke out from time to time in pogroms (such as in Lyons in 177) or individual martyrdoms (such as that of Polycarp, ca. 155). From the various accounts of these martyrdoms, the literature known collectively as Acts of the Martyrs, it is clear that the sufferings, tortures, and executions which Christians experienced were seen by many of them, and by the church at large, as the supreme arena for the development and perfection of Christian faith and character. Here Christians battled not only unbelievers but the devil himself on his own territory.

Like Ignatius of Antioch, they identified themselves completely with Jesus in His torture, cruel death, and burial, keeping their faith resolutely fixed on the reality of the resurrection, an eternal and imperishable victory which cannot be gained except through death (Ignatius, *To the Romans* [Ignatius, 1953, pp. 102–106]). The *Letter of the Churches of Lyons and Vienna* and the *Martyrdom of Perpetua and Felicitas* (Anonymous, 1972a, 1972c) both speak of the increasing display of Christian character in joy, peace, and love on the part of those who kept their faith fixed on Christ through the most excruciating suffering. In the *Martyrdom of Polycarp*, Polycarp testifies that it is Christ who will give him the grace to willingly accept and submit to the execution which has been decreed for him *(Martyrdom,* 13 [Anonymous, 1972b, p. 13]).

After the Edict of Milan in 313, the officially sanctioned martyrdoms ceased. And it was not long before bishops found themselves honored with social class privileges. But the peace that ensued brought an ambiguity to Christian life. Christians could be found compromising with the remnants of pagan culture — astrology, magic, festivals for the dead — which remained a large part of everyday life.

The importance of liturgy and especially of preaching (e.g., Chrysostom, Ambrose, Augustine) which related Scripture to daily life was crucial for the formation of Christian character at this time (Fontaine, 1986, p. 465). However, we also see the rise of the monastic movement, which offered for many the solitude and support for concentrated spiritual discipline in contrast to the tempting compromises of daily life.

SPIRITUAL FORMATION IN SOLITUDE

Spiritual formation could never be merely a collective or community endeavor. The focus, even in community nurture, is the transformation of individual human beings. However, neither was spiritual formation a wholly individual matter. The transformed lives of individual Christians flowed together in the formation of the Christian community which in turn nurtured the development of new spiritual offspring.

Scripture

This personal and individual responsibility in spiritual formation began in the liturgical worship of the community. It was incumbent on each Christian to participate in the liturgy by faith, so that the prayers and praise became one's own. The readings, expositions, and homilies of Scripture were also meant to be internalized personally by the hearers.

This last point was given special emphasis by Origen of Alexandria, the most famous expositor in the third century. Origen developed a theology of reading and meditating on Scripture which answered the Greek philosophical concern for the education (formation) of the soul. Briefly put, it is the personal Word of God who is given to us in the Scripture. Those who have the Spirit of God are brought by that Spirit into communion with the Word Himself, Jesus Christ, when they meditate upon Him by faith in the reading of the Scripture. And this communion nourishes and edifies their souls in preparation for eternity.[4]

This was Origen's purpose in his expository ministry in the churches. But this objective was also applicable in personal and private meditations as well. In the fourth-century, Athanasius, bishop of Alexandria, wrote a manual for the devotional use of the Psalms which essentially follows Origen's theology of reading the Bible (Athanasius, *Letter to Marcellinus* [Athanasius, 1980]).

Continued meditation on Scripture kept its teachings present in one's mind. This presence served to order and guide one's responses and inclinations in the daily activities of life. But it also helped to identify temptation and reveal sin, leading in the latter case to repentance and in the former to acts of rejection and denial.

Asceticism

This brings us to asceticism, the rigorous practice of self-denial, which was another important aspect of personal spiritual formation in the early church. It was also strongly encouraged by Origen both by teaching and by example. Christian asceticism was the discipline of regularly denying "the desire of the flesh, the desire of the eyes, the pride in riches" (1 John 2:16, NRSV). Practically this meant giving one's wealth to the poor and adopting a simple lifestyle — simple clothes (perhaps without shoes), the refusal of ordinary comforts (such as a soft bed), celibacy, and acts of service to others. The goal was conformity to Jesus Christ.

Monasticism

Personal prayer and meditation along with ascetic discipline found its fullest expression in the movement of the fourth-century monastics. On the one hand, some sought complete solitude to struggle with the devil and gain victory in their souls over passions of the flesh. While some went to extremes, many, like the famous Anthony of the Egyptian desert, became spiritual guides and examples to thousands of Christians seeking a life of holiness.

On the other hand, some sought solitude in a community of similarly dedicated souls. Some of these were isolated, remote, withdrawn from outside society, like the cenobitic communities in upper Egypt. Others maintained regular contact with the broader church community, such as the monastic societies organized by Basil of Caesarea. These latter communities provided ministerial leadership for many churches.

In this communal form of monasticism, the practice of prayer and meditation was supplemented with the fellowship of sharing together insights and blessings from the Lord. The discipline of asceticism could be supplemented by the practice of learning to care for others.

Not every Christian became a monk, although thousands did. But the monks became the spiritual heroes of the day, taking the role which the martyrs played in earlier times. Theirs was the "unbloody" martyrdom, the act of complete identification with Jesus Christ in the absence of execution. For many they were the exemplary "aliens and strangers in the world" who did "abstain from sinful desires, which war against [the] soul" (1 Peter 2:11). They demonstrated the possibilities of spiritual formation which ordinary Christians sought to emulate while living in the world and regularly participating in community worship.

CONCLUSION

Spiritual formation was the focus of Christian ministry in the early church. It began with a period of teaching from the Bible and discipling for those seeking salvation in Jesus Christ. It took special focus in the reception of baptism, which was the time of a Christian's public profession of faith in which he or she was united with Christ and given the seal of the indwelling Holy Spirit.

This process of formation continued through regular fellowship with the church, participating with brothers and sisters in the liturgy of worship, establishing habits of praise, prayer, singing, and internalizing the Scripture. But this nurture also took place in the hostile worldly context in which most Christians lived. Faith was put to the test and brought to its fullness in the necessity of participating in the sufferings of Christ, even to the point of death.

And finally, spiritual formation continued with the internal struggle of temptation and evil desire. The personal practice of prayer and meditation on Scripture was meant to bring one into ever closer communion and conformity with the will of Jesus Christ. The practice of an ascetic lifestyle disciplined the will to reject evil desires. Some sought solitude in various forms of monasticism to pursue the development of a holy life. But the challenge of Christlikeness, of being progressively conformed to His perfect image, confronted all Christians, in every location and in all walks of life.

Notes

1. Irenaeus gives the illustration of someone taking a mosaic representation of a king and rearranging the pieces into the image of a dog or a fox. This he says is what Gnostics do to the biblical presentation of Christ. Catechetical instruction in the rule of faith, however, protects one from this kind of distortion (Irenaeus, *Adversus Haereses,* 1.8 [Irenaeus, 1985, p. 326]).

2. To fully approximate Christ's example, the earliest Christians preferred to be baptized in a river or stream. According to *Didache,* an early church manual, Christians should "baptize in running water, in the name of the Father and of the Son and of the Holy Spirit. If you do not have running water, baptize in some other." *(Didache* 7 [Anonymous, 1953, p. 175]).

3. Cyprian, *Ad Donatum.* The entire letter speaks to this matter, but see especially sections 5 and 15. On this matter and regarding Christian life in pagan society in general, I am especially indebted to Jacques Fontaine in his excellent article, "The Practice of Christian Life: The Birth of the Laity." See Fontaine, J. (1986). The practice of Christian life: The birth of the laity. In B. McGinn & J. Meyendorff (Eds.), *Christian spirituality, vol. 1: Origins to the twelfth century (pp. 453-491).* New York: Crossroad.

4. Origen's method of reading Scripture is explained at length in Torjesen, K. (1986). *Hermeneutical procedure and theological method in Origen's exegesis.* Berlin: Walter De Gruyter.

For Further Reading

Bouyer, L. (1963). *The spirituality of the New Testament and the fathers.* The history of Christian spirituality, vol. 1. (Mary P. Ryan, Trans.). New York: Desclee, 1963. A classic history of spirituality.

Chitty, D. (1966). *The desert a city.* Oxford: Blackwell. The classic study of monastic spirituality.

Finn, T. (Ed.). (1992). *Early Christian baptism and the catechumenate: West and east Syria* and *Early Christian baptism and the catechumenate: Italy, North Africa, and Egypt.* Message of the Fathers of the Church, Vols. 5 and 6. Collegeville, MN: Liturgical. These are collections of patristic readings on the subjects of catechesis and baptism, the most accessible collection of such readings. Both volumes are preceded by the same general introduction offering a very helpful summary of the general order of initiation and baptism.

McGinn, B., & Meyendorff, J. (Eds.). (1986). *Christian spirituality: Origins to the twelfth century.* World Spirituality: An Encyclopedic History of the Religious Quest, Vol. 16. New York: Crossroad. This is the most helpful volume on the nature of Christian spirituality in the early church.

Merriman, M. (Ed.). (1990). *The baptismal mystery and the catechumenate.* New York: Church Hymnal Corporation. Some articles bear on the early church.

Weitzmann, K. (Ed.). (1980). *Age of spirituality: A symposium.* New York: Metropolitan Museum of Art. An excellent discussion of the themes and forms of early Christian art.

White, J. (1993). *A brief history of Christian worship.* Nashville: Abingdon. This is the best survey of the history of liturgical worship. One chapter is devoted to the early church.

SALVATION AND SPIRITUAL FORMATION
Robert P. Lightner

The Bible is a book about God, about humanity, and about the relationship between God and humanity. Its central plot line describes God's work in salvation, a deliverance from sin's condemnation, which is the greatest thing that could ever happen to any human being. But salvation is a broad term expressing a host of activities of God's grace. A chapter like this one could include paragraphs about substitutionary atonement, redemption, reconciliation, propitiation, forgiveness, and justification, and at points we must look at some of these crucial concepts in the broad doctrine of salvation. But essentially we want to focus on the relationship between regeneration and ongoing spiritual growth. Once a person has been delivered from sin, he or she is called by Scripture to live a life pleasing to God. The new birth (regeneration) gives rise to the new growth (spiritual formation), two dimensions of God's work in our lives inseparably related to a proper understanding of salvation.

The relationship between the initial work of grace in the human heart and how Christians live out their faith for a lifetime must be understood by those who want to walk with the Savior. Indeed, if we do not understand it, great frustration and anxiety usually result. Schaeffer wrote clearly about the past, future, and present (note the interesting arrangement) of salvation.

Salvation, as the word is used in Scripture, is wider than justification. There is a past, a future, and just as really, a present. The infinite work of Christ upon the cross brings to the Christian more than justification. In the *future,* there is glorification. When Christ returns there will be the resurrection of the body and eternity. But there is also a *present* aspect of salvation. Sanctification is our present relationship to our Lord, the present tense (Schaeffer, 1971, pp. 73–74).

Schaeffer's "present tense" helps us get a handle on the concept of spiritual formation in relation to justification and regeneration. But before looking at how these two important dimensions of our salvation relate to each other, we need some basic definitions.

MEANINGS

Soteriology (the doctrine of salvation) includes a number of very important works of God. Three of these divine gifts are especially significant and closely related to spiritual formation: regeneration, justification, and positional sanctification. *Regeneration* imparts divine life to the one dead in trespasses and sins. This aspect of the salvation scheme makes possible all the rest. It is this aspect of the Spirit's work in salvation that this chapter links with justification.

Justification means that the Savior declares regenerated sinners righteous before the tribunal of heaven. Enns describes it well.

Justification is a gift given through the grace of God (Rom. 3:24) and takes place the moment the individual has faith in Christ (Rom. 4:2; 5:1). The ground of justification is the death of Christ (Rom. 5:9) apart from any works (Rom. 4:5). The means of justification is faith (Rom. 5:1). Through justification God maintains His integrity and His standard, yet is able to enter into fellowship with sinners because they have the very righteousness of Christ imputed to them (Enns, 1989, p. 326).

Positional sanctification describes the believing sinner as set apart for God, His peculiar possession. These marvelous works of God take place at the same time—when a sinner, drawn by the Spirit, receives the Lord Jesus Christ as substitute for sin. At that moment God's justice has been satisfied, a place in heaven has been assured, and the process of spiritual formation has begun.

Spiritual formation describes the continuing work of the Holy Spirit in the life of a believer which conforms the child of God more and more to the image of Christ (2 Cor. 3:18). This work of the Spirit is possible only as we cooperate with God by walking "in the light as He is in the light" (1 John 1:7); by setting our hearts "on things above" (Col. 3:1); by ridding ourselves of the deeds of the flesh (Col. 3:8); and by putting on a heart of "compassion, kindness, humility, gentleness, and patience (Col. 3:12).

God does not treat His people as robots. He does not force His desires or His ways upon us. The necessity of human response to God's gracious invitation to walk with Him hand in hand, to obey Him, to live according to Scripture, appears everywhere throughout Scripture. In these ways God makes us more and more like His Son.

But all this raises a question: How does spiritual formation relate to regeneration? What connection exists between deliverance from sin's condemnation (Rom. 8:1) and spiritual growth? Between passing from death to life (1 John 3:14) and living out the new life we enjoy in Christ?

NEEDS

Need of Salvation
Scripture repeatedly warns us that all humankind is spiritually lost and therefore needs to be found or saved. This has always been a foundational doctrine of the historic orthodox Christian faith.

There is a threefold reason why God considers us all sinners who need salvation. First, either representatively or seminally or both, the whole human race sinned when Adam sinned (Rom. 5:12). Theologians call this *imputed* sin. Second, except Christ, everyone comes into the world with a sin nature, which means everyone has the capacity and tendency to sin from birth. This *inherited* sin results from imputed sin (Jer. 17:9; Eph. 2:3). Third, each person commits personal sins as soon as he or she knows right from wrong (Rom. 3:10). No one needs any instruction on how to sin. It comes automatically because of the inherited sin nature. This is *individual* sin.

Need of Spiritual Formation

The most basic reason why spiritual formation or growth in grace should be true of the believer is because we still possess what Paul calls "the flesh." Though the term "sin nature" is not common in Scripture, the concept permeates it throughout.

Sin nature can still lead Christians to the same wickedness as before salvation. Even though believing sinners have a whole new position in Christ and positionally possess all the riches of divine grace put to their accounts, they still have the sinful capacity and tendency with which they were born.

The saved sinner's sins are completely forgiven. Every believer is completely regenerated and justified, but needs to learn how to practice life on earth in harmony with a position in heaven. All believers need spiritual formation. None of us ever reaches the place in this life at which we no longer need to grow in God's grace. Only when we see Christ will we be made like Him (1 John 3:1-2) and have no more need of spiritual formation.

These two realities—spiritual formation and regeneration—stand in contrast with each other in several ways, and yet they also relate to each other. We will look first at contrasts. Throughout the rest of this chapter I will use the term *salvation* to refer to the deliverance God brings from sin's penalty at the time of faith, the point of regeneration and justification. There is a sense in which the believer finds continual deliverance from the power of sin. And there will eventually be deliverance from the very presence of sin when we see Christ. Primarily this discussion will focus on the first of these aspects.

Some have called this "faith development." Fowler's "stages of faith" must not be understood as stages in salvation, the way we are describing the aspects of God's working grace in this chapter. Fowler himself emphasizes that a person standing in one or another of these stages of faith is not thereby more or less related to Christ. But let him speak for himself.

Insofar as faith development theory makes any contribution to our dealing with salvation, it comes in relation to the way each stage adds to the realization of further aspects of a person's divine prepotentiation for growth in relation to the love of God and of the neighbor and in covenantal partnership with God. Faith development theory is closest to an understanding of salvation that relates the term to its Latin root *salus,* which means *wholeness* or *health,* or to the Greek term, *telios,* which means *perfection* in the sense of *completion* or *wholeness.* Faith development theory relates most readily to the understanding of *eternal life* found in John's gospel. There the term "eternal life" refers not only to one's assurance of life with God beyond physical death, but also to a *quality of this life* in which one's belief in Christ, and in the love and light disclosed in Christ, mediates communion with the one Christ called "Father" (Fowler, 1992, p. 19).

CONTRASTS

The Bible suggests three major contrasts between regeneration and spiritual formation.

Regeneration describes a work completely carried out by God whereas spiritual formation requires the believer's cooperation with God.

Justification does not result from God and the sinner each making a contribution. It is all of God — Father, Son, and Holy Spirit; the sinner contributes nothing. Faith in Christ alone, though absolutely essential, does not add anything to what God has done. Like the straw through which we sip a cold drink on a blistering day, faith provides the means by which salvation comes. Faith does not save sinners any more than the straw quenches thirst.

The New Testament describes salvation as spiritual birth (John 3:5-6; Titus 3:5). Neither physical nor spiritual birth is accomplished by the effort of the newborn. God the Father, God the Son, and God the Holy Spirit are each involved every time a sinner becomes a saint.

41

But in spiritual formation, God and humanity are both involved, each having an indispensable part to play. Growth becomes the key word here. Of course, only those born of God can grow up into Christ (Eph. 4:15). Scripture repeatedly exhorts God's people to set their affection on things above, to put to death the deeds of the flesh (things characteristic of the old sin nature), and to clothe themselves with the Christian graces produced by the Spirit of God. Clearly, God and His children cooperate in spiritual formation.

Regeneration is instantaneous and complete while spiritual formation is progressive and incomplete.

At the moment of faith in Christ, the believing sinner has no more condemnation (Rom. 8:1). The saved sinner is complete in Christ (Col. 2:10). Forgiveness, cleansing, justification, regeneration, reconciliation with God, and all the other wonderful things which take place at the time of salvation come to the believer immediately and fully. The riches of God's grace in Christ Jesus (Eph. 1:7) occur in all their fullness at the instant of faith.

The opposite is true in spiritual formation. Growth in grace takes time. Maturing in the things of God does not happen immediately. One does not become holy in a hurry. All through the New Testament, Bible writers urge the child of God to "grow in grace" (2 Peter 3:18); "walk in the light" (1 John 1:7); "draw near to God" (Heb. 10:22); "throw off" what hinders Christian growth (Heb. 12:1); "run with perseverance" (Heb. 12:1); this is spiritual formation. At salvation believers possess all the riches of grace, but we must appropriate them in daily life.

At the time of salvation the believing sinner is completely sanctified, set apart as God's possession positionally (1 Cor. 6:11). When the believer sees Christ either at death or when He returns, he or she will be perfectly sanctified, that is, completely set apart forever (1 Thes. 3:12-13). Between these two time periods, however, Christians must be progressively sanctified (2 Cor. 7:1), and that is spiritual formation. When a baby is born a new life enters the world. As the baby receives nourishment there is growth into childhood and eventual adulthood. Salvation is birth; spiritual formation is growth.

The meaning of sanctification and aspects of it may be visualized as follows:

Perfect (With Christ in heaven)
Progressive (Spiritual Formation)
Positional (Regeneration and Justification)

Regeneration is a gift from God and spiritual formation results in part from obedience and faithfulness to Him.

"The gift of God is eternal life" (Rom. 6:23), Paul told the Roman Christians. "By grace you have been saved through faith . . . it is the gift of God" (Eph. 2:8), he wrote to the Ephesian believers. Salvation is totally apart from human effort. God alone does the saving, the regenerating. To be sure, the sinner must believe, must receive, must trust; but that act of faith contributes nothing to the salvation God gives.

Spiritual formation, on the other hand, comes only from a positive response to God's call to obedience and holiness. As believers obey, accepting God's gracious invitations and exhortations, the mind of Christ is formed in us (1 Cor. 2:16) and we grow up in Christ (1 Peter 2:2). God's sanctifying grace utilizes the spiritual disciplines to facilitate the Spirit's work in us.

Westerhoff offers an interesting paragraph describing spiritual formation in this progressive mode.

Formation aids persons to acquire Christian faith (understood as a particular perception of life and our lives), Christian character (understood as identity and appropriate behavioral dispositions), and Christian consciousness (understood as that interior subjective awareness or temperament that predisposes persons to particular experiences). For example, Christian formation is the participation in and the practice of the Christian life of faith (Westerhoff, 1992, p. 10).

RELATIONSHIPS

Spiritual Formation Is Inseparable from Salvation

Salvation serves spiritual formation as a foundation serves a building. No matter how beautiful in appearance, a building will not stand the ravages of time and the storms of life unless built upon a solid foundation. Likewise, life, no matter how beautifully adorned and lived, will not stand in face of divine tests unless that life has been made new in Christ.

Salvation and spiritual formation might also be viewed as a biblical marriage. One partner makes possible and is incomplete without the other. Salvation involves the reception of divine life. This God-given life cannot be hidden completely forever. It will manifest itself someway, somehow, sometime.

Charles Ryrie wrote of three caveats one must take into account when thinking about fruit-bearing among Christians. First, believers are not *always* fruitful. The Apostles Paul and Peter both challenged their readers to engage in good works so they would not be unfruitful (Titus 3:14; 2 Peter 1:8). Second, the fruit which the child of God bears may not be outwardly evident. For example, we may not be able to see the aching heart of a believer exhibiting the gift of mercy in behalf of a brother or sister undergoing deep pain. But that is no less the fruit of God's work in one's life just because it remains invisible to the human eye. Third, our understanding of what fruit is and therefore what to expect in others may be either faulty, incomplete, or both (Ryrie, 1989, p. 45). The very nature of the gift of eternal life means growth, advance, action. Where none of these adorn the life, God's Spirit does not likely dwell.

The difficulty comes when we set up our own standards or tests to validate life. Just because we see no evidence of what we consider "proof" of divine life does not mean there is none. God has not made us the judges of this. True, believers often cite Matthew 7:20 ("by their fruit you will recognize them"), but a "fruit inspector" is very different from a judge of another's relation to God.

Spiritual Formation Is an Important Reason for Our Salvation

We could ask, "Why does God save sinners?" More personally, why did God save me? Several reasons can clearly be drawn from Scripture. Often we say, God saved me so that I might not spend eternity in hell but rather in heaven with Him. And this, of course, does highlight a reason for Christ's rescue. But it probably should not be thought of as the highest or most important reason. God also redeems sinners so that they might be conformed to the image of His Son. He saves so that we might bring Him praise, honor, and glory now and forever (Eph. 1:12, 14). We bring praise to Him in this life through our spiritual formation, through our walk with Him.

By means of God's grace and through the sinner's faith, God saves (Eph. 2:8). The believing sinner becomes God's "workmanship" created in Christ "to do good works" (v. 10). Formation and the good works for which God saves are inseparable; they always accompany each other in the Christian life.

Spiritual formation involves the working out of our salvation which God calls for (Phil. 2:12). God never tells sinners to work *for* salvation. After all, salvation is a gift and gifts can't be earned or they are no longer gifts. God does exhort His own to work out the salvation He has worked in their hearts. Apart from spiritual formation this cannot be done and spirituality as a lifestyle is impossible. Bloesch is clear here.

> The word *spirituality* refers to living out our lives in relation to the Eternal, appropriating redeeming grace in trust and obedience. If revelation involved only objective truths, the religious affections would be quenched and the religious yearning suppressed. Christians are spiritual, as well as rational, beings, and this means being in contact with the Spirit of God as well as with truths revealed by God.
>
> A *true* spirituality, however, will be grounded in the promises of God in holy Scripture. It will celebrate the glory of God, not the self-aggrandizement of the creature. In the midst of a rising tide of paganism and pseudo-spirituality, we need to recover the biblical pattern. This means not only immersing ourselves in the Bible itself, but also learning from the ongoing commentary on Scripture in the life of the church. It is especially important for us to rediscover the abiding insights of the sixteenth-century Reformers as well as of the Pietists and Puritans (Bloesch, 1991, p. 24).

Spiritual Formation and Salvation Are Both Grounded in the Finished Work of Christ

All evangelicals agree the salvation of sinners takes place only because Christ died in the sinner's place. In His death the Son of God was made sin for us (2 Cor. 5:21). On the cross the Lord Jesus Christ bore our sins in His own body (1 Peter 2:24). The very heart of the Gospel stresses that "Christ died for our sins" (1 Cor. 15:3). The very foundation of the Gospel is the efficacious, atoning death of Christ.

What we often overlook is that the believer's restoration to fellowship with God, one's forgiveness as a child of God, rests upon the same cross-work of Christ. The same is true of growth in grace, of spiritual formation. The Apostle Paul made this very clear in his words to the Roman Christians.

Romans 6 begins with a question related to the believer's walk and its answer. "Shall we go on sinning so that grace may increase?" (Rom. 6:1) The answer is "By no means! We died to sin; how can we live in it any longer?" (v. 2) What follows in that chapter describes the believer's co-crucifixion and co-resurrection with Christ (vv. 3-5). Paul's argument underscores our identification with Christ's finished work on the Cross. Because of this we need not be slaves to sin any longer (v. 6); we have been "freed from sin" (v. 7).

Because of their position in Christ, Christians can therefore consider themselves dead to sin (Rom. 6:11). No longer must we obey native lusts. Sin does not need to reign as a ruling monarch in our bodies (v. 12). Christians dare never forget that the work of spiritual formation requires considering ourselves dead to sin and yielding to the work of the Spirit of God in all areas of our lives. Charles Ryrie sees this as the key and puts it this way:

> If maturity is a key facet in spirituality, then the Holy Spirit must play a major role in producing it. To be able to discern involves knowledge of God's will and perspective. This the Spirit produces through His ministry of teaching (John 16:12-15). It will also include praying according to the will of God which is directed by the Spirit (Rom. 8:26; Eph. 6:18). The spiritual believer will surely be exercising the spiritual gifts which the Spirit gives and empowers (1 Cor. 12:7). He or she will learn to war victoriously against the flesh by the power of the Spirit (Rom. 8:13; Gal. 5:16-17). In short, the fullness of the Spirit is key to producing spirituality in the believer (Ryrie, 1986, p. 375).

SUMMARY

One's entire personality is affected in salvation. Not only does a person's position before God change, one's person changes too. Before salvation the sinner has what might be described as the old mind (intellect), the old heart (emotions), and the old will (self-determination). Each of these areas of personality has been affected by the Fall. Each is also made new in Christ. At regeneration the child of God receives a new mind, a new heart, and a new will (Pentecost, 1966, pp. 11–84).

In brief, everyone saved by God's free grace is a new creature in Christ. He or she is made whole again. Just as salvation affects the whole person, so spiritual formation affects the totality of the person. The new person grows in the grace and knowledge of Christ and becomes more Christlike. The saved sinner's walk also affects other believers. But we often overlook the fact that the one in whom the mind of Christ is being formed will have and show compassion to all, not just to other believers.

When we see human needs which we can help meet, we should get involved. When we are unable to help with tangible things—food, clothing, shelter—we should do our best to find help somewhere. In other words, the redemption God gives heightens in the redeemed an awareness of the needs of others. Christians recognize and act upon the need of humankind, not only to be redeemed, but also to be released from bondage resulting from the curse that rests upon the world because of sin.

Does spiritual formation relate to salvation? Indeed it does. So definite and integral is the relationship that there can be no spiritual formation where there has been no regeneration. Where there is no life there can be no growth; where there is no growth, there, no life exists.

For Further Reading

Bloesch, D. (1991). Lost in the mystical myths. *Christianity Today, 35,* 22-24. An insightful evaluation of modern spiritualities.

Enns, P. (1989). *The Moody handbook of theology.* Chicago: Moody. A good objective analysis of the areas covered.

Fowler, J. (1992). Stages of faith: Reflections on a decade of dialogue. *Christian Education Journal, 13,* 13–23. A helpful historical analysis.

Pentecost, J. (1966). *Pattern for maturity.* Chicago: Moody. The stress here is upon the biblical teaching.

Ryrie, C. (1986). *Basic theology.* Wheaton, IL: Victor. An introduction to theology, this primer is known for its precise distinctions and clear statements.

_____. (1989). *So great salvation.* Wheaton, IL: Victor. Offers response to lordship salvation issues.

Schaeffer, F. (1972). *True spirituality.* Wheaton, IL: Tyndale. An important book by Schaeffer on the nature of authentic spirituality.

Westerhoff, J. (1992). Fashioning Christians in our day. *Faculty Dialogue, 17,* 5-25. Thoughtful treatment of issues involved in faith development.

THE PURITAN MODEL OF SPIRITUAL FORMATION
Leland Ryken

"Where is God?" asks the *Westminster Children's Catechism.*
My own inclination is to answer, "God is in heaven." Traditions
of spirituality have generally agreed. The dominant model of
spirituality through the centuries has been an aspiration of the
human soul from earth to heaven. In this paradigm, spirituality
is most likely to be nurtured by a special set of activities apart
from one's ordinary daily routine, such as prayer, Bible reading, contemplation, and worship.

Such a conception of the spiritual life need not disparage
active life in the world, though an incipient sacred-secular dichotomy is often discernible. The "secular" life is either a diversion from true spirituality, or it is of secondary importance.
To the extent that spirituality is linked with the active life, it is
viewed as something to balance it, not as something identified
with it.

There is much to commend in this theory of spiritual formation. But it also runs certain risks—risks that the English and
American Puritans of the sixteenth and seventeenth centuries
can help us to counteract. Their distinctive contribution to our
thinking about spiritual formation is the claim that all of life is
God's.

"Where is God?" asks the catechism. And its answer catches
us by surprise: "God is everywhere." In such an outlook, the
goal of spirituality is not to raise the individual soul above
earthly pursuits to heaven, but instead to bring heaven down
into earthly pursuits.

Puritan piety began with a rejection of the centuries-old dichotomy that divided life into the categories of sacred and secular. For the Puritans, all of life was potentially sacred. Puritan John Cotton theorized, "Not only my spiritual life but even my civil life in this world, and all the life I live, is by the faith of the Son of God; He exempts no life from the agency of his faith" (Cotton, 1963, p. 312). What does this theory look like when put into practice?

DAILY WORK AND THE GOD-CENTERED LIFE

We can begin with attitudes toward work, by which the Puritans meant not only the job through which one earns a livelihood but also such daily tasks as washing dishes and mowing the lawn. In kernel form, the Puritan doctrine of vocation, or calling, held that God calls people to their tasks and that the performance of these tasks can become a form of stewardship to God. The Puritan divine Richard Steele sounded the keynote when he wrote that "God doth call every man and woman . . . to serve him in some peculiar [particular] employment in this world, both for their own and the common good" (Ryken, 1991, p. 26).

Several corollaries follow from the belief that God calls people to their tasks. One is that work ceases to be impersonal, becoming instead a means by which a person lives out his or her personal relationship to God. "Whatsoever our callings be," claimed a Puritan source, "we serve the Lord Jesus Christ in them" (Ryken, 1991, p. 27). If God is the one who calls people to their work, such work can be a form of service to God. John Cotton thus claimed that a person who "serves Christ in serving of men . . . doth his work sincerely as in God's presence, and as one that hath an heavenly business in hand" (Cotton, 1963, p. 322). In a similar vein, American Puritan Cotton Mather exclaimed, "Oh, let every Christian walk with God when he works at his calling, act in his occupation with an eye to God, act as under the eye of God" (Ryken, 1991, p. 27).

To relate the Puritan doctrine of calling to the idea of Christian formation, we can say that a Christian's work in the world itself provides the occasion for forming Christian character and is the arena within which to exercise Christian virtue. According to Thomas Gouge, Christians should "so spiritualize our hearts and affections that we may have heavenly hearts in earthly employments" (Ryken, 1991, p. 208). Instead of linking spirituality with a retreat to some "sacred space," the Puritan ideal was that a person might know that "his shop as well as his chapel is holy ground" (Ryken, 1991, p. 208). While most Christians have seen the possibility of serving God in their work, the Puritan ideal was to serve God through or by that work. And while many traditions have implicitly linked piety with the contemplative life, the Puritans associated piety equally with the active life.

SEEING GOD IN THE COMMONPLACE

A second ingredient of spiritual formation for the Puritans was their practice of sanctifying the common. Because the Puritans viewed life through the wide-angle lens of God's sovereignty, everything in life became a potential pointer to God and carrier of grace. The Puritans were the true sacramentalists of their day, much more so than traditions that multiplied ritual within the church building.

The sanctity of the common was a constant Puritan theme. John Bunyan asked in the preface to *Grace Abounding,* "Have you forgot . . . the Milk-house, the Stable, the Barn, and the like, where God did visit your soul?" (Bunyan, 1966, p. 5) "Canst thou not think on the several places thou hast lived in and remember that they have each had their several mercies?" asked Richard Baxter (Kaufmann, 1966, p. 216). Walter Pringle told his children the exact places at which certain things happened to him: his first experience of prayer came "at the northeast of Stitchel Hall," and years later he committed his newly born son to God "at the plum tree on the north side of the garden door" (Watkins, 1972, p. 64).

In such a framework, there are no "trivial" events, and life itself provides a continuous means of spiritual formation. Nathaniel Mather claimed that even the simplest activities, such as "a man's loving his wife or child," could become "gracious acts . . . of great account in the eyes of God" (Ryken, 1991, p. 209). God "sanc-

51

tified John Winthrop's "dangerous hot malignant fever" in such a way that Winthrop "never had more sweet communion with him than in that affliction" (McGee, 1976, pp. 15–16).

For the Puritans, anything in life might become a channel of God's grace. The young Robert Blair looked out of the window one day to see "the sun brightly shining, and a cow with a full udder"; he remembered that the sun was made to give light and the cow to give milk, which made him realize how little he understood the purpose of his own life (Watkins, 1972, p. 65).

The Puritan view of the sanctity of the common rested partly on an extraordinary awareness of God's providence. This, in turn, produced the Puritan practice of keeping diaries. "If we were well read in the story of our own lives," said Richard Sibbes, "we might have a divinity [theology] of our own, drawn out of the observations of God's particular dealing toward us" (Ryken, 1991, p. 209). John Bartlet advised Christians to "meditate on the experience you have had of God's faithfulness, and [the] goodness you have had in all his providences. . . . To help you herein, you shall do well to make a catalogue and keep a diary of God's special providences" (Kaufmann, 1966, p. 213). Isaac Ambrose used the provocative phrase "a sanctified memory" in urging the same practice (Ryken, 1991, p. 310).

The doctrine of nature likewise led the Puritans to see God in the commonplace. Thomas Taylor said that "the voice of God is in all the creatures and by them all speaketh unto us always and everywhere" (Ryken, 1991, p. 310). Thomas Shepard asked, "Can we, when we behold the stately theater of heaven and earth, conclude other but that the finger, arms, and wisdom of God hath been here?" (Ryken, 1991, p. 310)

In such a climate of living, virtually any daily event might become a "teachable moment." For Cambridge University student Thomas Goodwin, it was a spur-of-the-moment decision to attend a funeral service instead of going partying with his friends. John Bunyan's teachable moment came when his work took him to Bedford, where he overheard "three or four poor women sitting at a door in the sun, and talking about the things of God" (Bunyan, 1966, pp. 16–17).

There was, in short, no place where the Puritans could not potentially find God. They were continuously open to what Richard Baxter called "a drop of glory" that God might allow to fall upon their souls (Baxter, 1966, p. 173). Spirituality, in this view, is not so much the story of the soul's seeking God as it is the story of seeing God — recognizing the presence of God in all of life.

THE FAMILY AS AGENT OF SPIRITUAL FORMATION

One of the hallmarks of Puritanism was its genius for maintaining a balance between competing poles. The personal and individual aspect of spiritual formation that I have discussed thus far was balanced by communal dimensions that fed the practice of personal piety. The family was the primary context for such spiritual formation, and much of what we might say about the subject is encapsulated in a chapter title that Puritan scholar Christopher Hill gave to a discussion of the topic — "the spiritualization of the household" (Hill, 1964, p. 443).

The Puritans' favorite image for the family was that of a miniature church. Richard Baxter wrote that "a Christian family . . . is a church . . . a society of Christians combined for the better worshipping and serving God" (Ryken, 1991, p. 84). William Gouge said that the family is "a little church" (George, 1961, p. 275), while William Perkins wrote, "These families wherein this service of God is performed are, as it were, little churches, yea even a kind of Paradise upon earth" (George, 1961, p. 275).

The picture of the family as a miniature church goes far toward explaining the exact forms of spiritual nurture that the Puritans exercised in their homes. To begin, worship was a regular part of the household routine. Nicholas Byfield advised, "Parents should carefully set up the worship of God in the family that from their cradles [children] may see the practice of piety" (Ryken, 1991, p. 85). Increase Mather's church in Boston made the following commitment: "We promise (by the help of Christ) that we will endeavor to walk before God in our houses, with a perfect heart; and that we will uphold the worship of God therein continually, according as he in his word requires, both in respect of prayer and reading the Scriptures, that so the word of Christ may dwell richly in us" (Morgan, 1966, p. 140).

In viewing the family as a church, the Puritans made family

devotions a standard feature of their life. According to Richard Baxter's *Christian Directory,* family worship should be held twice each weekday: "It is seasonable every morning to give thanks for the rest of the night past . . . and to beg directions, protection and provisions and blessing for the following day . . . and that the evening is a fit season to give God thanks for the mercies of the day, and to confess the sins of the day, and ask forgiveness, and to pray for rest and protection in the night" (Ryken, 1991, p. 86).

The Puritans regarded the family, no less than the church, as a center for instruction in Christian doctrine and morals. Thomas Taylor, for example, expressed the need "to instruct everyone of [a] family in the fear of God" (Hill, 1964, p. 455). Several Puritan practices fostered such instruction. Personal Bible reading is almost synonymous with the Puritan movement. "Repeating the sermon" at home was a common practice on Sundays. A contemporary observer of the Puritans recorded that "what [the Puritan] heard in public" was "repeated in private, to whet it upon himself and family" (Collinson, 1990, p. 377). Theophilus Eaton, a typical Puritan in this regard, assembled his whole family on Sunday evenings, "and in an obliging manner conferred with them about the things with which they had been entertained in the house of God, shutting up all with a prayer for the blessing of God upon them all" (Morgan, 1966, p. 102).

The technique that Puritans found most effective in Christian instruction of children was catechizing. Richard Baxter devoted a section of *The Reformed Pastor* to "the duty of personal catechizing and instructing the flock." Richard Stock, John Milton's boyhood pastor in London, catechized the children of his parish during the week, boys and girls on alternate days (Parker, 1968, p. 9). The goal of such catechizing was not memorization but understanding. Cotton Mather cautioned parents not to let "the children patter out by rote the words of the catechism, like parrots; but be inquisitive how far their understandings do take in the things of God" (Morgan, 1966, p. 98).

Yet another activity that made the Puritan home a keystone of spiritual formation for every member of the family was the endearing practice of families' calling their private thanksgiving days and fast days, attended by friends and neighbors. A specimen entry in a diary catches some of the flavor of such gatherings initiated by individual families: "We had a solemn day of thanksgiving at my house for my wife's and son's recovery; my son Eliezer began, Mr. Dawson, John proceeded, I concluded with preaching, prayer; we feasted 50 persons and upwards, blessed be God" (Davies, 1948, p. 282).

It is obvious that Hill is right in speaking of "the spiritualization of the household" that was a hallmark of Puritanism. Lawrence Stone similarly speaks of the "general tendency to substitute the household for the church," concluding that "the essence of Puritanism was a family church" (Stone, 1977, p. 141).

PURITAN CHURCH LIFE AND SPIRITUAL FORMATION

Our picture of Puritan church life will be clarified if we pause to consider the historical situation. The Protestant Reformation was a protest movement governed by a strong anti-Catholic strain. The Puritans were profoundly distrustful of external institutional religion, and they rejected Catholic notions of church rituals as a requirement for salvation and of priestly intermediaries between the believer and God. In England, moreover, the Puritans were a persecuted minority who had to practice their communal religious life in relative secrecy.

Practical constraints thus made it necessary for the Puritans to think of their church as a church-within-the-church. This dual allegiance to the local church and the smaller group within it determined much of the weekly church life of a typical Puritan.

The Puritans did not conceive of spiritual formation apart from church attendance on Sunday, when they typically attended two worship services. The heart of the public worship service, moreover, was the sermon.

It is impossible to overstate the importance of preaching to the Puritan conception of spiritual formation. Historian Michael Walzer calls the preacher "the hero of sixteenth-century Puritanism" (Walzer, 1965, p. 119). George Walker, a Lancashire-born London preacher, gave this description of Puritan zeal for attending sermons: the people of his native county, he said, "are ready and willing to run many miles to hear sermons when they have them not at home, and lay aside all care of profit, leaving their labour and work on weekdays to frequent meetings for prophecy and expounding of God's word" (Richardson, 1972, p. 84). Christopher Hill has adduced evidence that having a good preacher was an economic asset to a market town because it drew crowds to hear the preacher's market-day sermon (Hill, 1964, pp. 98–99).

Puritan sermons were a blend of head and heart. They placed immense demands on the intellect of the listeners, yet their aim was affective — to move the believer to action. Notetaking at sermons was a standard Puritan practice. It is also relevant to the theme of this volume to note that the Puritans placed particular emphasis on the application part of the sermon — the "uses" of the doctrine, as they called it.

This insatiable capacity for sermons produced two distinctive Puritan practices. One was "prophesyings," which were preaching seminars or workshops attended by ministers of a district to upgrade the quality of their preaching. Balancing these clerical workshops were "lectureships" designed to improve the laity's grasp of the content of the Christian faith. Puritan lecturers were free-lance clergy privately supported by the laity and therefore beyond control of the state church. A modern historian calls these lectureships "a sort of grand-parent of our modern Bible-study: a preaching service of considerable length and great depth, usually being attended by pastors and members from neighboring Puritan congregations" (Lewis, 1977, pp. 61–62).

To such prophesyings and lectureships we can add another quaint Puritan term — "conventicles." These were home prayer meetings and Bible studies held for the most part secretly to avoid prosecution from the Anglican Church. Patrick Collinson's book *The Elizabethan Puritan Movement* includes an important chapter on "The Meetings of the Godly" that surveys the remarkable range of ways in which the Puritan laity took the initiative in finding spiritual sustenance, often in defiance of state and church officials (Collinson, 1967, pp. 372–382).

Refusing to define the church in predominantly institutional terms, the Puritans instead regarded it as a fellowship. An accompanying emphasis was the beneficial influence that Christians can have on each other. "Christian conference" was a prized activity, by which the Puritans meant conversation with Christians of like mind and soul on spiritual matters. American Puritan John Winthrop recorded a "conference with a Christian friend or two," adding that "God so blessed it unto us, as we were all much quickened and refreshed by it" (McGee, 1976, p. 196). Thomas Watson urged Christians to associate with each other, on the ground that "they may, by their counsel, prayers, and holy example, be a means to make you holy" (McGee, 1976, p. 202).

A final institutional foundation of spiritual formation for the Puritans was education. Founding schools was a hallmark of the Puritans. Education, moreover, was conceived in terms of Christian formation. Milton defined the end of education as being "to repair the ruins of our first parents by regaining to know God aright, and out of that knowledge to love him, to imitate him, to be like him" (Ryken, 1991, p. 163). When Harvard College was founded to ensure an educated clergy, one rule observed at the college was this: "Let every student be plainly instructed and earnestly pressed to consider well the main end of his life and studies is to know God and Jesus Christ which is eternal life, John 17:3, and therefore to lay Christ in the bottom, as the only foundation of all sound knowledge and learning" (Miller & Johnson, 1963, p. 702).

CONCLUSION

Three concepts sum up Puritan theory and practice of spiritual formation. One is *the primacy of the spiritual.* The Puritans believed that a person's spiritual life was the great priority in life. "In a divine commonwealth," wrote Richard Baxter, "holiness must have the principal honor and encouragement" (Ryken, 1991, p. 207). Samuel Willard claimed that "the generality of men take their measures from the observation of outward providence: if there be outward peace and plenty, they call them happy days . . . but we have a better rule. . . . The more of Christ that a people enjoy, the happier are they, and the less he is known and acknowledged . . . the greater is the infelicity of such a people" (Ryken, 1991, p. 206).

A second mainstay of Puritan thinking about Christian formation can be summed up by the notion of *the balanced Christian life*. For example, spiritual nurture was at its heart personal and individual, but it occurred only within broader contexts of family, church, and school. It included a blend of head and heart: a major thrust of the Puritans was to insist on preachers who were "godly and learned," but at the same time the Puritans spoke at length about cultivating godly "affections," by which they meant emotions.

Finally, the Puritan concept of spiritual formation was founded on the principle that *all of life is God's*. The spiritual life was rooted in such specifically devotional acts as Bible reading, prayer, and church attendance, but it extended equally to the daily routine of work and family living.

Much of what we might say on the subject is captured admirably in Patrick Collinson's statement that "the life of the Puritan was in one sense a continuous act of worship, pursued under an unremitting and lively sense of God's providential purposes and constantly refreshed by religious activity, personal, domestic and public" (Collinson, 1967, p. 356).

For Further Reading

George, C. and K. George. (1961). *The protestant mind of the english reformation, 1570–1640*. Princeton: Princeton Univ. Press. A survey of Puritan ideas, including such issues as theology, politics, economics, church, and family.

Hambrick-Stowe, C. (1982). *The practice of piety: Puritan devotional disciplines in seventeenth-century New England*. Chapel Hill: Univ. of North Carolina. A description of the public and private devotional life of the Puritans.

Hill, C. (1964). *Society and puritanism in pre-revolutionary England*. New York: Schocken. A historical survey focused particularly on the religious life (broadly defined) of the English Puritans.

McGee, J. (1976). *The godly man in Stuart England: Anglicans, puritans, and the two tables, 1620–1670*. New Haven: Yale Univ. Press. A description of key Puritan emphases, developed through a contrast with Anglican views on the same subjects.

Ryken, L. (1986). *Worldly saints: The puritans as they really were*. Grand Rapids: Zondervan. An overview of what the Puritans believed and practiced. Topics include work, marriage and sex, money, family, preaching, church and worship, the Bible, education, and social action, concluding with a chapter on "The Genius of Puritanism: What the Puritans Did Best."

Watkins, O. (1972). *The puritan experience: Studies in spiritual autobiography*. New York: Schocken. An analysis of the Puritan experience through a study of such genres as diaries, biographies, and autobiographies.

COUNTERFEIT SPIRITUALITY
Timothy R. Phillips & Donald G. Bloesch

At a recent United Church of Christ conference on "Health and Spirituality: The Abundant Life" in Danvers, Masachusetts, Dominican Matthew Fox led the participants in a song and ritual dance drawn from native tribal traditions (Lavos, 1990, p. 4). More than 400 people danced around their tables singing "I walk with beauty before me, behind me, above me, below me, all around me." Meditation techniques were recommended for inner healing, such as, repeating a word, phrase, or muscular activity while blithely disregarding all thoughts. The speakers conveyed the impression that "anyone can have mystical experiences by using the tools of ritual and gratitude." M. Scott Peck, the noted psychiatrist and author of *The Road Less Traveled,* assured the conferees, "We have the technology to welcome God into our organizations. There is nothing magical about this technology. It follows the rules of love."

Throughout the Christian church and even our society, interest in spirituality is burgeoning. But much of the current fascination with spirituality simply reflects our cultural ethos. Amid this rising tide of spiritual options and confusion, our piety must constantly be evaluated by Scripture. The focus of Scripture is Jesus Christ and His benefits, which redeem us from the power of sin and guilt. True spirituality is living out one's life through faith in Jesus Christ, making His gift of salvation the basis for every aspect of our existence so He is truly acknowledged as Lord over all. Through this process Christians are transformed into His image. God's reconciling and justifying work outside us in Jesus Christ and His regenerating and sanctifying work within us by His Spirit identify the contours of Christian spirituality. An anthropocentric orientation whereby salvation becomes basically a human achievement characterizes the perennial counterfeits that subvert true spirituality.

SPIRITUALITY IS ESTABLISHED BY GOD IN JESUS CHRIST

Despite humankind's rebellion and bondage in sin, God acted in history to call a people to Himself. Through this historical revelation God identified who He is in contrast to this fallen cosmos, demonstrated His graciousness to the sinner, and promised Israel that He would reestablish His kingdom over creation. Jesus Christ fulfilled this promise. In this One, God assumed human flesh, took on our guilt, created a new humanity, and brought about the reconciliation of creation. In Jesus Christ God has descended to our condition, meeting us where we are and offering us a personal relationship with Him whereby we may grow into His image. In Him are found "all the treasures of wisdom and knowledge" (Col. 2:3). True spirituality must live from God's salvific words and deeds which culminate in Jesus Christ.

The Spiritual Counterfeits of Subjectivism and Mysticism
The human proclivity, however, is to define God not by His own objective revelation in history outside us, but from within through subjective criteria. For instance, much popular evangelicalism portrays Christ as the great therapist for enhancing self-esteem. As a result, sanctity is redefined as sanity, and holiness as healthfulness. Nor is subjectivism a recent innovation. During the Gilded Age, many evangelicals concurred with Russell Conwell: "to make money honestly is to preach the gospel" (Conwell, 1976, p. 237). In other words, the picture of Christ is formed more by the individual's own cherished images than by God's Word.

New Age writers enshrine this subjective turn by repudiating God's self-revelation in unique historical events for a nature mysticism. They see all nature as alive, filled with divine energy. Nature is not simply the handiwork, but the very body of God.

61

Pictured as a verb rather than a noun, God is the process of cosmic becoming. God is resymbolized as "the Life Force," "the Power of Creative Transformation," "the Flowing River of Nature," "the Divine Eros," "the Womb of Being," and "the Infinite Abyss." Divine immanence and process displace God's personhood.

Since humans are defined as part of this divine "Mother Earth," "to be in touch with ourselves is to be in touch with the word of God that is ourselves" (Larkin, 1981, p. 60). The resulting spirituality explores the reservoir of unlimited power within us. Many encourage the practice of centering—focusing attention on the inner core of the self to commune with "the infinite ground of being." Others urge us to rise above words and images until we are lost in the pulsating vitality of life or the abysmal silence. The promise is that "higher potentials of Divine life" or the "Christ energies" are waiting to be released (Spangler, 1976, pp. 117-118).

While some of these techniques are found in the mystical heritage of the church, several features differentiate New Age spirituality from Christianity. Most dangerous is the devolution of Jesus from Savior to spiritual guide. The New Age etherealizes Christ into a symbol for "a universal experience, [and] not an exclusively Christian one" (Spangler & Thompson, 1991, pp. 133–134). Jay McDaniel's claim (1990, p. 193) is characteristic: "As long as the fruits . . . are a love of life and a commitment to shalom, there is no reason for Christians to insist that one type of spirituality is higher, deeper, or more revelatory than another."

Affirming Christ as the only way is condemned as ethnocentric and arrogant "in a world . . . [in which] there are many worthwhile religious ways" (McDaniel, 1990, p. 4). But the Jesus of Scripture—the only Jesus we can ever know—did not discover humanity's latent possibilities for ascent. Christ claimed to be God's own condescension to sinners in history, and was confessed and worshiped as such by the apostolic church. This point undergirds all of Christ's claims, distinguishing Him from every other religious figure. If Christ is not the Savior, He offers only a repackaging of the old, not a new humanity. That is why our hope lies in what God has done for us in the person of Jesus Christ, not in what humans can do.

Undergirding the New Age and other subjective spiritualities is an *eros* conception of love, that is, the desire to possess the highest good and thereby perfect the self. The existentialist Miguel de Unamuno candidly admits: "My longing is not to be submerged in the vast All . . . or in God" but "to become myself God, yet without ceasing to be I myself" (White, 1983, p. 111). Peck insists that "we are growing toward godhood. God is the goal of evolution. It is God who is the source of the evolutionary force and God who is the destination" (Peck, 1978, pp. 269–270). This stands in glaring contradiction to Scripture. In Christianity, God descends to us rebels, and enables us to enter a personal relationship with Him. And Christian spirituality reflects God's *agape* love, His willingness to serve unconditionally. By contrast New Age spirituality values self-affirmation more highly than supplication and service (Bloesch, 1991).

Finally, in this subjective religion the individual's optimistic aspirations obscure reality. Focusing solely upon the evolutionary goal of the whole, it readily accepts all aspects and energies, even the shadowy, as essential to the symbiosis which propels this higher end. Evil and rebellion consequently are recast as good. By contrast, the Christian maintains that without God's demonstration in history of His gracious love and sovereignty, we can only consider ourselves forsaken specks in a foreboding cosmos which returns us to dust. Instead of prizing the creative imagination, Christian spirituality is grounded upon a confrontation with God through His words and acts in history.

SPIRITUALITY IS DEPENDENT UPON GOD'S SUPERNATURAL ACT OF REGENERATION

The human person was created as a relational being, dependent upon a loving fellowship with the Infinite as the meaning for all life. But rebellion against God as Lord corrupted human nature. Our incessant desire to satiate this infinite vacuum with finite things reflects the sinner's quest to be god. Humans cannot choose the spiritual good, only their egocentric good. Our actions may elicit admiration from others, but not God. Simply put, "the heart is deceitful above all things" (Jer. 17:9) and in bondage to sin.

We are changed not by entering a new social situation or observing new practices, but only through God's supernatural action. Jesus maintained that "unless one is born again, he cannot see the kingdom of God" (John 3:3, NKJV). John Wesley explains that the unregenerate "has, in a spiritual sense, eyes and sees not. . . . He has no true knowledge of the things of God. . . . But as soon as he is born of God, there is a total change. . . . The 'eyes of his understanding are opened' . . . 'he sees the light of the glory of God,' His glorious love, 'in the face of Jesus Christ'" (Wesley, 1955, p. 233). With new desires and powers, the believer perceives God's spiritual reality and acknowledges His Kingship. As Jonathan Edwards elaborates, the regenerate are taken by the excellency of Jesus Christ in Himself, while others are engaged in divine things only insofar as they enhance self-interest. John Calvin and Ignatius Loyola make this point through the motto *Soli Deo Gloria* (glory to God alone). God's regeneration enables spirituality to move beyond self-interest to self-sacrificial service for Christ (Rom. 12:14ff).

The Spiritual Counterfeit of Pelagianism

The perennial spiritual counterfeit called pelagianism dismisses the need for God's regenerative work, claiming that humans intrinsically have the power to change the direction of their lives and attain righteousness. It sustains this thesis by restricting God's glory to human goals and possibilities. Consequently pelagian spirituality becomes the means for achieving a culturally defined standard of decency by appealing to the individual's self-interest. Because it exalts the individual's achievements, this spirituality divides the saved from the lost on the basis of privilege and perspiration.

For instance, eighteenth-century Britain adapted the Gospel to the unregenerate and produced a self-interested moralism. "Let them be kind, and honest, let them be sober on market days," one pastor proclaimed, "and then they will certainly go to heaven, and will probably reap a good harvest" (Sykes, 1934, p. 262). This boot-strap spirituality scorned the alienated masses, on whom society preyed, as mere "wretches" and "deservedly unhappy" (Swift, 1957, p. 191). In nineteenth-century liberalism, this pelagian spirituality identified "human values with the divine, proclaimed the glad tidings of progress and hallowed man's moral efforts though they led to civil, international and class war" (Niebuhr, 1937, p. 195). Therapeutic America is no different. "A therapist told me," one journalist recently recorded, "that my grief at seeing a homeless man my age was really a feeling of sorrow for myself" (Stafford, 1993, p. 29). Contemporary culture encourages us to indulge ourselves and disregard those unlike us, including the Third World. In sum, pelagianism represents a descent into self-interest and elitism masquerading as morality.

Similar difficulties beset humanitarianism, the most attractive form of unregenerate spirituality. Humanitarianism's vision for rebuilding society replaces God's purposes for humanity with the Western vision of religious and moral toleration. Without a universally verifiable method for identifying true values, the Western world treats religious statements as simply the individual's private right to pursue happiness, however he or she desires. Values are restricted to the arena of private and subjective preferences, prohibited from impacting public life. This division between the public and private arena, which the modern state guards as protective of human rights, reveals secularism's tyranny. For it regards spirituality and morality as tangential to human life and simply a matter of relative taste. Moreover, love is confined to these limits. Love ends where the humanitarian's own rights and freedoms are infringed.

In the midst of this counterfeit spirituality, we need to recover the biblical pattern. Scripture insists that we are slaves to sin, even dead in our sins. Only God can enlist us into His kingdom and rule. What this world needs is not persons who are neighborly but new, due to God's regenerating work. Then, instead of neglecting those outside the bounds of our self-interest, we will demonstrate a readiness to serve unconditionally, gladly making ourselves expendable for Jesus Christ—who alone ought to be the unifying center for humanity.

SPIRITUALITY IS BASED UPON JUSTIFICATION

Humankind's rebellion against God's moral rule issues not only in enslavement but also in God's judgment for guilt. This judgment is not designed to rehabilitate the sinner, but to rectify and reestablish God's righteous rule. The sinner must pay the penalty God's law demands, a penalty as great as the one against whom the sin is directed. Since sin is first and foremost a rejection of God, the penalty is infinite. The more seriously we take God, the more quickly we must concede our desperate situation. We cannot pay the penalty for sin. As Paul confesses, we do not have a righteousness of our own "that comes from the law" (Phil. 3:9). Examined in the light of God's holiness, even the actions of the regenerate appear as "filthy rags" (Isa. 64:6).

Into this predicament God has entered in the person of Jesus whose death was a vicarious and substitutionary sacrifice for us. His cry, "My God, my God, why have you forsaken me?" (Matt. 27:46), is that of the holy and merciful Judge, the "Lord of glory" Himself, accepting the punishment due us (1 Cor. 2:8). By imputing Christ's alien righteousness to all who believe in Jesus, God forgives and embraces us with His love, despite who we are. In Jesus Christ, God declares the ungodly righteous, though they inwardly remain sinners (Rom. 4:5). Fellowship with God, then, is based on God's justification of the ungodly, not on personal progress toward holiness.

The Spiritual Counterfeit of Legalism

The Reformers profoundly contributed to evangelical spirituality by uncovering the reality of justification by faith alone. More often the Law has been transmuted into a ladder by which we merit closer fellowship with God. This is the spiritual counterfeit of legalism, in which the basis for fellowship is conditional on our cooperative moral and spiritual achievements. Foremost in the legalist's mind is oneself: do I come up to God's standard? Many ladders have been devised: ascetic discipline, a life restricted by taboos and enculturated rules, even the performance of external pieties. But the spirituality that lives through these achievements is either crippled by anxiety over continuing sin or elevated to a smug self-righteousness.

If one never attains these standards, anxiety besets the believer. As Luther confessed:

[I]f ever a monk could get to heaven through monastic discipline, I was that monk. . . . And yet my conscience would not give me certainty, but I always doubted and said, "You didn't do that right. You weren't contrite enough. You left that out of your confession." The more I tried to remedy an uncertain, weak and troubled conscience . . . the more I daily found it more uncertain, weaker and more troubled (McGrath, 1988, p. 72).

The experience taught Luther that the "godly trust not to their own righteousness" but "look unto Christ their reconciler, who gave his life for their sins" (Dillenberger, 1961, p. 149).

More often in the history of the church, God's holy demands have been manipulated and trivialized to advance the individual's pride and self-righteousness. Such was Jesus' indictment of the Pharisees: while appearing virtuous by tithing even mint and rue, inside they were "full of greed and wickedness" (Luke 11:39-42). Historically, evangelicals have employed taboos on certain behaviors to identify "true" believers, oblivious to their own materialism and racism.

Self-righteousness short-circuits the Law; it provides solace instead of sorrow. God intends for the Law to shatter the sinner's illusions so we recognize that there is no inherent difference between us and any other, and thereby drive us to Christ. Not only does legalism fail to resolve the problem of righteousness before God, it does not enhance the believer's internal virtue. Most people are too fixated upon securing their own status before God to abandon themselves in love to one another.

Together with Calvin and Luther we must reaffirm the apostolic message. Our hope and salvation are certain, said Luther, because they carry us

out of ourselves, that we should not lean to our own strength, our own conscience, our own feeling, our own person, and our own works, but to that which is without us, that is to say, the promise and truth of God which cannot deceive us (Luther, 1953, p. 372).

SPIRITUALITY LIVES THROUGH FAITH IN JESUS CHRIST

The salvation Jesus Christ has established outside us must take root in us. The Spirit's reviving moves us to trust wholly in

Jesus Christ as Lord and Savior. In the biblical sense, faith means entering into a personal relationship with Christ in which the objective realities of salvation become our own. We apprehend God the Judge, and in repentance we confess our sinfulness and desperation before Him. God in Christ personally encounters us, crying out, "I have not come to call the righteous, but sinners" (Matt. 9:13). The believer flees to Christ and His cross, taking refuge in His righteousness. Empowered by the Spirit, faith lays hold of Jesus' benefits. The role of the Spirit in creating and sustaining fellowship between Christ and the believer is essential to biblical spirituality.

The Spiritual Counterfeit of Formalism

The loss of the Spirit's internal reality constantly endangers spirituality. Without the living reality of faith, an external component supplants Christian spirituality and the spiritual counterfeit of formalism follows. Mistaking the constant repetition of a phrase or sentences for prayer and using religious ceremonies to preserve ethnic identity are classic examples. Scripture warns against this perversion: it is not the sacrifices of burnt offerings but the sacrifices of a broken spirit that are acceptable before God (Ps. 51:16-17).

Fear of formalism motivated the early Reformed Protestants to purify their sanctuaries and ceremonies. The pageantry of ritual, they recognized, may be aesthetically seductive, and while providing the appearance of spirituality actually divert attention from God's revelation. Renewal movements within the sacramental churches readily acknowledge this danger: "Christians do not need a *new* church. But we certainly do need a *renewed* church" (Schreck, 1993, p. 5). Actually, formalism appears under many guises and endangers all churches. As the slogan, "God has no grandchildren," suggests, only the Spirit brings godly sorrow and a new heart committed to Christ.

Within the Reformation churches, the absence of Christ's living presence usually means that faith fixates upon correct knowledge. The evangelical Hermann Sasse exemplified this dogmatism when he refused to sign the Barmen Declaration. Like others at Barmen, Sasse rejected Nazism and their apologists, the "German Christians." But he refused to join in this common cause, because the "Confessing Churches" were not properly constituted to make doctrinal pronouncements for the Lutheran Church (Cochrane, 1962). Dogmatism reigns when Christians are more concerned with advancing their own institutions than countering threats to the life of the church. The Spirit instead revives us to pursue God's ends, not exalt our own.

Other manifestations of formalism include sermons that buttress the tradition and target only the grievous sin of the outsider. God's Word is not "living and active" here, judging the "thoughts and attitudes of the heart" (Heb. 4:12). The unique reality of the Spirit does not consecrate the *status quo*, but takes faith beyond self-interest to Christ's lordship.

Authoritarian forms of Christianity, in which biblical truth is used to shield leadership from criticism, reflect formalism. For the living reality of faith points beyond itself to the life found in our Lord Jesus Christ. Christ alone persuades, leading us by a heart-changing force. Even though colored with a divine aura, authoritarian religion has no power to spiritually persuade; it can only be tyrannical. By contrast, a living faith recognizes that a believer is not simply a servant of the Lord, but belongs to His family, and thus must be treated "better than" a servant, "as a dear brother" (Phile. 16).

SPIRITUALITY IS A PROCESS OF BEING SANCTIFIED

God created humankind, body and soul, in His image. The Christian, as a result, understands historical and embodied creatureliness as decisive for spirituality. Not only is the future judgment based upon "things done . . . in the body" (2 Cor. 5:10; Matt. 25:31-46). More important, the reality of salvation—the acknowledgment of our sin, and the joyous gratitude to Jesus Christ for our justification—carries forth in concrete acts of love to others, exemplifying the love He has shown us. This pattern of crucifying the old nature and rising with Christ to a developing life of holiness outlines the lifelong process for sanctification. The goal of sanctification is to transform believers into Christ's image (Col. 3:10). For no one, as Calvin points out, "can be an heir of heaven who has not first been conformed to the only begotten Son of God" (Calvin, 1961, p. 181). In fact, those without a desire for a holy life lack the fruit and even the evidence of regeneration and justification. While we cannot earn or merit God's forgiveness, we do demonstrate it through deeds of self-giving love.

The church is the indispensable context for sanctification which is carried forward by the Word written and proclaimed, the sacraments, our life together, and bearing the cross through spiritual disciplines. This is where we are prepared for "works of service," become "mature, attaining to the whole measure of the fullness of Christ" (Eph. 4:12-16). But the church is not to be isolated from culture. This body of believers is called to take up the cross and follow Christ to the lost and derelict. Being tangible witnesses of His reconciliation and redemption is integral to the process that transforms us into His image.

The Spiritual Counterfeit of Gnosticism

In our day, the Gospel is being reinterpreted as a means for promoting the individual's own sensuality and self-realization, detached from a concern for others. Here spirituality severs sanctifying from justifying grace. We see this in Heinrich Heine's comment: "Things are admirably arranged. God likes forgiving sins, and I like committing them" (Lovelace, 1988). But this antinomianism—the rejection of God's holy law—is actually rooted much deeper. This counterfeit spirituality reflects the perennial heresy of gnosticism, which disdains embodied existence and offers freedom from the prison of history.

Like the gnostics who troubled the church at Corinth, American culture also elevates the real self above history. At the heart of much American religion is the vision of the self, existing independently of creation, with whom God is ever present. Salvation is gained within "by oneself without ambassador" (Ralph Waldo Emerson) through the knowledge of one's divine origin. An individualism dangerously free from history and others ensues (Bloom, 1992). Responsibility to others and the community is deemed inconsequential to the self. Gnosticism even maintains that actions in history—whether immorality, sensuality, enmities, jealousy (Gal. 5:19ff)—have no repercussions upon the individual. For the real self is invulnerable to creaturely influences.

A recent manifestation of gnostic spirituality was the glitz and greed of the 1980s, which fulfilled individual avarice while scorning the distress and needs of the commonweal. Gnostic traits are also infiltrating evangelical circles. The phenomenon of church-shopping and the reticence to be engaged in a local church reflect an individualistic spirituality rooted in a gnostic outlook. The complacency regarding our wealth and the facile acceptance of cultural mores regarding divorce, and even immorality, demonstrate gnosticism's impact.

This gnostic disdain of creatureliness is futile. We are embodied and inextricably enmeshed in the web of history, which shapes us just as we shape it. Actions have eternal consequences for our character and the destiny of others. That is why Scripture places so much emphasis upon the spiritual disciplines by which we replace the habits of sin with the habits of righteousness by following the example of Christ (Gal. 5:22ff).

Furthermore, this gnostic attitude patently contradicts the biblical pattern of God's action. For in Jesus Christ, God humbled Himself, descended to our place, and was obedient, even to the point of death (Phil. 2). This is the biblical understanding of *agape* love: "not that we loved God, but that he loved us and sent his Son as an atoning sacrifice for our sins" (1 John 4:10). Because Christ has secured our destiny through justification, evangelical spirituality can reflect this readiness to serve others unconditionally, gladly, making oneself expendable for God.

In the contemporary world, we desperately need to listen to Jesus' imperative: "Anyone who does not carry his cross and follow me cannot be my disciple" (Luke 14:27). Our mission is not to elevate or perfect ourselves but to elevate Him who died and rose again so we might live. With John the Baptist our motto should be, "He must increase, but I must decrease" (John 3:30, NKJV). Through this holy vocation of imitating and following Christ, we are being shaped and even remade in His image — "created in Christ Jesus to do good works" (Eph. 2:10).

CONCLUSION

True biblical or evangelical spirituality is an obedient response to the holiness won for us by God's personal incursion into history. Without these words and acts, spirituality reverts to subjectivism and mysticism. Without God's regeneration, spirituality continues to celebrate the sinner's self-aggrandizement, not God's glory. Without God's act of justification on account of Jesus' work, spirituality is hopelessly mired in legalism. Faith is an awakening and empowering by the Spirit for commitment to Jesus Christ and service under the cross; otherwise ritualism, dogmatism, authoritarianism, and other instances of formalism masquerade as faith. If spirituality does not demonstrate Christ's redemptive work through deeds of self-giving love, it reflects a gnostic disdain for others and this world. In contrast to these counterfeit spiritualities, biblical spirituality involves living out one's life through faith in Jesus Christ, appropriating the gift of redeeming grace in trust and obedience for service in His kingdom.

For Further Reading
(compiled by Timothy R. Phillips)

Bloesch, D. (1981). *Faith and its counterfeits.* Downers Grove, IL: Inter-Varsity. Excellent work, expands this chapter and includes other historical illustrations.

Bloesch, D. (1988). *The crisis of piety.* Colorado Springs: Helmers & Howard. Chapter 7, "Two Types of Spirituality," pp. 95–124, provides a helpful differentiation of mystical and Christian spiritualities.

Bloesch, D. (1988). *The struggle of prayer.* Colorado Springs: Helmers and Howard. Theological explication of prayer, the heart of Christian spirituality, with careful consideration of its distortions.

Bloom, H. (1992). *The American religion.* New York: Simon & Schuster. Helpful analysis of the gnosticism implicit in much American belief.

Heiler, F. (1958). *Prayer.* (S. McComb, Trans.). New York: Oxford Univ. Press. A classic analysis of prayer, distinguishing prophetic, mystical, ritualistic, and philosophical types.

Lovelace, R. (1979). *Dynamics of spiritual life.* Downers Grove, IL: Inter-Varsity. Explicates Christian spirituality's theological foundation in regeneration, justification, and sanctification, and incisively analyzes their distortions.

Niebuhr, H.R. (1937). *The kingdom of God in America.* New York: Harper & Row. Classic study of the devolution of Puritan spirituality into pelagianism.

Nygren, A. (1982). *Agape and eros.* (P. Watson, Trans.). Chicago: Univ. of Chicago Press. Excellent work, explicating Christian love over against its competitors.

Peters, T. (1991). *The cosmic self: A penetrating look at today's new age movement.* San Francisco: HarperCollins. A helpful and incisive analysis of the New Age.

GOD IS MOST GLORIFIED IN US WHEN WE ARE MOST SATISFIED IN HIM
John Piper

The biblical aim of life is the glory of God: "So whether you eat or drink or whatever you do, do it all for the glory of God" (1 Cor. 10:31). The aim of spiritual maturity is to magnify God's glory for people to see and admire. But the surprising thing for many of us is to realize that we magnify God's glory not by supplementing it with effort, but by savoring it with joy.

The way to glorify a self-replenishing, all-satisfying mountain spring is not to add buckets of brackish water from our valley streams, but to kneel down and drink until we are refreshed and happy and strong. God is most glorified in us when we are most satisfied in Him. Therefore the essence of all biblical spirituality is being satisfied with all that God is for us in Christ.

This is extremely good news because it means that our passion to be satisfied and *God's* purpose to be glorified are not at odds. We can leave behind once and for all the fear that our quest for joy is self-exalting and God-belittling. It is the opposite. Our quest confesses that we are empty and God is full. We are needy and He is rich. We are sick and He is the great physician. We are hungry, and He is the Bread of Life. We are thirsty, and He is Living Water. The quest for joy in God is not self-exalting; it humbles us as poverty-stricken and honors God as all-sufficient. We may pursue this quest with a clear conscience and with God's approval.

This pursuit is the process of Christian spiritual formation. Being satisfied with God is the aim and essence of that formation. It's the *aim* of spiritual formation because the glory of

God is the aim of all things. And it's the *essence* of spiritual formation because what makes every action spiritual is the Spirit-given element of satisfaction with God at its core. In other words, satisfaction with all that God is for us in Christ is both the *motive* that prompts the pursuit of spiritual formation and the *matter* that makes up the heart of that formation. Joy in God is the heart of spirituality and its final reward.

We can show this from Scripture by looking briefly at some of the steps of spiritual formation.

CONTRITION

Simon Peter's contrition in Luke 5:8-10 has a startling source. Jesus had told the fishermen to push out into the deep and let down their nets for a catch.

Peter protested, "Master, we've worked hard all night and haven't caught anything" (5:5). But he obeyed (unenthusiastically) anyway. When the nets went down they filled with so many fish that they started to break. Peter's response was remarkable, very unlike our modern self-enhancing response to grace. "When Simon Peter saw this, he fell at Jesus' knees and said, 'Go away from me, Lord; I am a sinful man!' " (5:8)

What is remarkable here is that a miracle of grace, not a word of judgment, broke Peter's heart and brought him to contrition. There is a great discovery we can make here.

When David Brainerd preached to the Indians in the woods of Crossweeksung, New Jersey in 1745, he discovered that brokenheartedness for sin was aroused in an unexpected way. He wrote in his journal on August 9:

> There were many tears among them while I was discoursing publicly . . . some were much affected with a few words spoken to them in a powerful manner, which caused the persons to cry out in anguish of soul, although I spoke not a word of terror, but on the contrary, set before them the fullness and all-sufficiency of Christ's merits, and his willingness to save all that come to him; and thereupon pressed them to come without delay (Pettit, 1985, p. 310).

Again on November 30 he preached on Luke 16:19-26 concerning the rich man and Lazarus.

> The Word made powerful impressions upon many in the assembly, especially while I discoursed of the blessedness of Lazarus "in Abraham's bosom. . . ." They have almost always appeared much more affected with the comfortable than the dreadful truths of God's Word. And that which has distressed many of them under convictions, is that they found they wanted, and could not obtain, the happiness of the godly (Pettit, 1985, p. 342).

This points to something very remarkable about the spiritual basis of evangelical contrition, the beginning of all true spiritual formation. The basis of contrition is the discovery of joy. The tears of these Indians flowed not so much from fear of punishment as from loss of God's grace. Not so much because of the threatened pain in hell as because of the forfeited pleasure of heaven. The quickening of spiritual taste for the pleasures at God's right hand (Ps. 16:11) created contrition for the folly of sin.

However, not all weeping over sin is evangelical contrition. It is possible to weep over sin not because we love God and want to enjoy all that He is for us in Christ, but because we fear punishment. Many a criminal will weep when his sentence is read, not because he has come to love righteousness but because his freedom to do more unrighteousness is being taken away. That kind of weeping is not evangelical contrition.

What Brainerd discovered is that the root of true contrition for sin is the awakening of joy in God. Savoring God precedes sorrow for falling short of His glory. It was a strange discovery: awakened pleasure is the essence of evangelical penitence. And yet it is not so strange, for everyone knows a man must fall in love with a woman before estrangement truly hurts.

REPENTANCE AND FAITH

Besides contrition, repentance and faith are rooted in this same awakening of joy in God. Repentance and faith are opposite sides of the same coin: repentance turns from sin and faith turns to God. There cannot be one without the other. What we discover from Scripture is that the essential thing about this turning is that it is owing to a change in what one takes pleasure in.

In Jeremiah 2:12-13 God describes the condition of sinners: "Be appalled at this, O heavens, and shudder with great horror," declares the Lord. "My people have committed two sins: They have forsaken me, the spring of living water, and have dug their own cisterns, broken cisterns that cannot hold water."

What is the source of repentance implied in these verses? It is awakening to the fact that you can't satisfy the thirst of your soul at a broken cistern. The essence of sin is failing to experience God as a spring of living, satisfying water. *The essence of repentance is turning from the broken cisterns of the world back to the all-satisfying fountain of God.* The root of that turning is the awakening of a new taste for God that makes Him more desirable than anything in the universe.

Faith is rooted in this same awakening. In John 6:35 Jesus says, "I am the bread of life. He who comes to me will never go hungry and *he who believes in me will never be thirsty.*" This promise shows that faith means being satisfied with Jesus. It is a spiritual drinking of all that God is for us in Christ.

"Whoever drinks of the water I give him will never thirst. . . . If a man is thirsty, let him come to me and drink. Whoever believes in me, as the Scripture has said, streams of living water will flow from within him" (John 7:37-38). Believing in Jesus means having the deepest cravings of our hearts satisfied with all that God is for us in Him.

For the Apostles Paul and Peter, joy was at the very heart of genuine faith. Paul said, for example, "Not that we lord it over your *faith,* but we work with you for your *joy,* because it is by *faith* that you stand firm" (2 Cor. 1:24). Joy is virtually interchangeable with faith in that verse. Again he said to the Philippian church, "I know that I shall abide and continue with you all for your furtherance and *joy of faith*" (Phil. 1:25, KJV). The phrase "joy of faith" shows that joy is enmeshed in the experience of faith. Romans 15:13 shows that joy is experienced in the act of believing: "May the God of hope fill you with all *joy* and peace *in believing*" (RSV). Similarly Peter says, *"Believing, you rejoice* with joy unspeakable and full of glory" (1 Peter 1:8, NKJV).

Faith cannot be defined biblically without including this dimension of delight. It means being satisfied with all that God is for us in Jesus. Definitions of faith limited to endorsing doctrinal facts or making religious decisions are one of the reasons that so little spiritual formation follows from such evangelism. The transforming power of faith is precisely the triumph of true pleasure over the fleeting pleasures of sin.

OVERCOMING SIN

The battle to overcome sin in our lives is a battle to stay satisfied with all that God is for us in Jesus. In other words it is a "fight of the faith" (1 Tim. 6:12, NASB). We fight the fleeting pleasures of sin with the long-term, infinitely superior pleasures of God.

Hebrews 11:24-26 gives Moses as an illustration of how faith overcomes sin in this way: "By faith Moses, when he had grown up, refused to be known as the son of Pharaoh's daughter. He chose to be mistreated along with the people of God rather than to enjoy the pleasures of sin for a short time. He regarded disgrace for the sake of Christ as of greater value than the treasures of Egypt, because he was looking ahead to his reward."

The power of sin was broken in Moses' life "by faith." But what did that mean? How was the power of sin's pleasure broken? It was broken because Moses looked to the reward. That is, he contemplated how short and inadequate the pleasures of Egypt; then he contemplated how lasting and deep the pleasures at God's right hand (Ps. 16:11). Overcoming sin "by faith" meant overcoming it "by a greater satisfaction in God."

THE SACRIFICE OF LOVE

This same satisfaction in all that God is for us not only overcomes the alluring power of sin; it also impels us into acts of sacrificial love. Paul gives an example of this in the Macedonian churches. "And now, brothers, we want you to know about the grace that God has given the Macedonian churches. Out of the most severe trial, their overflowing joy and their extreme poverty welled up in rich generosity'' (2 Cor. 8:1-2).

Where did their "rich generosity" come from? Not from their material wealth. They were in "extreme poverty." It came from "their overflowing joy." That is exactly what the text says, "Their overflowing joy . . . welled up in rich generosity." And what caused this overflow of joy? Answer: "the grace God has given." In other words, because of God's grace, the Macedonian Christians were overflowingly satisfied with God and could sacrifice even the little material substance they had for the poor.

God is very pleased with this kind of generosity—the kind that comes from overflowing joy. In the very next chapter Paul makes this explicit: "Each man should give what he has decided in his heart to give, not reluctantly or under compulsion, *for God loves a cheerful giver*" (2 Cor. 9:7). The kind of love that God delights in is the kind that comes from a delight in Him.

Love is costly. But the cost bears no comparison to the reward. And it is not unloving to believe this and to bank on it. Jesus said, "Love your enemies, do good to them, and lend to them without expecting to get anything back. *Then your reward will be great,* and you will be sons of the Most High, because he is kind to the ungrateful and wicked" (Luke 6:35). The power to expect nothing in return on earth is the assurance of the reward of infinite satisfaction in heaven with God.

An actual instance of how this assurance of joy in God produces self-sacrificing love is given in Hebrews 10:32-35.

> Remember those earlier days after you had received the light, when you stood your ground in a great contest in the face of suffering. Sometimes you were publicly exposed to insult and persecution; at other times you stood side by side with those who were so treated. You sympathized with those in prison and joyfully *accepted the confiscation of your property, because you knew that you yourselves had better and lasting possessions.* So do not throw away your confidence which will be richly rewarded.

Evidently the early Christians had been faced with a situation in which some of them were in prison. They had to decide, "Do we go underground and play it safe? Or do we go visit our brothers and sisters in prison and risk the loss of our property and our lives?" They decided to visit the prison. The result was "the confiscation" of their property. But this did not deter them. In fact, they "joyfully accepted" it. Where did they get the power to do that? From the assurance that they had "better and lasting possessions." They were satisfied with all that God was for them in Jesus Christ. This joy was the power that impelled them into sacrificial service for the sake of suffering saints in need.

Jesus said that "the kingdom of heaven is like treasure hidden in a field. When a man found it, he hid it again, and then *in his joy* went and sold all he had and bought that field" (Matt. 13:44). The point of this parable is that the presence and rule of God in our lives is more valuable than everything else in the world. It means that the "sacrifice" of love may look radical to the world, but in fact it is no ultimate sacrifice. It is sustained and empowered by the deepest satisfaction possible — satisfaction with all that God is for us in Jesus.

Peter once said to Jesus, "We have left everything and followed you!" This sounded a bit self-pitying. So Jesus replied, "I tell you the truth . . . no one who has left home or brothers or sisters or mother or father or children or fields for me and the gospel will fail to receive a hundred times as much in this present age . . . and in the age to come, eternal life" (Mark 10:29-30). The point of Jesus' response is to remind Peter that his "sacrifice" in "leaving everything" is not an ultimate sacrifice. There is no room for self-pity in the sacrifice of Christian love.

This has been the experience of all the saints that have sacrificed most in the cause of Christ. David Livingstone gave his testimony to this effect on December 4, 1857. The great pioneer missionary to Africa was making an appeal to the students of Cambridge University.

People talk of the sacrifice I have made in spending so much of my life in Africa. . . . Is that a sacrifice which brings its own blest reward in healthful activity, the consciousness of doing good, peace of mind, and a bright hope of a glorious destiny hereafter? Away with the word in such a view, and with such a thought! It *is emphatically no sacrifice.* Say rather it is a privilege. Anxiety, sickness, suffering, or danger, now and then, with a foregoing of the common conveniences and charities of this life, may make us pause, and cause the spirit to waver, and the soul to sink; but let this only be for a moment. All these are nothing when compared with the glory which shall be revealed in and for us. *I never made a sacrifice* (Winter & Hawthorne, 1981, p. 259).

The sacrifices of love are at the heart of spiritual formation. But the spring of these acts is not merely a sense of duty, but a sense of delight in all that God is for us in Christ. Which means that the spring of love is faith. "The only thing that counts is *faith expressing itself in love"* (Gal. 5:6). And the meaning of that faith is "being sure of what we hope for" (Heb. 11:1). And that assurance of eternal joy in God is the power to endure hardship for the sake of love. "Let us fix our eyes on Jesus . . . who *for the joy set before him endured the cross"* (Heb. 12:2).

PRAYER

How shall we become the kind of people so satisfied in God that we can "let goods and kindred go, this mortal life also" in a lifestyle of simplicity and love? One crucial part of the answer is prayer.

If we long to experience this freeing satisfaction in God, we should ask for it the way Moses did in Psalm 90:14-15: "Satisfy us in the morning with your unfailing love, that we may sing for joy and be glad all our days. Make us glad for as many days as you have afflicted us, for as many years as we have seen trouble."

If we want to be satisfied with God's love and be glad in His goodness, we should cry out for it in prayer. We often have not because we ask not (James 4:2).

Prayer is designed to fulfill our joy and give the glory to God. That's why Jesus said, "Until now you have not asked for anything in my name. Ask and you will receive, *and your joy will be complete."* "I will do whatever you ask in my name, *so that the Son may bring glory to the Father"* (John 16:24; 14:13). Prayer is the admission of our weakness and the Father's strength, our emptiness and His fullness, our need and His all-sufficiency. That's why prayer is designed to give us the joy and give God the glory.

MEDITATION ON GOD'S WORD

Prayer does one of its most deep and satisfying works when it intersects with the Word of God in our lives. Without prayer the Word lies before us as a blank page. We must cry out again and again with the psalmist, "Open my eyes that I may see wonderful things in your law" (Ps. 119:18). "Praise be to you, O Lord; teach me your decrees" (Ps. 119:12).

When God draws near to a person and answers these prayers, the Word becomes a source of life-changing delight. "His delight is in the law of the Lord, and on his law he meditates day and night" (Ps. 1:2).

"The precepts of the Lord are right, giving joy to the heart" (Ps. 19:8). "The ordinances of the Lord are sure and altogether righteous. They are more precious than gold, than much pure gold; they are sweeter than honey, than honey from the comb" (Ps. 19:9-10).

Meditating on the Word of God in a spirit of prayer is the primary means of replenishing the satisfaction in God which frees us for sacrificial love. The Word gives life (James 1:18; 1 Peter 1:23); it begets and sustains faith (Rom. 10:17; John 20:31); it encourages hope (Rom. 15:4); it sets us free (John 8:32); it works holiness (John 17:17); it revives the soul (Ps. 19:7); it gives light to the eyes (Ps. 19:8); it nourishes assurance (1 John 5:13); it defeats the devil (Eph. 6:16; 1 John 2:14).

It is no wonder that Jesus said of His own words, "These things I have spoken to you that my joy may be in you and that your joy may be full" (John 15:11, RSV). And no wonder Jeremiah and the psalmists exulted to know and "eat" the Word of God. "Oh, how I love your law! I meditate on it all day long" (Ps. 119:97). "Your statutes are my heritage forever; they are the joy of my heart" (Ps. 119:111). "When your words came, I ate them; they were my joy and my heart's delight" (Jer. 15:16).

This experience has been true for God's people all through the centuries. Consider, for example, the story of "Little Bilney," one of the early English Reformers, born in 1495. He was outwardly rigorous in his efforts at religion. But there was no life within. Then he happened to receive a Latin translation of Erasmus' Greek New Testament.

> I chanced upon this sentence of St. Paul (O most sweet and comfortable sentence to my soul!) in 1 Timothy 1: "It is a true saying, and worthy of all men to be embraced, that Christ Jesus came into the world to save sinners; of whom I am the chief and principal." This one sentence, through God's instruction and inward working, which I did not then perceive, did so exhilarate my heart, being before wounded with the guilt of my sins, and being almost in despair, that . . . immediately I . . . felt a marvelous comfort and quietness, insomuch that "my bruised bones leaped for joy." After this, the Scriptures began to be more pleasant to me than the honey or the honey comb (Anderson, 1981, p. 25).

Another great man of prayer and faith discovered the satisfying and sanctifying power of the Word in his own devotions. George Mueller lived from 1805 to 1898 and is famous for establishing orphanages in England and for depending on God for all his needs. In his *Autobiography* he told how he discovered using the Scriptures to satisfy his soul every morning.

> I saw more clearly than ever, that the first great and primary business to which I ought to attend every day was, to have my soul happy in the Lord. The first thing to be concerned about was not, how much I might serve the Lord, how I might glorify the Lord; but how I might get my soul into a happy state, and how my inner man might be nourished. . . .

> I saw, that the most important thing I had to do was to give myself to the reading of the Word of God and to

meditation on it, that thus my heart might be comforted, encouraged, warned, reproved, instructed; and that thus, whilst meditating, my heart might be brought into experimental communion with the Lord. I began therefore, to meditate on the New Testament, from the beginning, early in the morning (Bergen, 1906, pp. 152–154).

CONCLUSION

Having our souls "happy in the Lord," as Mueller says, is not mere icing on the cake of Christian commitment. It is the spring of all true spiritual formation, all true Christlikeness, all true holiness.

The quest for holiness and the quest for happiness are one. And the good news is that they are not at odds. Just as there is a holiness without which we will not see the Lord (Heb. 12:14), so there is a happiness without which we are not holy. This happiness is the happiness of faith—a happiness of being satisfied with all that God is for us in Jesus. It is not glib or trite or superficial. It is not naive about the pain and suffering in the lives of the saints. It knows the apostolic experience of "sorrowful, yet always rejoicing" (2 Cor. 6:10). It knows how to "weep with those who weep." But it insists that the weeping of compassion is the weeping of joy impeded in the extension of itself to another.

This holy happiness cannot be finally shaken because it is rooted in God and in the glory that will surely be revealed. "I consider that our present sufferings are not worth comparing with the glory that will be revealed in us" (Rom. 8:18). Thus Paul says, "We rejoice in the hope of the glory of God" (Rom. 5:2). And when he boils it down to its essence he simply says, "We also rejoice in God" (Rom. 5:11). This joy in God honors God, just as buying my wife a gift out of delight honors her more than if I buy it out of duty. A fountain is glorified best when we drink to satisfaction. This is the sum of the matter: God is most glorified in us when we are most satisfied in Him.

For Further Reading

Lloyd-Jones, M. (1965). *Spiritual depression: Its causes and cures.* Grand Rapids: Eerdmans. This great preacher from a generation ago shows us from Scripture how to "talk to ourselves" with truth about God, rather than "listen to ourselves." His burden is to build a more joyful, and therefore more powerful and winsome, church for God's glory.

Piper, J. (1987). *Desiring God: Meditations of a Christian hedonist.* Portland, OR: Multnomah. A good book for anyone serious about maturing in faith. This book sketches out the purpose for Christian living and in doing so challenges many stereotypes about the spiritual or deeper life. It is a call to living a life built on the foundation of enjoying God.

Richards, L. (1987). *A practical theology of spirituality.* Grand Rapids: Zondervan. A very readable and practical introduction into the whole area of developing a deeper spiritual life.

Whitney, D. (1991). *Spiritual disciplines for the Christian life.* Colorado Springs: NavPress. An evangelical survey of the major disciplines. The book places a strong emphasis on the practice of the disciplines and their biblical rationale. It is particularly strong on topics related to personal Bible study and meditation.

SEVEN

LONGING FOR EDEN AND SINNING ON THE WAY TO HEAVEN*
Larry Crabb

This chapter is adapted from Larry Crabb's book Inside Out. *In this chapter he provides a helpful critique of some contemporary Christian teachings which offer believers a relief from our current afflictions, if they perform certain duties and exercise faith. However, Crabb asserts that the Bible reserves such relief for heaven alone and that as humans we are a thirsty people who long for the quality relationships, meaningful work, and justice which we were designed to enjoy in Eden. Crabb believes that many Christians think that their various problems of living stem from following these thirsts and that if they could extinguish their longings they would be free from pain and various problems. According to Scripture the problem is not with our thirsts, but with the strategies we use to meet them. There is nothing intrinsically wrong with a thirst for human intimacy, but seeking to meet that thirst through casual sex rather than through time with God and friendships is wrong. The distinction between the thirsts and the strategies is important because some well-meaning teachers tell believers to stop being thirsty rather than showing them better strategies for meeting their thirsts.*

Modern Christianity, in dramatic reversal of its biblical form, promises to relieve the pain of living in a fallen world. The

---

*From: Larry Crabb (1988). *Inside Out*. Colorado Springs: NavPress. Used by permission.

message, whether it is from fundamentalists requiring us to live by a favored set of rules or from charismatics urging a deeper surrender to the Spirit's power, is too often the same: The promise of bliss is for NOW! Complete satisfaction can be ours this side of heaven.

Some speak of the joys of fellowship and obedience, others of a rich awareness of their value and worth. The language may be reassuringly biblical or it may reflect the influence of current psychological thought. Either way, the point of living the Christian life has shifted from knowing and serving Christ until He returns to soothing, or at least learning to ignore, the ache in our souls.

THE FALSE HOPE:
WE NEED NOT FEEL OUR DISAPPOINTMENTS

We are told, sometimes explicitly but more often by example, that it is simply not necessary to feel the impact of family tensions, frightening possibilities, or discouraging news. An inexpressible joy is available which, rather than *supporting* us through hard times, can actually *eliminate* pressure, worry, and pain from our experience. Life may have its rough spots, but the reality of Christ's presence and blessing can so thrill our soul that pain is virtually unfelt. It simply is not necessary to wrestle with internal struggle and disorder. Just trust, surrender, persevere, obey.

The effect of such teaching is to blunt the painful reality of what it is like to live as part of an imperfect, and sometimes evil, community. We learn to pretend that we feel now what we cannot feel until heaven.

But not all of us are good at playing the game. Those whose integrity makes such pretense difficult sometimes worry over their apparent lack of faith. "Why don't I feel as happy and together as others? Something must be wrong with my spiritual life." To make matters worse, these people of integrity often appear less mature and their lives less inviting than folks more skilled at denial. And churches tend to reward their members who more convincingly create the illusion of intactness by parading them as examples of what every Christian should be.

PAIN IS UNIVERSAL

Beneath the surface of everyone's life, especially the more mature, is an ache that will not go away. It can be ignored, disguised, mislabeled, or submerged by a torrent of activity, but it will not disappear. And for good reason. We were designed to enjoy a better world than this. And until that better world comes along, we will groan for what we do not have. *An aching soul is evidence not of neurosis or spiritual immaturity, but of realism.*

The experience of groaning, however, is precisely what modern Christianity so often tries to help us escape. The gospel of health and wealth appeals to our legitimate longing for relief by skipping over the call to endure suffering. Faith becomes the means not to learning contentment regardless of circumstances, but rather to rearranging one's circumstances to provide more comfort.

Orthodox Bible preachers rarely are lured into proclaiming a prosperity gospel, but still they appeal to that same desire for relief from groaning. They tell us that more knowledge, more commitment, more giving, more prayer—some combination of Christian disciplines—will eliminate our need to struggle with deeply felt realities. Yet there is no escape from an aching soul, only denial of it. The promise of one day being with Jesus in a perfect world is the Christian's only hope for complete relief. Until then we either groan or pretend we do not.

The effect of widespread pretense, whether maintained by rigidly living on the surface of life or by being consumed with emotionalism, has been traumatic for the church. Rather than being salt and light, we have become a theologically diverse community of powerless Pharisees, penetrating very little of society because we refuse to grapple honestly with the experience of life.

WE LACK CONFIDENCE IN CHRIST

Beneath much of our claim to orthodoxy, there is a moral cowardice that reflects poorly on our confidence in Christ. We trust Him to forgive our sins and to keep us more or less in line as a community of decent people, but is He enough to deal with things as they really are? Do we know how to face the confusing reality of a world where good parents sometimes have rebellious children and bad parents produce committed missionaries? Can we plunge into the disturbing facts of life and emerge, as the writer of the seventy-third Psalm did, with a renewed confidence in God and a deeper thirst for Him? Can we enter those hidden inner regions of our soul where emptiness is more the reality than a consuming awareness of His presence and where an honest look reveals that self-serving motives stain even our noblest deeds? Is Christ enough to deal with that kind of internal mess? Or is it better to never look at all that and just get on with the Christian life?

When we reflect deeply on how life really is, both inside our soul and outside in our world, a quiet terror threatens to overwhelm us. We worry that we simply will not be able to make it if we face all that is there. In those moments, retreat into denial does not seem cowardly, it seems necessary and smart. Just keep going, get your act together, stop feeling sorry for yourself, renew your commitment to trust God, get more serious about obedience. Things really are not as bad as you intuitively sense they are. You have simply lost your perspective and must regain it through more time in the Word and increased moral effort.

There is something terribly attractive about knowing what to do to make things better. If we can explain why we feel so bad in terms of something specific and correctable (like not spending enough time in devotions), then we can do something about it. And we like that. Nothing is more terrifying than staring at a problem for which we have no solutions under our direct control. Trusting another is perhaps the most difficult requirement of the Christian life. We hate to be dependent because we have learned to trust no one, not fully. We know better. Everyone in whom we have placed our confidence has in some way disappointed us. To trust fully, we conclude, is suicide.

WE PROVIDE OUR OWN RELIEF

The fallen person takes command of his or her own life, determined above all else to prove who is adequate for the job. And like the teen who feels rich until he starts paying for his own car insurance, we remain confident of our ability to manage life until we face the reality of our own soul. Nothing is more humbling than the recognition of (1) a deep thirst that makes us entirely dependent on someone else for satisfaction and (2) a depth of corruption that stains everything we do—even our efforts to reform—with selfishness. To realistically face what is true within us puts us in touch with a level of helplessness we do not care to experience.

A woman admitted to herself that she had lost all romantic feeling for her kind and thoughtful husband. On the advice of her pastor, she was praying to regain her warmth while at the same time moving toward her husband in chosen obedience. She wanted to believe that the spark was rekindling, but it was not. She then tried to convince herself that it did not matter how she felt; obedience was all that counted. But her lack of romantic feeling for a man who treated her well troubled her deeply. There was nothing she knew to do that could change her internal condition. She felt hopeless.

If awareness of what is inside forces me to admit that I am utterly dependent on resources outside my control for the kind of change I desire, if helplessness really is at the core of my existence, I prefer to live on the surface of things. It is far more comfortable. To admit I cannot deal with all that is within me strikes a death blow to my claim to self-sufficiency. To deny the frightening realities within my soul seems as necessary to life as breathing.

It must be said that this state of affairs is thoroughly understandable. We do not like to hurt. And there is no worse pain for fallen people than facing an emptiness we cannot fill. To enter into pain seems rather foolish when we can run from it through denial. We simply cannot get it through our head that, with a nature twisted by sin, the route to joy always involves the very worst sort of internal suffering we can imagine. We rebel at that thought. We were not designed to hurt. The physical and personal capacities to feel that God built into us were intended to provide pleasure, like good health and close relationships. When they do not, when our head throbs with tension and our heart is broken by rejection, we want relief. With deep passion, we long to experience what we were designed to enjoy.

In the midst of that groaning, the idea that relief may not come is unbearable. It is horrible. How can we continue to live with the ache in our soul provoked by a daughter's abortion or a wife's coldness? How can life go on with a husband who looks for every opportunity to be mean while convinced of his own righteousness? How do we cope with disfiguring illness, with guilt over the bitterness we feel as we care for an elderly, helpless parent, with an income that never lets us get ahead?

Into that personal agitation comes the soothing message of modern Christianity: *Relief is available!* Either the disturbing elements in your world will settle down when you develop enough faith, or you can enter a level of spiritual experience in which the struggle to cope is replaced by a fullness of soul. Satisfaction, one way or another, is available, and it is available now.

Better still, it is within our power to arrange for the relief we long for. We can learn to claim promises with more faith; we can classify sin into manageable categories and then scrupulously avoid it, thereby guaranteeing the blessings we covet; we can practice new forms of meditation; we can become more involved in church activities and Bible study. *Something we can do will advance us to a level of spirituality that eliminates pain and struggle as ongoing, deeply felt realities.*

DIGGING OUR OWN WELLS

The appeal is great. When our souls are thirsty, we can dig our own well. Christian leaders provide the shovels and point out likely spots to dig, and off we go. Discipleship programs, witnessing strategies, Bible memory systems, new forms of community, richer experiences of the Spirit, renewed commitment: the list goes on. Good things to do, but the energy to pursue them is often supplied by the expectation that I will find water that will end all thirst. No more struggle, disappointment, or heartache. Heaven now.

Not everyone, of course, teaches this theology. But many do, and many more communicate the same hope by neither sharing honestly their own current struggles nor realistically addressing the struggles of others. It is tempting to stay removed from the problems for which we have no ready answers. It is much easier to preach that we need less counseling and more obedience than to involve ourself in the messy details of life where obedience comes hard. One result of extricating ourself from the tangled complexity of life is simplistic preaching that fails to deal with life as it is. Rather than penetrating life with liberating truth, such preaching maintains a conspiracy of pretense that things are better than they are or ever can be until Christ returns. We end up unprepared to live but strengthened in our denial.

A deeply ingrained passion for independence, a legacy left to us by Adam, and a legitimate thirst to enjoy the perfect relationships for which we were designed make us respond eagerly to the hope that heaven's joys are available now—and on demand. When teenagers rebel, hurting parents would love to believe there is a way to replace the terrible heartache with happy confidence. When singleness seems more a prison than an opportunity for expanded service, it would be wonderful to quickly transform the loneliness into a contentment that feels no loss.

But maybe these understandable desires are not within reach. Perhaps the anchor that enables people to weather life's storms and grow through them is gratitude for what happened at the cross of Christ and passionate confidence in what will yet take place at His coming. Could it be that the only source of real stability in the *present* (a kind of stability that does not require the character-weakening mechanism of denial) is appreciation for the *past* and hope for the *future?* Maybe the presence of Christ now, in His Word and Spirit, can be enjoyed only to the degree that it causes us to take both a backward and a forward look.

But such talk seems hopelessly non-immediate, a pie-in-the-sky kind of comfort. We want something *now!* And something is available now, something wonderful and real. But we will find only its counterfeit until we realize that the intensity of our disappointment with life coupled with a Christianity that promises to relieve that disappointment now has radically shifted the foundation of our faith. No longer do we resolutely bank everything on the coming of a nail-scarred Christ for His groaning but faithfully waiting people. Our hope has switched to a responsive Christ who satisfies His hurting people by quickly granting them the relief they demand.

That hope, however, is a lie, an appealing but grotesque perversion of the good news of Christ. That lie has led thousands of seeking people into either a powerless lifestyle of denial and fabricated joy or a turning away from Christianity in disillusionment and disgust. That lie blocks the path to the deep transformation of character available now. *We can* enter into a rich awareness of being alive as a Christian; *we can* taste His goodness in a way that whets our appetite for more. But to demand that our groaning end before heaven keeps us from all that is available now.

GOD WANTS TO CHANGE US

God wants to change us into people who are truly noble, people who reflect an unswerving confidence in who equips us to face all of life and still remain faithful. Spirituality built on pretense is not spirituality at all. God wants us to be courageous people who are deeply bothered by the horrors of living as part of a fallen race, people who look honestly at every struggle, who feel overwhelmed by what we see, yet emerge prepared to live. Scarred, still troubled, but deeply loving. When the fact is faced that life is profoundly disappointing, the only way to make it is to learn to love. And only those who are no longer consumed with finding satisfaction now are able to love. Only when we commit our yearnings for perfect joy to a Father we have learned to deeply trust are we free to live for others despite the reality of a perpetual ache.

This chapter is not about relief; it is about change. Its message is not, "Here's how to feel better now." Rather, it deals with the route to transformation of character.

That route, it should be noted, takes a surprising twist that cannot be seen from the narrow gate leading into it. After traveling the route for some time (one never knows how much time, but certainly more than those who are committed to immediate relief would ever endure), something unexpected and wonderful occurs. A hint of one's substance develops and a glimpse of what it means to be *alive* awakens the soul to its unrealized potential for joy. And that glimpse so clearly reflects the beauty of Christ's involvement with us that a self-sufficient pride in one's value becomes unthinkable.

The ache remains and even intensifies as more of the fallen reality of our own soul is exposed. But the notion that our present suffering is nothing in comparison with the glory ahead begins to make sense.

I am not very far along the path to deeply felt life and joy in Christ, but I think I am on it. Consider with me what is available in this life: a change of character that enables us to taste enough of God now to whet our appetite for the banquet later.

The kind of internal change that permits a richer taste of God is possible, but it requires surgery. The disease blocking our enjoyment of God has spread beyond the point where more effort to think right will be enough. And there is no anesthetic as the knife penetrates our souls.

DEEP LONGINGS AND WRONG STRATEGIES

In the rest of this chapter, I want to get us started on our inward look. A helpful place to begin is with a record of what God saw when He looked deeply into the hearts of His people during a time in their history when they were slipping far away from Him. Listen to His comments in Jeremiah 2:13: "My people have committed two sins: They have forsaken me, the spring of living water, and have dug their own cisterns, broken cisterns that cannot hold water."

Notice two observations that text suggests. First, *people are thirsty.* Although the fact of universal thirst is not directly stated, it is clearly assumed. Frequent references to thirsty hearts in the Bible, as well as to the fact that people were designed to enjoy satisfaction available only in God, support the idea that every person is thirsty. We all long for that which God designed us to enjoy: tension-free relationships filled with deep, loving acceptance and with opportunities to make a difference to someone else. Observe carefully that in our text, God assumes His people are thirsty but He never condemns them for that thirst. Thirst is not the problem. Neither of the two sins He rebukes them for involves the fact that people are thirsty.

Second, *people are moving in wrong directions in response*

to their thirst. They refuse to trust God to look after their thirst. Instead, they insist on maintaining control of finding their own satisfaction. They are all moving about determined to satisfy the longings of their hearts by picking up a shovel, looking for a likely spot to dig, and then searching for a fulfillment they can generate. To put it simply, people want to run their own lives. The fallen person is both terrified of vulnerability and committed to maintaining independence.

The human race got off on a seriously wrong foot when Eve yielded to Satan's lie that more satisfaction was available if she took matters into her own hands. When Adam joined her in looking for life outside of God's revealed will, he infected all his descendants with the disease of self-management. Now no one seeks after God in an effort to find life. The most natural thing for us to do is to develop strategies for finding life that reflect our commitment to depending on our own resources. Simple trust is out of fashion. Self-protection has become the norm.

The Scriptures consistently expose people as both thirsty and foolish. We long for the satisfaction we were built to enjoy, but we all move away from God to find it. An inside look, then, can be expected to uncover two elements imbedded deeply in our heart: (1) thirst or *deep longings* for what we do not have; and (2) stubborn independence reflected in *wrong strategies* for finding the life we desire.

It is with an understanding of these two fundamental elements that we can productively explore beneath the surface of our everyday problems. The first element, deep longings, reflects our humanness and all the dignity accorded to us as bearers of God's image. We long for a quality of relationship and meaning that no other creature has the capacity to enjoy. We were designed to richly enjoy the person of God as well as His provisions.

The second element, wrong strategies, exists because we are sinful. Only foolish, rebellious, proud people would move away from the Source of life in search of fulfillment they can control. And that is exactly what we have done—and do. Spouses demand certain responses from one another as a condition for life. People require that they never hurt again the way they once did in some previous trauma. We devise strategies designed to keep us warmly involved with each other at a safe distance. We live to gain life from others and to protect ourselves from whatever we think is life-threatening.

An inside look must anticipate uncovering both deep, unsatisfied longings that bear testimony to our *dignity*, as well as foolish and ineffective strategies for keeping ourselves out of pain that reflect our *depravity*. Each of us is a glorious ruin. And the further we look into our heart, the more clearly we can see the wonder of our ability to enjoy relationship alongside the tragedy of our determination to arrange for our own protection from hurt.

TAKING AN INSIDE LOOK

One brief illustration may clarify how these two elements operate beneath the surface. A couple wonders what to do with their twenty-two-year-old son who has dropped out of college with a drinking problem and wants to return home. The usual Christian approach to resolving their question would be to consult a few "experts" to see whether there is a consensus in how biblical principles might apply. After consulting with their advisers and praying that God would overrule any wrong decision they might make, they decide either to forbid their son to return home to teach him responsibility, or to welcome him back to demonstrate grace.

But suppose we were to take an inside look before arriving at the decision. Perhaps the young man's longings for respect and involvement have gone unmet in a family where Dad is distant, hostile, and uninvolved, and where Mom clings protectively to her son for the intimacy her husband denies her. In that situation, perhaps the son should be received home with both an apology from Dad for his cold distance and a commitment to learn how to warmly relate, and a commitment from Mom to healthily back away from her son as she learns to more openly share her pain with her husband.

In order to make these changes, both parents would need to look inside themselves to see their own unsatisfied thirst and their self-protective styles of relating. For example, Dad might need to face how deeply inadequate he feels to give of himself with any hope of finding respect. Perhaps *his* father never valued him for anything other than his work habits. As a result, he may have learned to work hard and give little of himself, hoping this style of relating would bring him everything he wanted. When his son began giving him trouble during his teen years, Dad likely withdrew into working harder, feeling anger at his son for letting him down but being unwilling to share openly his concern and affection for fear that what he shared of himself would not be well received by his son. His longings for respect and for relationship with his son are legitimate; his strategy of keeping his distance to protect himself from rejection is sinful.

Perhaps Mom, after years of living with a man who never gave himself to her, had become a hard woman, a mother who matter-of-factly performed her maternal duties. Her feminine soul may have been aching with the pain of loneliness and neglect, a pain so terrible that her only solution (in her mind) was to never again be close enough to anyone to be hurt. The deep love she felt for her son may have been hidden behind the barricade of self-protective coolness. To make it even more complex, perhaps Mom, although dutiful in her approach to mothering, yielded to her unquenchable desires for intimacy by becoming manipulatively involved with her son, much like Rebekah with Jacob. The boy may have felt unwanted by his father and controlled by his mother.

Without for a moment excusing his sinful behavior by focusing on his parents' failures, I would still want to see the family face their relational problems if the young man were to return home. If, on the other hand, the family was characterized by a soft-touch father who granted his son's every wish and a docile mother who could never say no to anything, then it might be wise to require certain evidence of responsibility in their son before offering to welcome him home.

No amount of looking inside will yield perfect certainty about what to do. But some understanding of what is going on within us will often help us see what changes must occur on the inside before effective external change can be expected.

Spiritual formation must be concerned about promoting change from the inside out. Outer factors do influence the deepest part of our lives, but true freedom from destructive habits and patterns of self-protection only come from a deep inner transformation. Larry Crabb's distinction between thirsts and the strategies used to meet them is essential to any formation program which seeks to move beyond mere sin management.

For Further Reading

Benner, D. (1988). *Psychotherapy and the spiritual quest.* Grand Rapids: Baker. A helpful work on the integration of psychotherapy and spirituality, accomplished in part by viewing therapy as soul care.

Crabb. L. (1993). *Finding God.* Grand Rapids: Zondervan. Themes found in this chapter are further refined in this thoughtful and personal reflection on pain and loss and the presence of God.

Lloyd-Jones, M. (1965). *Spiritual depression: Its causes and its cure.* Grand Rapids: Eerdmans. A collection of thoughtful sermons on the joylessness and lack of freedom common to so many Christians. His analysis is keen and compassionate, and his solution is wise and Christocentric.

Propst, R. (1988). *Psychotherapy in a religious framework: Spirituality in the emotional healing process.* New York: Human Sciences. A proposal for forming a healing partnership of cognitive therapy and religion.

Seamands, D. (1981). *Healing for damaged emotions.* Wheaton: Victor. A clear examination of how past hurts can affect us today and how we can overcome their power.

SPIRITUAL FORMATION THROUGH THE LITURGY
Lynn C. Bauman

From its beginnings liturgy has been a part of Christian worship, and spiritual formation through the liturgy a part of normative Christian experience. These two features of church life (worship through liturgy and spiritual formation in worship) form the focus of this chapter. To understand the power of liturgy to shape spiritual reality within us, however, it is important that we answer certain fundamental questions.

First, we need to know something about liturgy itself and its origins. Worship in the Christian community has characteristically supported elements of ritual and beauty. What is the purpose of ritual and role of beauty in Christian worship and spiritual formation? Why does God take the human proclivity toward worship and ritual, which together create the liturgy, and use it as a vehicle to fashion our inner lives? What does Christ seek to accomplish in His followers through this process? Finally we must also understand something of the specific shape of traditional Christian liturgy and its capacities for spiritual formation. We will examine each of these questions and concerns in the course of this study.

THE ORIGINS OF LITURGY IN CHRISTIAN WORSHIP

Synagogue Worship
Some imagine that the early Christians were "free form" in their manner of worship. Both tradition and historical inquiry,

however, indicate otherwise. The early Christians were for the most part Jews, familiar with the formal worship (for liturgy) of the synagogue service, as well as temple worship at Jerusalem. Early Christians, therefore, did not start out to create Christian worship afresh as they began to worship God in Christ; they simply adapted and built upon the forms of Jewish worship they already knew.[1]

The worship familiar to most Christians today, traditionally called the "Liturgy of the Word," comes to us from the synagogue service. Synagogue worship began with an opening invocation followed by the reading of texts from the Hebrew Scriptures and the chanting or singing of psalms. The readings were followed by teaching or preaching. The exposition of Scripture concluded with prayers for the life of the community and the coming of the Messiah.

Early Christian worship modified the liturgy of synagogue worship by reading from the writings of the apostles, singing hymns to Christ (fragments of which remain to this day preserved in the Scriptures and in the tradition of the church), and by praying prayers that addressed God the Father through Jesus Christ the Son. This basic form grounded early Christian worship, but was also expanded to include the service of Holy Communion.

The Passover Meal

On the night of His earthly passion, in a gathering with His disciples, Christ broke bread in the tradition of the Hebrews and said the prayer of blessing *(barakah)* over the bread and wine at the Passover meal. This "Liturgy of the Meal" was also a part of normal Jewish worship. Having sanctified it with His own prayer to the Father, Jesus made this form of worship a norm in early Christian worship, commanding its repetition. The Hebrew Prayer of Blessing or Thanksgiving *(eucharistia* or eucharist) was combined with the liturgy of the Word to form the primary liturgy of early Christian worship and became its standard through the centuries which followed.

The shape given to the liturgy and worship of the early church (the "liturgy of the Word" followed by the "liturgy of the Meal") was deemed a fitting way, therefore, to worship God in the beginning life of Christianity. Today the church still follows these same patterns, albeit in many different forms. Even those churches typically known for "free church" worship and who would disavow participation of any kind in liturgy per se, inadvertently adapt many of these ancient norms.

THE PLACE OF RITUAL AND BEAUTY
IN CHRISTIAN WORSHIP

Ritual and Significance

When human beings approach the most profoundly significant events of life, we commonly invest them with great ceremony. Ritualized events in human society usually indicate moments of great meaning for us, whereas the events of a more common variety are often "off the cuff." Humans of almost every culture and time show that some events are of extreme importance by putting them in the context of solemn ritual. We set out our best linens, silver sets, and lighted candles, for example, when we want a meal to stand out as memorable. A wedding is rarely solemnized without due ceremony. Music, art, and other creations of human beauty assist by raising such times out of the ordinary and the mundane into a higher realm of significance.

Christian worship is an act of supreme importance. In it we approach the greatest mystery of all—God as Ultimate Reality. We should not be surprised, therefore, that both Hebrews and Christians allowed their liturgies to be infused with great beauty, solemnity, and ritual. From early in its inception Christian liturgy and worship has had such accompaniments. For Christians, worship is not simply a beautiful human ritual, however magnificent and full of ceremony. It constitutes a meeting between the human and the divine. At such a meeting, through the ritual, something begins to change us. Worship through the liturgy is meant to take us beyond the experience of the event itself and advance the process of spiritual formation. The fact that we are drawn to this experience offers a sign of the transcendent within us.

Worship As the Sign of the Divine Image

From the dawn of history, testimony exists of an almost inescapable longing to worship. Human beings worship, in part, because they are hungry to find the One who can fill the inner void with a fullness saturated with eternal life and being. According to Christian teaching, the clear evidence of such a drawing to worship provides an unmistakable indication of the stamp of the divine image within us, a sign of the *imago dei*. We cannot become completely human without drawing spiritual breath *(ruah, pneuma)* in the presence of the One who created us for Himself. The longing to worship God, therefore, begins to draw us away from the narrow horizons of our selves toward the limitless domain of the divine transcendence.

An Invitation to Communion

In His closing prayer and final instructions, Jesus invited His disciples into intimate union with God. St. John records the final prayer before His death in which Jesus revealed the goal of human existence—to be one with the Father. No longer were the disciples meant to remain simply servants (slaves), now they would be regarded as intimate "friends," able to share in the inner life of God. At the heart of what is often called the "high priestly prayer of Christ" (John 17), we find the request that His disciples will join the fellowship which He shares with the Father at the heart of the divine life (John 17:20-26). He thus invited the disciples into the intimacy of communion with God, the same intimate union which Jesus Himself knows.

Throughout the New Testament the writers of epistles repeat these same themes of intimate union and worship at the level of the Spirit. St. Paul, for example, expresses this inner cry as "Abba, Father," which issues from the heart and voices the Spirit's desire to bring us into fellowship with God. In this union He makes us heirs of God and joint heirs with Christ (Rom. 8:15-17). The Spirit searches our hearts and intercedes for us. St. John makes the same point in his first epistle saying that we are invited into the inner circle of fellowship and united there with the Spirit (1 John 1:1-10; 3:24; 4:13). But the question remains, why does God wish for such worship? What purpose and effect does He intend?

Worship As the Way of Transformation

In the prayer life of Christ it is clear that His worship of God was not monological, but dialogical. He conversed with God,

His Father. Intimacy, fellowship, and dialogue take place between friends, which is precisely what Jesus calls His disciples at the end of His ministry to them (John 15). Mutual self-revelation and the sharing of burdens, thoughts, goals, and ideas always form the center of such a relationship.

On the human level we seek for similar communication with each other and our own children. Could this not also explain the use of the same metaphors in Scripture? Perhaps like the mother who has been with her children all day and hungers for adult communication, God also wishes to establish a dialogical relationship with adult sons and daughters who will share His nature, mind, and vision. He seeks a mature relationship with us. In their letters St. Paul and St. John make it clear, however, that we are not merely friends in conversation: God wants something more from us and "in" us. He desires to move us toward our destiny—the transformation of our being into His likeness.

Through worship God not only invites us into fellowship and friendship, He also brings us into conformity to the image of the Son of God (Rom. 8:26-29; 1 John 3:1-3). In a dialogical way God seeks permission to enter into the "deep structures" of our being, and begin there to do His work of remaking and transforming us (Rom. 8:15-16, 23; 1 Cor. 2:12-16). Our worship is one crucial way of welcoming God on the inside of us and allowing His Spirit to get on with the task of reforming and remaking us. In worship, particularly in liturgical worship as a vehicle, we are carried forward. The doors of intimacy are opened, and we move toward transformation of being. But how does liturgy facilitate such spiritual formation?

LITURGY AS A MEANS OF SPIRITUAL FORMATION

The Work of the People

The term "liturgy" comes from the language of the New Testament itself. It comprises two Greek words, *laos* meaning "people," and *ergon* meaning "work" (Luke 1:23; Phil. 2:17; Heb. 8:6). Together these terms signify that worship is a work that involves the whole people of God in the transforming sacrifice of Christ. By virtue of the one offering of Christ, we enter into His life and are remade.

103

The first important aspect of the "work" of worship is to awaken us to the presence of God and then to create within us a readiness for the creative process of spiritual formation. It is through the regular worship of God in the liturgy that this process of spiritual formation begins. Liturgy is designed to penetrate past the surface level, allowing us to be available to the divine Presence in such a way that God can reach the depths of the human heart. If, as has been traditionally taught by the church, the liturgy itself came into being as a result of the activity of the Spirit of God, then we can understand it as a "sacred structure" powerful enough to reshape our inner lives.

In the act of worship through the liturgy, we encounter a sacred structure which ultimately disciplines and forms us. Without such a spiritual formation we remain dispersed, unformed, and unmade. Through the structure of the liturgy, prayer can be understood as the gathering of our attention and recollection in such a way that it leads to transformation of being. But what is this structure and how does it act upon our attention?

The Shape of the Liturgy

As we have seen earlier, liturgy does not take any form we desire. From its beginning Christian liturgy has had a unique and specific "shape," and this shape has a specific purpose.[2] The experience of moving through the "shape of the liturgy" in worship takes us from our most unformed state and begins (or continues) the process of spiritual reformation. As the liturgy begins and we gather to worship, we are "called" to attention in the recreative presence of God through the *opening acclamations.*[3] These sentences invoke the divine Presence and turn our attention from the world we have just left to the divine Reality itself. In that Presence, our lives are challenged and refocused, and our energies concentrated.

The service moves from the opening invocation to the *hymn of praise* where heart and consciousness are elevated above this world into divine realities. In the ancient liturgies the hymn most often used was the *Gloria in excelsis* (Glory be to God on high). Other ancient hymns of praise were used as well: the *Kyrie Eleison* (Lord Have Mercy) and the *Trisagion* (Thrice Holy God). Once we have been reoriented and lifted into the presence of God through the acclamations and the hymns of praise, a prayer is offered asking for divine assistance so that human hearts be made ready to hear the Word of God.

The *oral reading of Scripture* (called "lessons") has been central to Christian worship from the beginning of the church, for in the hearing of the Word we start to understand the "will of heaven" revealed to us on earth. Typically the readings appear in four sections—an Old Testament passage, a Psalm, an Epistle, and finally a Gospel portion. The reading of the Gospel forms the high point in the liturgy of the Word, and it is given honor as all stand to hear it read from the center of the nave. After the reading of the Gospel text, the congregation sits to hear the Word of God expounded through preaching. Preaching is not a pause or diversion from the liturgy; it serves to attract our attention and instruct the soul, weaving the passages together to form a "net of understanding." The Word of God read and preached "informs" and nourishes us, and we begin to understand our need before the Almighty and His work to meet that need.

The *Creed* has been one of the essential features of the liturgy used to remind us of the entire scope of the Gospel in the redemptive work of God. Sunday by Sunday the church "remembers" the whole and places the instruction from the readings of Scripture and the sermon into its entirety. The Western church today typically uses two creeds: the shorter Apostles' Creed and the slightly longer Nicene Creed, referring to the Council of Nicaea in the fourth century.

Following the Creed, the whole congregation then offers the Prayers of the People which affirm the work of the priesthood of all believers in intercession for the world, the church universal, the local community, the parish, and its own special needs. Through these prayers, the people of the congregation also make a public act of the *Confession of Sin* whereby they acknowledge the fact that they have not carried out their responsibilities of priesthood to the world in full. In this manner both the sins of the people and of the world are lifted into God's presence. The celebrant speaks of the words of *Absolution* so that the people may be assured of God's forgiveness, and then the celebrant invites the congregation to exchange the Peace which sanctifies the gathering of the community as a unified body, ready to offer the entire world into the transforming power of Christ at the Eucharist.

The Liturgy of the Meal begins with the *Offertory*. The people bring the gifts forward in the form of bread, wine, offerings of treasure, and in the inner offerings of their prayer. They place these upon the altar and the congregation prepares the Great Thanksgiving (Holy Communion or the Mass). This central act of the liturgy is a long prayer begun by Christ and continued throughout the centuries. It includes the *Sursum Corda,* the *Sanctus* and *Benedictus,* and the *Prayer of Consecration* including the *Epiclesis,* which calls upon the Holy Spirit to sanctify the elements and the people who receive them. These terms are ancient in origin and refer to the various parts of the Eucharistic prayer which have been consecrated through time as the prayer of Christ Himself expressed through His people.

In this act the symbol and reality become one, for the Eucharist is the supreme sign of spiritual formation and at once its primary vehicle. Physically we experience communion (union) with God by receiving the elements, and spiritually we participate in the transforming work of Christ. In intimacy and union transformation of being begins and we are formed by the Spirit into the image of Christ.

The celebrant breaks the element and distributes Communion to the congregation. In this act God's people unite with the transformed body of Christ. From this moment also Christ makes Himself present and available through His body for the life of the world (John 6:33, 51). For many believers, Communion constitutes the "mystery of the sacrament" which not only transforms the people of God but makes them ready to extend the liturgy into the world where literally and figuratively they become "His body," carrying out His mission and work. For this reason the liturgy concludes when the people receive a benediction and blessing which releases them at the dismissal to carry out their task as "reformed" beings who through the worship itself have been recreated into worthy messengers of the Good News. In this cycle of dismissal and return back to the altar, week by week, the congregation performs the great work of the liturgy as the people of God bringing to realization the redemption of the world.

LITURGY AS LIFE, LIFE AS LITURGY

Many Christians, however, make the mistake of seeing the liturgy only in terms of what happens during worship on Sunday morning. This severely limits its significance and purpose. Perhaps one experience on Sunday morning concentrates the meaning of life itself for the Christian, but liturgy correctly understood as the "work of the people" is nothing less than life lived out day by day as a participation in the body of Christ. Experienced in this way, the liturgy reaches completeness.

The Liturgical Image

A full understanding of Christian ministry consists of two basic actions imaged in the liturgy. Week by week the laity are formed through worship into "offerers and gatherers" for the world. From the heart of the liturgy they go out into the world to offer the presence of Christ. There they meet the deep needs, concerns, troubles, and experiences of countless men and women as Christ did in His own day. Through His body Christ ministers to their needs in words of wisdom and life, acts of comfort and healing, and the invitation to life and liberty. As the people of God return from the world back into worship, they gather up these concerns, needs, troubles, and burdens and carry them to the altar as a part of their weekly offering.

Through the gifts of money, time, wine, and bread the celebrant "re-presents" all that is offered, lifting them into God's presence in the name of Christ. In that moment the Holy Spirit moves over these gifts and, as at the first creation, brings order out of chaos, carrying forward the redemption by recreating, sanctifying, restoring, and making all things new. The central mystery of the Eucharistic Prayer is that God takes all that we offer, touches and transforms it and gives it back to us as food, continuing His transforming and healing work. In this way Christ makes His one and eternal sacrifice available to the whole world. All that is brought to Him is received in order that it might be redeemed and restored.

True Bread for the Life of the World

This traditional understanding of the theology of Eucharist makes it clear how the Eternal Bread is broken and given to

107

feed the world (John 6:32-33). The feeding, however, cannot take place without the formation and response of the body of Christ. In the liturgy the members of Christ's body are fed the sacrament in order to carry it hidden within their own being out into the world. The great work and ministry of the church, therefore, is nothing less than Christ Himself feeding the multitudes. We have been fed in order that we might feed the world in Christ's name and make available to the world the "bread" of love, grace, and forgiveness.

The World As Parish
Often when laypeople begin to exercise ministry in response to the call of Christ, they center upon the church. This, however, restricts the full cycle of Christ's work imaged in the liturgy. The world, not the church, is the central focus of Christian ministry. Baptism confers this mission to the world as a special vocation of all laypersons. The ministry of Word and Sacrament forms the people of God for this ultimate vocation. The world becomes the parish of the believer—these people; these circumstances; these opportunities; these needs, hurts, troubles, and difficulties are the specific "parish responsibilities" which call us and for which the Sunday liturgy prepares and forms us.

CONCLUSION

Clearly the church offers other contemporary forms of worship and different shapes of liturgy. In some the emphasis shifts toward instruction through the preaching of the Word of God. In others the sacramental act seems more central. Each in its own context represents a form capable of bringing about spiritual formation to its own degree. However, worship without a "shape" may easily degenerate into a mere reflection of our basest proclivities, whether emotional or intellectual. On the other hand, a rigid and unyielding adherence to ritual for its own sake can become dead and spiritually stifling.

For that reason perhaps, the ancient liturgy properly celebrated survives as a balance and a corrective to our common human tendencies. The fundamental shape of the liturgy may be seen to represent a "transmission" from the Spirit, a gift given at the beginning of the church's life to empower and sustain it. It represents both then and today, a form of wisdom which, for many, receives special honor along with the transmission of Scriptures. Together they act to support and encourage spiritual life and growth, for the goal of each is the continuous renewal of the new creation into the image and likeness of the Son of God. To this creative energy, this spiritual formation, the church submits itself Sunday to Sunday in the power of its worship.

Notes

1. For an examination of the apostolic tradition of Christian worship see the study and translation of the text by Burton Scott Easton. *The apostolic tradition of Hippolytus* (Hamden, CT: Archon, 1962). This text is an early writing of the tradition of the apostles as it had been received and practiced in Rome, the see city of Peter. Hippolytus, a disciple of Irenaeus, was one of the early bishops, writing about A.D. 200. An alternative reading of Hippolytus can be found in P. Bradshaw (1992). *The search for the origins of Christian worship: Sources and methods for the study of early liturgy.* New York: Oxford Univ. Press.

2. In his classical work, *The shape of the liturgy,* Gregory Dix examines the historical development and universal employment of the "shape of the liturgy" in the life of the early church.

3. The particular expression of liturgy used in this article is the Anglican rite in the *Episcopal book of common prayer,* 1979. Although this rite has its own unique characteristics, it is representative of the universal "shape of the liturgy" expressed throughout the Catholic and Orthodox traditions.

For Further Reading

Casel, O. (1962). *The mystery of Christian worship.* Westminster, MD: Newman. For many Christians, worship through the Liturgy is more than a simple remembrance of past events. It is a calling of the redeeming work of Christ from out of eternity into the present. This mystery is explored in this volume.

Dix, G. (1945). *The shape of the liturgy.* London: Dacre. This is the classic work dealing with the historical development of Christian liturgy from its inception to the present. It compares the constituent parts of the liturgy in each of the traditions.

Dugmore, G. (1964). *The influence of the synagogue upon the divine office.* Westminster, MD: Faith. The obvious connection between early Christian worship and the Hebrew tradition is examined in this text.

Howard, T. (1981). *The liturgy explained.* Wilton, CT: Morehouse-Barlow. This small text is perhaps the best brief introduction to the traditional Christian liturgy. It gives a concise explanation of its many elements.

Jungmann, J. (1978). *Christian prayer through the centuries.* New York: Paulist. An important study of historical development of public Christian prayer. For those unfamiliar with liturgical history this volume would be invaluable.

Martimore, A. (Ed.) (1973). *The church at prayer: The eucharist.* New York: Desclee. Worship through the Liturgy of the Meal is the primary prayer of the church. This text examines the many dimensions of that celebration.

Price, C. (1979). *Liturgy for living.* New York: Seabury. This volume introduces the interested reader to many issues concerning liturgical worship; its origins, its contemporary use, and its theological foundations.

Schmemann, A. (1988). *For the life of the world: Sacraments and orthodoxy.* Crestwood, NY: St. Vladimir's Seminary Press. This text is a brilliant study by a Russian Orthodox theologian exploring the sacramental and cosmological dimensions of the liturgy. It places the ancient liturgy securely in the modern context as the prayer of the church which transforms the world.

Thompson, B. (1980). *Liturgies of the western church.* Minneapolis: Augusburg Fortress. The fundamental sourcebook on liturgies. It contains many Protestant liturgies with a discussion of their context and historical development.

SPIRITUAL FORMATION THROUGH PUBLIC WORSHIP
Kenneth O. Gangel

Early in 1992 a small evangelical denomination surveyed its clergy regarding the practice of the spiritual disciplines. Among those who responded, 85 percent or more indicated they were "making progress" or "firmly established" in nine of twelve disciplines listed. People ranked worship, prayer, study, and guidance rather high. Fasting, confession, and solitude drew the lowest ratings.

Among pastors, number of years in ministry seemed to favor practice of the disciplines. For example, 21 percent of those having ten years or less in ministry were "firmly established" in meditation, while pastors in the thirty-plus years averaged 47 percent. The same pattern held true for prayer. However, the averages for confession and celebration were relatively smaller among older pastors in comparison to younger (Rambo, 1992).

Interestingly, the pastors cited worship very high in their ratings of their own practice of spiritual disciplines. One wonders whether the congregants would make the same choices or whether their personal assessment of what kind of spiritual formation takes place during public worship might vary from that of their spiritual leaders.

Worship in evangelical churches today too often seems a congregational adaptation of good old American pragmatism — people do what they like and they like what they do. Worship experience has become a means to an end as hymns, Scripture reading, and prayer serve as "preliminary activities" leading up to the focal point of worship, the preaching of God's Word.

Without diminishing the importance of exposition, one could argue that one person's comments about the Bible may be no more important than the worship pattern, no more truth-serving than singing God's Word or listening to it read in its purest, uninterrupted form.

Biblical worship is often corrupted by boredom, lack of purpose, and nonparticipational behavior which leads a congregation through the motions without genuine heart involvement. The opposite extreme offers little more than secular entertainment with a religious veneer, a packaged plastic program so perfect and professional that even the most sincere worshiper can scarcely break through its shrink-wrapped design to get his hands on true worship.

WHAT IS WORSHIP?

Webber defines worship as "a meeting between God and His people" and calls for renewal of worship based on the Scriptures and the history of the church (Webber, 1982, p. 11). He suggests that evangelicals actually suffer from an illness of which the failure to worship is a symptom. He warns that "the remedy consists of repentance, a *metanoia,* a turning away from all shallow and uninformed approaches to worship" (Webber, 1982, p. 20).

Many people think the Gospel of John focuses on evangelism, the message that "whosoever will may come." But in his presentation of Jesus Christ the Son of God, John is concerned that people recognize His deity and bow before Him in worship. A blind beggar came to faith in the Savior after his sightless eyes saw light for the first time. Within hours he fell before the One who created sight "and he worshiped Him" (9:38).

Johannine Foundations

In the Lord's encounter with the woman of Samaria (John 4) John mentioned "worship," "worshiped," or "worshipers" ten times (out of its thirteen occurrences in his Gospel). The ten usages appear within five verses (4:20-24), dramatically demonstrating the difference between religion and Christianity. The Samaritan woman was deeply religious and knew precisely the appropriate place of worship which, in her view, was Mount Gerizim. The Lord Jesus shoved aside the discussion of both place and time. Religion may emphasize the human struggle to find God but the message of John's Gospel identifies how God has revealed Himself to people. True worshipers need not seek a hidden God; the self-revealed God actively seeks the right kind of worshipers.

God is Spirit and His people must worship Him "in spirit and truth" (John 4:23). The word "spirit" refers not to the Holy Spirit but to the spirit of the worshiper. One's posture in worship (kneeling, standing, bowing) plays a minor role; God is concerned with attitude before act because wrong attitudes produce wrong acts.

To worship "in truth" means to be concerned for honesty before God and man. It also suggests that believers must be biblical in their worship.

Small wonder that Paul affirmed, "God highly exalted Him, and bestowed on Him the name which is above every name, that at the name of Jesus every knee should bow, of those who are in heaven and on earth and under the earth, and that every tongue should confess that Jesus Christ is Lord, to the glory of God the Father" (Phil. 2:9-11).

To the confused woman by the well the Lord offered the only voluntary declaration of messiahship in the entire New Testament—"I who speak to you am he" (John 4:26).

Essential Components

How then shall we define worship? Worship is affirmation. In worship a believer acknowledges that God's revelation of Himself in Jesus Christ demands response. The self-revealed God awaits the reaction of His creation and that response represents a duty for God's redeemed people, not some kind of emotion sweeping over them in a certain hour on a certain day. In true worship believers affirm their relationship to God because worship looks above.

Worship is also conservation. The corporate worship of the people of God preserves and transmits the faith. Christians identify themselves with the redeemed of all times and places. The Word and the words used to communicate faith form a foundation to conserving and transmitting God's truth.

113

Worship is also *edification.* The worshiper gains increasing understanding of God's person and truth because proper worship teaches theology. In this sense biblical worship serves both vertical and horizontal dimensions, though the latter should not be placed ahead of or even on a level with the former.

Worship is *celebration.* Believers celebrate their union with the Creator of the universe and with the Father of His people. They celebrate His marvelous works. They celebrate the birth, life, death, resurrection, and coming reign of the victorious Savior. And they invite others to join in their homage.

In all four of these components worship shows itself a true spiritual discipline. One grows in these behaviors as they are learned. Leaders can teach these processes and the body can practice its collective growth and formation in as simple a way as cultivating these essential ingredients of worship.

> All people that on earth do dwell.
> Sing to the Lord with cheerful voice;
> Him serve with fear, His praise forth tell.
> Come ye before Him and rejoice.
>
> For why? The Lord our God is good,
> His mercy is forever sure;
> His truth at all times firmly stood.
> And shall from age to age endure.
> William Kethe, "All People That
on Earth Do Dwell" (1561)

NEED FOR SPIRITUAL FORMATION IN PUBLIC WORSHIP

Everything we know about adult education focuses on the centrality of need awareness, and spiritual formation in public worship will not likely vary from that pattern. Several spiritual needs can be met through properly conducted public worship.

Spiritual Growth of the Body
Certainly one obvious need consists of the corporate spiritual growth of the body. In the pastoral survey mentioned above, the focus centered on individuals as does much of our under-

SPIRITUAL FORMATION THROUGH PUBLIC WORSHIP

standing of spiritual formation. But group growth, the spiritual maturation of people whom God has brought together in what we call a congregation, truly represents a major need in this disconnected society. We could ask whether each component of the worship service contributes to the goal of corporate unity and spiritual growth. Does it draw men and women closer to the Heavenly Father or have we injected it for entertainment or activity purposes only?

Instructional Awareness

A second contemporary need for spiritual formation in public worship deals with an instructional awareness. Too often the church has separated these intimately related ingredients of Christian life—worship and learning. To be sure, not all worship is learning and not all learning, worship. The emphasis here centers on recognizing the instructional aspects of a corporate worship experience and making use of learning opportunities for spiritual growth. Johnson reminds us that

> formation equips us to be critically self-aware of the culture in which we participate, to know the difference between the Christian Story and the many stories of our culture that bid for our commitment and loyalty. . . .
>
> Formation requires a community that is intentional and disciplined in its spiritual life and that includes in the process of Christian initiation training in praying and meditation, searching the Scriptures, repentance and confession, praise and proclamation, works of mercy and justice (Johnson, 1989, p. 158).

Surely in our corporate worship we must learn how to conduct a worshipful life *outside* the boundaries of the sanctuary. Biblical worship should result from conversion since the cross makes possible obedience to God built upon repentance. God uses Law and Gospel to drive people toward the Savior and the fellowship of believers.

Participation

Still a third need forces us to recognize the paucity of participation not only in order of service, but through intentional spiritual formation in public worship. In the practice of spiritual formation we bring something to God, even if it be only our wretched sinful selves in desperate need for forgiveness. We also bring praise and adoration in whereas the former tends to be a private discipline, the latter binds us together in participation.

Perhaps corporate worship will take a nudge toward progress if Christians begin to realize that worship does not consist merely of Bible study or any other single activity. Certainly *prayer* will be involved, as will *praise*, but a third word beginning with that letter clamors for more attention—*participation.*

Balancing Content and Process

The fourth need in many evangelical churches is a better balance between content and process. Because of our commitment to absolute truth and the authority of Scripture, we tend to focus on the cognitive product (particularly the sermon) rather than the spiritual formation of the worshipers through the entire worship experience. But worship concentrates one's faculties on corporate self-giving to God in response to His love and in praise to His glory. It is both sacramental and sacrificial and though it may be an oversimplification, the ACTS emphasis on worship process is still helpful: Awareness, Commitment, Transformation, Self-sacrifice.

We do not wish to encourage formality and certainly not legalism. Ignatius of Antioch once wrote, "Those who had walked in ancient practices attained unto a newness of hope, no longer observing Sabbaths but fashioning their lives after the Lord's day, on which our life also arose through Him." Jesus made very plain that the Sabbath was made for people and not people for the Sabbath. So keeping the seven-day system of the Old Covenant, the early Christians changed the emphasis from the seventh to the first day (John 20:1, 19, 26; 1 Cor. 16:2; Acts 20:7). By the end of the first century, the first day had become "the Lord's day" (Rev. 1:10).

Focus on day, time, procedure, or attire can never produce the process of spiritual formation through worship nor can that balance be achieved by overemphasizing any one dimension of the worship experience.

Spontaneity and Freedom

Finally, we must address the need for spontaneity and freedom in worship. To be sure, one must be careful here to avoid the trap of license while trying to combat legalism. But liberty offers the happy middle ground on that continuum. As Howard put it, "The ancient church talked about the Dance. The saints are the men and women who enjoy the liberty and bliss of that Dance because they have submitted their mere spontaneity to the choreography, and lo, have been set free to enjoy a new kind of spontaneity (Howard, 1977, p. 21).

But in his provocative article Howard really attacks a careless lack of self-control which scorns tradition and genuine spontaneity. This chapter simply emphasizes a voluntary involvement in spiritual formation through public worship; the adult choice to give oneself to God without external force compelling that surrender. Sincere fulfillment of form is fine but represents only the beginning of worship. The psalms surely teach us that God expects worshipers to offer a personal, unique expression of their own response to deity.

OBJECTIVES OF SPIRITUAL FORMATION THROUGH PUBLIC WORSHIP

"There is no life," wrote T.S. Eliot in his poem "The Rock," "that is not in community, and no community not lived in praise of God." In ancient Israel the act of assembling focused on collectivity, the people of God in congregation. To be sure, there existed a focus on place (tabernacle or temple). Sacred shrines and pious personnel are not essential ingredients of biblical worship, but the gathering of God's people, congregated in His presence, began at Mount Sinai where the assembling involved the actual formulation of a nation.

Communication – practising God's presence

Surely a major focus in public worship is communication. God communicates with me; I communicate with God. When I concentrate on growth of inner life in balance with my upper look during corporate worship, I practice God's presence.

Many New Testament words express the act of gathering and

117

reflect the sense of community so strategic in Paul's teachings, but none more descriptively than *ekklēsia*. Used more than 100 times by New Testament writers, it speaks of people who are gathered out of the world.

Modern-day individualism has diminished and diluted the communication emphasis in Scripture. Piety has become compartmentalized, relegated to a private personal pocket of life, resulting in a religious consumerism which describes worship as "attending the church of your choice." Western culture drowns in humanistic religion with its focus on "getting something out of the service."

Biblical worship, on the other hand, sees the Shepherd gathering the sheep, the Father gathering the children. The relational unity which God's people have with Him is, by its very strength, an antidote to individual loneliness (Ps. 106:47; Isa. 11:12; John 11:52; Eph. 1:7-10).

When Christians gather for worship they practice God's presence by affirming His plan in their lives and in the entire world (Col. 1:15-20). People gather in groups for all kinds of reasons—fellowship, learning, hospitality, fun, and even mutual service—but none other than worship exalts the glory of the triune God.

Many Christians have come to think of "orthodoxy" as correct doctrine when, as a matter of fact, a more specific use of the word would be "right worship." As the disciples gathered with Jesus in informal ways and places, He certainly taught them correct doctrine. But their communion with the Master stressed a relationship to cultivate rather than merely a volume of truth to learn. Worship is "theatric," or in other words, people and God coming together in a unique communication designed and sustained by the Holy Spirit.

Practicing God's presence emphasizes the spirit of worship, not its forms—the church as inn, not fort. The gathered body itself, even apart from its teaching and preaching, provides an act of evangelism, a symbol, a demonstration to an unbelieving world that the good news has been communicated and received (Acts 2:42-47). That fact does not minimize the teaching role as the church's educational leaders explain the many ways in which communication with God in public worship heightens our spiritual formation.

118

We gather together to ask the Lord's blessing;
He chastens and hastens His will to make known;
The wicked oppressing now cease from distressing,
Sing praises to His name; He forgets not His own.
                    Dutch folk hymn, "We Gather Together,"
                          Translated by Theodore Baker, 1874

Celebration

A second objective many have identified in public worship
is celebration. It may not be too much to say that Christians
celebrate their own spirituality during corporate worship and,
in so doing, share their relationship to God with others. Worship is neither simultaneous private devotions nor sanctified
spectatorism. Only when we appropriately and actively involve
ourselves in the worship process can spiritual formation take
place.

Celebration and joy afford appropriate faith responses to
God's work in His world. In ancient times Israel's leaders called
the people to a festal mentality at times of worship.

> Then Nehemiah the governor, Ezra the priest and scribe,
> and the Levites who were instructing the people said to
> them all, "This day is sacred to the Lord your God. Do not
> mourn or weep." For all the people had been weeping as
> they listened to the words of the Law. Nehemiah said, "Go
> and enjoy choice food and sweet drinks, and send some to
> those who have nothing prepared. This day is sacred to
> our Lord. Do not grieve, for the joy of the Lord is your
> strength" (Neh. 8:9-10).

How much more do New Covenant believers have reason to
respond to God's grace as they speak "to one another in
psalms, hymns and spiritual songs" (Eph. 5:19). They rejoice in
God's people as well as in God Himself, for their life together
in the community of believers offers cause for celebration. Not
only this, but they also rejoice in their expectation of the Lord's
return and the establishment of His kingdom on earth. True
worship concentrates all one's physical, emotional, and spiritual faculties on corporate self-giving to God in response to His
love and in praise to His glory.

119

So dominant is the reality of grace that believers find it extremely difficult to separate who God is from what God does. The question then becomes, what can one give to someone who *gives* everything? God's gifts provide an occasion to celebrate the giver, and worship stimulates spiritual reaction. As Langdon Gilkey put it, "Worship is a response to the presence of God, our reaction to the appearance of the holy" (Gilkey, 1964, p. 108).

When worship takes the form of response to a giving God, it honors grace by affirming that the Heavenly Father has taken the initiative. The ultimate gift, of course, was the Cross. Response to Calvary adorns the worship of the New Testament, causing it to stand in contrast to the cultic worship of first-century Mediterranean paganism. Christians "decultified" worship. Rather than secret rites practiced in darkened, scented cathedrals, worship became a normal, natural, and lifelike part of everyday behavior.

At certain times during the week Christians gather for collective praise. As Flynn (1983) put it in a book title, "together we celebrate." This corporate response of celebration does three things for the church:

(1) It acknowledges God's supremacy by affirming who He is and what He has done. It agrees with God, honors Him, and says yes to His Word.

(2) It rehearses God's goodness by affiliating with His great plan for the world in natural, personal, and special revelation (Ps. 100).

(3) It proclaims God's truth by accenting that His message includes more than just "Gospel"; the total scope of truth always has its source in God (Ps. 93).

> I sing th' almighty pow'r of God
> That made the mountains rise,
> That spread the flowing seas abroad
> And built the lofty skies.
> I sing the wisdom that ordained
> The sun to rule the day;
> The moon shines full at His command
> And all the stars obey.

I sing the goodness of the Lord
That filled the earth with food;
He formed the creatures with His word
And then pronounced them good.
Lord, how Thy wonders are displayed
Where e'er I turn my eye,
If I survey the ground I tread
Or gaze upon the sky!

There's not a plant or flow'r below
But makes Thy glories known;
And clouds arise and tempests blow
By order from Thy throne;
While all that borrows life from Thee
Is ever in Thy care,
And everywhere that man can be,
Thou, God, are present there.
    Isaac Watts, "I Sing the Mighty Power of God" (1715)

Comprehension

Certainly a third formational objective we want to see achieved in our lives and the lives of those we lead in public worship is comprehension. God forbid that worshipers should go through repetitious acts like heathens chanting before an idol. To put it most simply, people should learn theology as they worship, and that learning should provide a foundation for life change and transformation.

Obviously the quality of that experience and the capacity it might have to produce spiritual formation depends upon the biblical quality of the worship experience itself. We know that behavior change begins with knowledge, moves to belief, then to value, and only finally to behavior. People must first know God, trust His revelation of Himself, value their relationship to Him, then attitudinal and behavioral transformation can take place.

WORSHIP AS SERVICE

The Germans say it well with their word *Gottesdienst*, commonly used for worship but literally meaning "service of God."

121

Central to a New Testament understanding of service is the word *diakeneō*, from which comes the English word "deacon." It denotes more an act of service than the state of servitude (Luke 22:27; 1 Peter 1:12; Heb. 6:10). Common acts of self-abasement translate in New Testament theology into acts of service for each other. As Jesus put it to the disciples on the night of His crucifixion, the true guest takes the role of a waiter (Luke 22:24-27).

Worship as service describes people allowing God to work through them in order to create a spiritual community. Worship as service involves the understanding and application of spiritual gifts and their role in the body of Christ (Rom. 12:6-8). The unity, diversity, and mutuality of the church abound when worshipers serve and servants worship. The worship affirmation in Romans 11:33-36 is followed by the appeal in 12:1 for "reasonable service" (NKJV) or "logical liturgy" ("spiritual worship"). The apostle then describes the unity of Christ's body ("each member belongs to all the others," 12:5), details some of the spiritual gifts which carry out this worship-service, and discusses the whole lifestyle of the church active in worship and service.

The practical application of all this activates the involvement of the entire church congregation in worship. Did the Apostle Paul scold the Corinthian believers when he said, "When you assemble, each one has a psalm, has a teaching, has a revelation, has a tongue, has an interpretation. Let all things be done for edification" (1 Cor. 14:26, NASB)? Or did he simply suggest that this kind of mutual sharing had taken on a dimension of disorder at the church at Corinth and needed to be brought back into proper perspective and practice? Perhaps the discipline required to participate decently and in order in public worship makes up part of the formational dimensions of that experience.

Holy God, we praise Thy name;
Lord of all, we bow before Thee;
All on earth Thy scepter claim,
All in heav'n above adore Thee.
Infinite Thy vast domain,
Everlasting is Thy reign.

Lo! the apostolic train
Join Thy sacred name to hallow;
Prophets swell the glad refrain,
And the white-robed martyrs follow;
And from morn to set of sun,
Through the Church the song goes on.

Holy Father, Holy Son,
Holy Spirit, Three we name Thee;
While in essence only One,
Undivided God we claim Thee,
And adoring bend the knee,
While we sing our praise to Thee.

> Attributed to Ignace Franz,
> "Holy God, We Praise Thy Name" (1774)

STRATEGIES FOR SPIRITUAL FORMATION

We have neither space nor intent to offer an exhaustive study of inclusions and exclusions of worship strategies calculated to produce spiritual formation. Nevertheless, it may be safe to suggest that contemporary evangelical worship include some portion of the following almost weekly.

Hymnody

Worship music exists to glorify God and edify others. Based on God-given ability and skill (1 Chron. 15:16-24), those who serve the church in this capacity must develop their ministry most carefully (1 Chron. 16:4-6) and above all focus a doctrinal understanding of what they and we hear and sing (1 Chron. 29:20-21). We render all this in the power of God's Spirit (Col. 3:15-17) and focus on hymns, that reflect simplicity, singability, sound doctrine, clarity of message, and God-centeredness. In a fascinating study of New Testament hymns, Martin concludes that the early believers developed their theology in precisely this way.

Yet as Christ's saving achievement in bringing the world back to God implies that He has done what God alone can do, it was a natural step for a "functional" Christology to take on a trinitarian formulation. And that implies too that the first Christians made in *worship* the decisive step of setting the exalted Christ on a par with God as the recipient of their praise. Hymnody and Christology thus merged in the worship of the one Lord (Martin, 1983, pp. 132–136).

Public Prayer

Prayer in worship should be both corporate and individual though many evangelical worship services lack the sufficient quiet for either. Public prayer often seems improvised, marked by needless repetition and empty language ("Lord, we just really pray"), too often "us" focused. Huxhold talks about the place of pastoral prayer in the context of worship, contrasting the economy of ancient prayer with the embellishment of modern performances.

> Some of the most pointed prayers in the church's treasury of prayers are succinct and extremely relevant to the Lessons they put into petition. One can easily detect how new or how modern the prayers of the church may be often by their failure to practice an economy of words and also because of their strained attempts at being novel. Just to enjoy the restraint, beauty, and brevity of the prayers that have survived the ages is good enough reason to be loyal to the church's book of prayer (Huxhold, 1982, pp. 395–400).

Huxhold emphasizes that public prayer ought not resemble preaching. We might also add that public prayer need not announce nor inform God about events happening in church or community. It is instead a focused exercise through which one member of the body speaks to God in behalf of others, usually expressing collective repentance, praise, and petition.

Confession of Sin

Certainly confession of sin marks true worship. Old Testament priests washed their hands before entering the tabernacle, and an emphasis on cleansing dominates Old and New Testaments alike. Too often the freedom of many churches generates a happy fellowship which makes the worship room sound like a busy airport before services are officially begun. Can we not learn to use prelude time as personal preparation for true worship? Corporate worship as formation of the gathered body must be taught in the church during its gathered meetings.

Immortal, invisible, God only wise,
In light inaccessible hid from our eyes,
Most blessed, most glorious, the Ancient of Days,
Almighty, victorious, Thy great name we praise.

Unresting, unhasting, and silent as light,
Nor wanting, nor wasting, thou rulest in might;
Thy justice like mountains high soaring above
Thy clouds, which are fountains of goodness and love.

To all, life Thou givest, to both great and small.
In all life Thou livest, the true life of all.
We blossom and flourish as leaves on the tree,
And wither and perish—but naught changeth Thee.

Great Father of glory, pure Father of light,
Thine angels adore Thee, all veiling their sight;
All praise we would render; O help us to see
'Tis only the splendor of light hideth Thee!
Walter C. Smith, "Immortal, Invisible God Only Wise" (1867)

Creedal Recitation/Affirmation
Some congregations never let a Sunday slip by without the recitation of one or more creedal statements. Others consider the public recitation of the Apostles' or Nicene Creeds a formality alien to the freedom they seek. Hanko defines creedal recitation and bemoans its loss in the church.

Many actively oppose the use of creeds and the doctrines taught in the creeds; but an even greater problem is that of neglect of the creeds. Whether this neglect is the fault of the leaders or of the laymen is really "a moot question" — the fact is that the creeds are neglected by both pulpit and pew. The creeds have become dusty archives because the church is silent concerning them. And where silence rules, ignorance follows (Hanko, 1983, pp. 236–238).

Preaching

Surely many evangelical congregations view the sermon as the central and perhaps singular source of spiritual formation in a public worship service. The emphasis in this chapter on other forms and processes should not detract from the fact that sound exposition of the Scriptures can surely provide foundation for spiritual growth. But we can achieve that better if we design participational strategies and offer practical application of biblical truth which places the text within contemporary context. Spiritual formation can never develop from preaching which does not answer what Leroy Ford likes to call the "so what" questions. Nor can a dogmatic, demanding, dour condemnation assist struggling saints in their quest for nurture.

Ordinances

In the Passover feast, devout Jews remind themselves of who and whose they are. And though the Lord's Supper is no more a Christian Passover than Sunday is a Christian Sabbath, the worship life of the church inseparably relates to eating and drinking. Indeed, spiritual hunger and thirst rest at the foundation of the life in Christ (Ps. 23:5). We share meals both in family and church. Animals grab a morsel and slink off to chew it alone. Believers fellowship together at food, both physical and spiritual. The English word "Lord" comes from the Old English words for "loaf" (hlāf) and "keeper" (weard) (Oxford English Dictionary); He is the Keeper of the bread, the One to whom believers look to be fed. Promises of future gatherings for feasting abound in New Testament teaching (Matt. 8:11; Rev. 19:9).

As the Lord's Supper, Communion focuses on Him and therefore celebration and affirmation become proclamation (1 Cor. 11:23-26). A spirit of duty or requirement rather than joy and freedom detracts from the reality of the worship experience.

The New Testament suggests that this meal sanctifies all others. Every Communion meal offers an occasion for worship, an acknowledgment that believers are guests in the world of their divine Host. All worship gatherings of believers do not observe ordinances, nor are all gatherings the sharing of a bounteous physical feast. But in reality, all such gatherings recognize hunger and thirst, a desire to come to the table of the Lord and be refreshed from His hand with song, prayer, Scripture, and other elements of the worship "meal."

As a fellowship feast, the Lord's Supper emphasizes what the Lord's people have in common ("communion"). The elements may be distributed in varying forms, but they emphasize one loaf and one cup. Eating in unison focuses the celebration of the whole church without regard to denominational or even congregational boundaries.

Deep formational significance underlies the celebration of the Communion as a traditional thanksgiving to God, a form of prayer. The remembrance provides opportunity to proclaim the reality of the Cross in daily existence. As believers partake in the elements of worship, they acknowledge a giving of themselves to God in response to what He gave and continues to give.

Here, O my Lord, I see Thee face to face;
Here would I touch and handle things unseen,
Here grasp with firmer hand the eternal grace,
And all my weariness upon Thee lean.

This is the hour of banquet and of song,
This is the heavenly table spread for me,
Here, let me feast and feasting still prolong
The brief bright hour of fellowship with Thee.

Feast after feast thus comes and passes by,
Yet passing points to the glad feast above,
Giving sweet foretaste of the festal joy
The Lamb's great bridal feast of bliss and love.

> Horatius Bonar,
"Here, O My Lord, I See Thee Face to Face" (1855)

True worship must be offered to God alone in deep appreciation of His majesty and rulership in the world and in believers' lives. The worshiper engages God on a spiritual rather than physical level and the worship experience, private or public, must be *dominated by God's Spirit*.

An attitude of settled dependence on the Holy Spirit leads to cleansing, readiness, and a cultivation of the proper mind and heart attitude for worship. Worship then becomes a *total response* in which spiritual, emotional, and physical factors tune together to draw attention to the Heavenly Father.

Biblical worshipers see themselves as Paul described in Ephesians 1, recipients of a vast undeserved bounty of spiritual riches provided entirely by the grace of God. They worship in truth regarding the Triune Godhead and particularly Jesus Christ the atoning Son. The preaching of the Word of God does not conflict with the solitude of quiet meditation, for both have their distinctive roles in the total worship experience. As God's people worship they focus their attention on the worthiness (worth-ship) of God. Consequently song and other forms of praise should flow almost spontaneously from God's adoring, joyful people.

What finer atmosphere exists to provoke and promote spiritual formation? The pathway of Christian growth climbs upward from its beginning at the hour of corporate worship when believers bow together before Christ's cross and crown.

For Further Reading

Allen, R. & Borror, G. (1982). *Worship — rediscovering the missing jewel.* Portland: Multnomah. A thoroughly evangelical and tightly written volume which offers helpful information on the definition, program, and a variety of aspects of worship in Christian congregations.

Erickson, C. (1989). *Participating in worship.* Louisville: Westminster/John Knox. Erickson takes a totally different approach to worship than do Allen and Borror, as he argues for a balance of participation in the symmetry of word and sacrament. He attempts to deal comprehensively with various trends as well as traditional approaches to worship from Catholic and Eastern Orthodox to Pentecostal Protestantism.

MacArthur, Jr., J. (1983). *The ultimate priority.* Chicago: Moody. This lay level paperback is a helpful summary of biblical information on worship with special focus on personal rather than public.

Senn, F. (1983). *Christian worship and its cultural setting.* Philadelphia: Fortress. Senn wants to help pastors and other worship leaders avoid cultural capitulation while at the same time remaining culturally relevant in handling worship and liturgy. He argues that the interplay between theology and culture should transform the kind of culture appropriated in Christian worship. The book is written from a Lutheran point of view.

Webber, R. (1985). *Worship is a verb.* Waco, TX: Word. Webber's work in this area is well-known and highly respected. As the title implies, this particular work focuses on participation and the active involvement of the worshiper at all points in the worship experience.

White, J. (1980). *Introduction to Christian worship.* Nashville: Abingdon. White emphasizes historical theological and pastoral dimensions of Christian worship with interesting chapters on "The Language of Space" and the role of "Initiation and Reconciliation" in worship.

LIVING AND GROWING
IN THE CHRISTIAN YEAR
D. Bruce Lockerbie

Our principal distinctiveness as human beings derives from the fact that we are made in the image of God. From this created condition, we obtain our consciousness of time and our need for its sanctified observance in rituals of faith. Massey H. Shepherd, Jr. concurs that "time is an inevitable condition of our creatureliness. It is part of the givenness of our human existence. God has set us within the mysterious ordering of time that we may grow with it in His grace and spend it to His glory" (Shepherd, 1952, p. 91). Since time is also an instrument of cultural memory and religious significance, through festival and ceremony we develop the rhythm of our religious experience.

For thousands of years the people of God have understood, as John H. Westerhoff says, "the stories we celebrate shape our faith and life" (Hauerwas & Westerhoff, 1992, p. 274). One of the ways of reclaiming the stories of our redemption has been to mark the days and seasons of the Christian Year (hereafter, called the Year).

THE DIFFERENCES AMONG US

If "liturgy" means "the work of the people"—and if the purpose of that work intends to assist our spiritual formation and growth—then on any given Sunday throughout Christendom, but especially in the United States of America and Canada, three distinct patterns of liturgy may be perceived in acts of worship.

In one church, the public reading of Scripture, singing of hymns and spiritual songs, and proclamation of the Word are all bound together by a common theme derived from paying heed to the calendar that sets forth the annual cycles of the Year.

Down the block, another church's Scripture, song, and sermon are also thematically joined but by some other thread: a local emphasis on world missions, Sunday School promotion, Thanksgiving Day, "every-member-canvass," or some similar event.

A third church across town has randomly selected Scripture lessons from the back of the hymnal; its choice of songs may be "favorites" called out by the congregation, while the pastor's sermon treats some current topic or proceeds verse-by-verse through an ongoing series of sermons, without regard for times or seasons.

Three assemblies of Christians gathered for communal worship; three different approaches to celebrating the mystery of union with God: *cyclical, occasional,* and *spontaneous.*

What difference does it make how a church chooses to worship? Why does it matter whether believers observe days and seasons? How might the recognition of holy days and holy seasons contribute more effectively to the spiritual formation of Christians, collectively in our churches and privately in our homes and families?

Evelyn Underhill notes that, while the difference between "ordered" and "free" worship has made them into "competing opposites," both are needed "if the full span and possibilities of Christian worship are to be realized; and it is one of the many tragedies of Church history that they have so often been regarded as hostile to one another" (Underhill, 1936, pp. 110–111).

ORIGINS OF THE LITURGICAL CALENDAR

The origins of the Year's cycle and its biblical warrants, of course, may be found in the assertion that, having finished his work of Creation, God rested, blessed the seventh day, and made it holy (Gen. 2:2-3). Thus one day in each seven was sanctified, set apart for holiness unto the Lord.

Old Testament Origins

Under Mosaic Law, observance of the Sabbath became mandatory as a sign between God and the Israelites (Ex. 31:12ff). Thereafter, other specific days, weeks, and months were set aside, with rituals established, for recalling God's special dealings with His people, notably Passover (Ex. 12:14ff) and the other recurring seasonal feasts detailed in Leviticus 23.

The God who ordained these festivals to His glory expected their celebration to honor His holiness. Their rituals reenacted God's personal concern for His people; their offerings represented wholehearted obedience and submission to God's will. But God also regarded the desecration of these days and seasons as an abomination (Isa. 1:13-14). Clearly, the cheapening of holy days into holidays is not an exclusively modern phenomenon.

New Testament Origins

Jesus of Nazareth lived by the Jewish calendar, including Sabbath observance, although He proclaimed a higher understanding of the Sabbath (Matt. 12:1-14). He also honored the major festivals, celebrated from boyhood—for instance, when He went to Jerusalem at age twelve, with Mary and Joseph (Luke 2:41ff) and again, just before the Crucifixion, to celebrate the Passover (John 12:1ff).

So too the apostles, following the Ascension. These devout Jews were in Jerusalem not only because of the expressed command of their risen Lord ("Do not leave Jerusalem," Acts 1:4), but also because they were to celebrate the Feast of Pentecost. In his account of St. Paul's missionary journeys, Luke notes that "we sailed from Philippi after the Feast of Unleavened Bread, and five days later joined the others at Troas, where we stayed seven days" (Acts 20:6). Such a passage reveals the pervasive nature of the religious calendar in governing common life, its dates and times; it also indicates that Paul and other Christians continued to mark the Sabbath and the major Jewish festivals.

But as Oscar Cullman shows, a dramatic change in observance occurred early in the growth of the Christian church, when Christians began to celebrate "the Lord's day" (Cullman, 1953, pp. 7–36). We know that Jesus' followers met on the day of Resurrection, the first day of the week, and again eight days later (John 20:1, 19, 26); we know that the early church met on "the first day of the week" (Acts 20:7-8); such meetings were not to be neglected (1 Cor. 16:1-2; Heb. 10:25). Before the end of the first century, "the first day of the week" had become known as "the Lord's day" (Rev. 1:10). So early Christians knew the discipline of a weekly reminder of the Resurrection.

THE LITURGICAL CALENDAR IN CHURCH HISTORY

Church history does not reveal precisely when and how weekly observance of the Resurrection on "the Lord's day" came to be highlighted as a festal season. By the third century, a three-day festival called Pascha — the Greek form of the Hebrew *pesach* or Passover — was being celebrated to commemorate both the Crucifixion and Resurrection.

After the Emperor Constantine's edict in 313 giving Christianity civil acceptance, the church began filling in the calendar with additional events in the life of Christ. Perhaps a visit to Jerusalem by the emperor's mother Helena in 327 helped increase interest in the sites and commemoration of biblical events.

As the sixth century ended, Pope Gregory I was sending out missionaries, such as Augustine to England. Gregory encouraged the ambassadors of Christ to capitalize on already existing festivals, accommodating the Gospel to their pagan converts' own myths and rites, proclaiming them fulfilled in Christ. Thus adopted and Christianized, Christmas occurred on December 25, replacing the pagan festival called Winterset. Epiphany, from January 6 onward, commemorated not only the arrival of the Magi but also the "showing forth" of Christ to the Gentiles, Jesus' baptism, and, eventually, His transfiguration.

During the reign of Charlemagne (768–814), canon law became institutionalized throughout the Holy Roman Empire, so that civil and religious calendars were as one. The seasons of Lent, Easter — including Ascension Day — and Pentecost followed closely the life and passion, death and burial, resurrection and exaltation of Jesus Christ; then the work of the Holy Spirit in the church. In the Western church, the season called Advent found its place at the beginning of the Church Year; in the Eastern church, Easter still begins the Year and is, ecclesiastically, "New Year's Day."

While the sixteenth Reformation disrupted uniform observance in some parts of Christendom, from Anchorage in the West to Vladivostok in the East, the daily and weekly rehearsal of biblical history and religious tradition have woven themselves into the tapestry of common life. Throughout Europe, where established religion flourished, the civil calendar still closely adheres to the Year. Even in North America, where neither Canada nor the United States has a state church, quasi-religious holidays such as St. Valentine's Day, St. Patrick's Day, and All Hallows' Eve (more familiarly, Halloween) are as well known as the more serious Christmas and Easter celebrations.

THE CHRISTIAN CALENDAR SEASON-BY-SEASON

In the Western church, the Year now takes this shape:

Advent	Four Sundays prior to Christmas Day
Christmas	December 25 through January 5 ("Twelve Days")
Epiphany	January 6 and possibly as many as nine Sundays following (depending on date of Easter, which determines Lent)
Ash Wednesday	First day of Lent
Lent	Five Sundays prior to Holy Week
Palm Sunday	Triumphal Entry (beginning of Holy Week)
Maundy Thursday	Institution of the Lord's Supper
Good Friday	Crucifixion
Easter Even	Initiation in baptism
Easter	The Resurrection and seven Sundays following
Ascension Day	Thursday of week between sixth and seventh Sunday
Pentecost	Eighth Sunday after Easter and all Sundays until Advent repeats the cycle

To these usual Sunday dates are added various Saint's Days, chosen to commemorate the martyrdom of a saint. For instance, St. Andrew is remembered on November 30, St. Mark on April 25, St. Helena on August 18. All Saints Day, one of three non-moveable feasts, is always celebrated on November 1, a day on which to give thanks "for all the saints who from their labors rest." The other two fixed dates are Christmas Day and Epiphany.

THE SIGNIFICANCE OF THE LECTIONARY

The Year is more than dates on a calendar; it is also a cycle of Scripture readings called the lectionary. Read together daily and on Sunday, these texts coordinate examples and lessons from selections representing, respectively, the Old Testament, Psalms, Gospels, and Epistles. Thus, for example, Christians observing Epiphany find the daily and Sunday lectionary leading through the New Testament accounts of the Wise Men, the Baptism of Jesus, the announcement of "the Lamb of God" by John the Baptist, various early appearances and teachings of Jesus, and always climaxing with the Transfiguration. These Gospel lessons are also accompanied by paralleling passages from the Pentateuch or the Prophets, from the Psalms and the Epistles.

Perhaps in no other common way does liturgy so well achieve its purpose than by the integration such reading of Scripture brings to worship. Together the day's lectionary readings develop a strong commitment to the authority of Scripture for all time; through these interdependent passages, the universality of the truth of God may be manifest to anyone who has ears to hear.

OPPOSING VIEWS

But while almost all orthodox Christians observe at least Christmas Day and Easter Sunday, many Christians are iconoclastic regarding the Year, rejecting its validity or value for both public worship and private devotion.

Presupposing that observance of the Year must be accompanied by a "high church" aura of incense-and-candles or other arcane liturgics, some Christians believe the Year too formal; worse, too rigid. To them, the Year represents an ecclesiastical hierarchy and authority outside the local congregation. Other Christians reject what they see in the celebration of a calendar day as a needless distraction from the central purpose of worship, which is the praise of God. Still others simply object to the imposition of structure of any sort, within or without the local congregation; adherents of planned spontaneity or strategic informality in worship often avoid any tradition or hint of formalism.

Underhill concedes that "the risks and difficulties, the constant menace of unreality, attending the obligatory use of such stylized devotion, and persistent use of traditional material, are obvious" (Underhill, 1936, p. 119). But she cautions against "those who assume that it can only result in a formal and meaningless worship."

Still others find a scriptural basis for their opposition to sacred days and seasons. Assuming all ritual to be evidence of spiritual decay, they cite the condemning passages in the Old and New Testament, including St. Paul's rebuking words (Gal. 4:9-11; Col. 2:16-17). Or they argue that Paul himself took no firm position regarding sacred days, except in support of personal liberty to observe or not observe them (Rom. 14:5ff).

For these and other reasons—including emotional comfort in familiarity with a spontaneity that ignores traditional observance or regard for ceremony—the worship of God goes forward without reference to the ecclesiastical Year.

BEYOND TRADITION INTO MEANING

For Westerhoff, the occasions we honor "provide structure for understanding the meaning and purpose of our behaviors" (Hauerwas & Westerhoff, 1992, p. 274). Within us resides a psychological need to order time, not only by means of clock or chronograph but also by recurring seasons. Christians believe that Jesus of Nazareth lived in time; the Creed declares that "He was crucified under Pontius Pilate," which fact locates His life in a specific era. So the celebration of the sacred takes on historical significance. Through time and its sanctified commemoration, *then* becomes *now;* the past fuses with the present; history merges into current meaning.

But if—as is being suggested here—observance of the Year contributes to spiritual formation and meaning, is it not also true that what Westerhoff identifies as "the Hallmark card calendar" (Hauerwas & Westerhoff, 1992, p. 274) conveys a different and spiritually inferior kind of meaning? Increasingly, secular traditions usurp the Year's observance as the secular world "orders time with occasions such as Mother's Day, Halloween, St. Patrick's Day, the Fourth of July (Independence Day), Memorial Day, birthdays, and so forth" (Hauerwas & Westerhoff, 1992, p. 274).

Even more distressing is the fact that "many churches celebrate such days and thereby encourage a secularization of the church. For Christians the celebration of baptism days and the church's year—Advent, Christmas, Epiphany, Lent, Easter, Pentecost, and so forth—are more important" (Hauerwas & Westerhoff, 1992, p. 274).

In what must be his most searching criticism, Westerhoff says, "One year when Mother's Day and Pentecost corresponded, many churches celebrated Mother's Day and then wondered why the Holy Spirit was not alive in their lives, or the church infused by its presence" (Hauerwas & Westerhoff, 1992, p. 274).

A CASE FOR OBSERVING THE CHRISTIAN YEAR

What reasonable case can be made for celebrating the Year? I offer the following from the perspective of someone who came to a personal appreciation of the Year at age forty, after an upbringing that ignored all but Christmas and Easter.

1. *Observing the Year provides each Christian with opportunity to fulfill one of the most basic human instincts, the chance to start all over again.*

Renewal is at the heart of the Gospel of Jesus Christ: new birth, new life, new hope. Shepherd reminds us that "the annually recurring seasons of the Christian Year also afford us ever new opportunities for a fresh start" (Shepherd, 1952, p. 103). Even as secular pagans resort to New Year's resolutions, so at the coming of each Advent our human frailty is aided in committing ourselves to new devotion by the calendar and its meaning.

2. *The Year's cycle provides those principles and discipline each Christian needs.*

Because we are weak creatures, we need whatever framework will support our faith and provide a context for its articulation. This supporting framework will consist of many parts, including diligent Bible study and Scripture memorization or reciting the Apostles' Creed as an exercise in condensed theology. But it may also include the consistent, ongoing study of the cycle of days and seasons that make up the Year and "the cloud of witnesses" whose example of faith we may emulate.

3. *We need to walk with God's people through history, to "walk today where Jesus walked," by means of observing the Year.*

God ordained the annual celebration of Passover so that Israel would remember; so Moses commanded, "Commemorate this day, the day you came out of Egypt" (Ex. 13:3). For the same reason, when instituting the Lord's Supper, Jesus said, "Do this in remembrance of me" (Luke 22:19). Ritual reenacts sacred events and helps the worshiper transcend time and, by entering into the past event, appropriate its meaning. Holding a palm branch and shouting "Hosanna" on Palm Sunday helps a modern Christian identify with those enthusiasts of 2,000 years ago; so too can meditation on the Transfiguration (August 6) or the witness of Andrew to his brother Simon Peter (November 30).

Furthermore, many Christians are simply uninformed about history, having never studied the Middle Ages, the Reformation, or even their own national history. The Year observes, in a day-by-day reference, such persons as Agnes, martyred at Rome in 304 (January 21), and Jackson Kemper, first missionary bishop to the United States in 1870 (May 24). Learning about such people and their service to God informs us about the world in which they lived.

4. *Observing the Year means marking a season of several days or weeks rather than just one day.*

Most sacred days are set within a season: four weeks of Advent, twelve days of Christmas, and so on. In our increasingly secular era, the last vestiges of Christendom's once pervading influence have been reduced to an occasional day here, a day there — except when an excuse can be found for a long weekend in the interests of leisure. But for the Christian who observes the Year, its cycle extends the otherwise-compressed day into a time for more than frenzied commercialism; it can become a period of prayer, study, learning, and growth.

5. *Observing the Year sets believers apart from secularists for whom the holy-day has become merely a holiday.*

While the rest of the world resumes its schedule in the aftermath of a holiday, Christians may be quietly about the business of trimming our lamps and keeping them shining in a dark place, simply by observing the full season. By declaring that one's annual life-cycle begins not on January 1, nor on the Labor Day weekend, but with the First Sunday in Advent, one may openly affirm why life is regulated by a different calendar from the common.

6. *Marking a season gives time to develop a biblical understanding or theology of the season.*

Consider, for instance, the season of Christmas, the season that celebrates *giving.* Its Twelve Days exist as more than the title of a song whose lyric confuses most of us. Each day, from December 25 to January 5, speaks of my True Love's full-hearted giving to me. Who else is my True Love but the one from whom comes every good and every perfect gift? The one who gives from every element of His creation "one blessing after another" (John 1:16)? So, during the full season of Christmas, a Christian might choose to mark each day in thanksgiving for specific blessings bestowed or anticipated.

PUBLIC AND PRIVATE OBSERVANCE OF THE YEAR

A worshiping community meeting as a church need not take on unfamiliar ecclesiastical trappings or abandon its preferred order of worship to begin observing the Year. Simply by using the lectionary as Scripture lessons and by correlating the hymns and other music (if not the pastor's sermon!) with those lessons, worship leaders can turn worshipers toward a fuller recognition of the progress and continuity of the presence of God in His dealings with Israel, in the life of Christ, and in the growth of the church.

Or a pastor might use the teaching role for some portion of the Year—Advent, Epiphany, Lent, or Easter—to develop within the congregation a deeper understanding of that particular season. For instance, once a year—most appropriately, on Maundy Thursday—a church might follow the example of Jesus Christ and engage in the ceremony of foot washing—or some contemporary, culturally equivalent menial task which makes clear the servant's role.

Whether or not one's church follows the Christian calendar, increasing numbers of evangelical Christians find comfort and nurture in observance through their private devotions. Some persons may adopt the Anglican *Book of Common Prayer*, whose Lectionary offers three years of readings; or its Daily Office, which offers a more extensive selection in two years of readings. Many other aids to personal worship are available, including daily devotional guides, such as *Forward Day by Day*, geared to the Year.

Non-Anglican adaptations of the Year and commentaries to accompany the Year are also readily available in bookstores.

A Christian may also invoke privately what a nonobserving church ignores: fasting and abstinence, prayer and confession during Lent; a servant's willingness to perform the most menial task on Maundy Thursday; a prayerful watch, as in Gethsemane, during the overnight leading to Good Friday morning.

A Christian family wishing children to catch the significance of the various seasons may celebrate by lighting an Advent wreath—four candles, one for each Sunday in Advent, set within a holly or evergreen wreath as a table centerpiece—to prepare for the coming Incarnation. If Christmas decorating includes a traditional creche, parents can teach a child what many Christmas cards do not know: the wise men's arrival comes at the end of the Christmas season—and never at the manger.

" ... KEEP BETWEEN YOURSELF AND GOD"

Does observance of the Year fall into the category of practices that belong to the right of private judgment, or is there an intrinsic spiritual value being missed by those who do not observe the Year?

A biblically enlightened understanding of the Year recognizes that "we live, through our liturgical year, literally between two worlds, marked by the two Advents of our Lord, His coming to us in time and His coming to us for all eternity" (Shepherd, p. 122). Whatever else, observance of the Year has as its purpose only to enhance our love and worship of God, not to become an object of love and worship itself. Any observance of the Year, therefore, intends to help focus spiritual insight and deepen understanding of redemptive history. No day—not this coming Sunday nor even next Easter—holds any obligation over the Christian; such teaching is a corruption from the days of Rome's authority and Henry VIII's Act of Uniformity. We worship in adoration, not upon threats of reprisal.

Furthermore, while there are spiritual benefits to be gained by living and growing through the Year's cycle, the Apostle Paul instructs us to respect both the person who "considers one day more sacred than another" and another who "considers every day alike"; each must be "fully convinced in his own mind" that he "does so to the Lord" (Rom. 14:5-6).

Celebrating the Year has helped many Christians become more spiritually mature. Those who have never experienced its joys may wish to expose themselves to some sample observation. Of course, judgmental attitudes on either side are dangerous (Rom. 14:22).

For Further Reading

Cullman, O. (1953). *Early Christian worship.* Naperville, IL: Alec R. Allenson. A monograph by the German scholar, this slim volume introduces basic characteristics of worship in the early church, then examines the nature of worship as found in John's Gospel.

Hatchett, M. (1976). *Sanctifying life, time, and space: An introduction to liturgical study.* New York: Seabury. A brief history of the development of Christian rituals marking birth-to-death, celebrating annually the mystery of God-in-Christ, and setting apart places of worship.

Hauerwas, S. & Westerhoff, J. (Eds.) (1992). *Schooling Christians: "Holy experiments" in American education.* Grand Rapids: Eerdmans. The final chapter of this symposium, "Fashioning Christians in Our Day," by Westerhoff, makes the case for "cultic life" as essential to the formation of Christians.

Job, R. and Sawchuck, N. (1983). *A guide to prayer for ministers and other servants*. Nashville: Upper Room. A devotional handbook structured upon the Christian Year yet not tied to any particular ecclesiastical liturgy and useful for both personal and corporate worship.

Webber, R. (1993). *The book of daily prayer*. Grand Rapids: Eerdmans. A practical and convenient guide to prayer, this daily devotional is organized around the Christian Year in order to carry Christians more fully into the experience of Christ.

NURTURING THE SPIRITUAL LIVES OF TEACHERS
Robert W. Pazmiño

Justo L. Gonzalez, a church historian, has aptly observed that spirituality

> . . . has to do with the manner in which the gospel is both "lived in" and "lived out." Spirituality is first of all living in the gospel—making faith the foundation for life. And it is also living out the gospel—making faith the foundation of action and structure (Gonzalez, 1990, p. 157).

If church leaders hope to nurture the spiritual life of teachers, they must consider how the Gospel is both lived in and lived out by those called to teaching ministries. They must also be clear in establishing the foundations for Christian teaching and spiritual nurture (Pazmiño, 1988). But prior to beginning a process of nurture, one must first discern the existing spirituality of teachers, leaders, and the entire faith community in which one is serving.

Recognizing that a diversity of spirituality exists today, Christian leaders can seek to help teachers to discern what in a given time and place is the faithful way of worshiping, witnessing to, and serving God. All true Christian spiritualities help those who follow Christ to walk and live in God's presence with body, mind, and soul. They help to maintain hope in the midst of the sufferings and struggles of this world (World Council of Churches, 1987, pp. 9–10).

"Christian spirituality encompasses all authentic ways of *fol-*

lowing Christ. It is a pilgrimage to God through Christ, a process of sanctification, a process of being formed in the image of God through the Jesus Christ" (World Council of Churches, 1987, p. 10). The call to Christian teachers, like the call to all believers, is to live by faith. The righteous will live by faith. In the Gospel a righteousness from God is revealed, a righteousness that is by faith and made available in Jesus Christ (Rom. 1:17). Christian spirituality for teachers implies a discipleship centered upon Jesus Christ as Lord and a walk with Christ's Spirit, the Holy Spirit. This Christian spirituality is best understood by exploring the experience of various persons in the Bible, the primary source for Christian faith.

OUR EXPERIENCE OF CHRISTIAN SPIRITUALITY

In the Bible we recognize a great diversity of spiritual life that directly relates to the particular context and experience of God's people. Different traditions of faith and experience fostered different spiritualities. The Old Testament provides a number of examples (World Council of Churches, 1987, p. 9). The peculiar spirituality of Israel found in the Exodus emphasized faithfulness to God's covenant in the midst of change and conflict. God called His people to commitment in the formation of a new community. Joshua and his household committed themselves to serve the Lord (Josh. 24:15). The royal traditions of the two kingdoms of Israel and Judah required faithfulness to God's values of righteousness and justice in the political, economic, and social affairs of state as suggested in Psalm 72 and Isaiah 58.

The priestly traditions in Jerusalem emphasized a spirituality that was sustained even after the Exile and modeled in the lives of both Nehemiah the lay leader and Ezra the priest. Ezra was dedicated to the study, living out, and teaching of God's Word (Ezra 7:10) that should also characterize those called to teaching today. The wisdom spirituality of the sages required a wholehearted listening and whole life response to wisdom as she called to persons in their daily walk (Prov. 8). Those who waited upon wisdom discovered fullness and joy in life even with their struggles and trials. This is particularly the case with the *anawim* (those who are poor, humble, and weak before God and others) whose spirituality challenges a culture of materialism and individualism.

The distinctive spirituality of the *anawim* is of particular significance for the majority of Christians around the globe, a spirituality incarnated in their lives and actions. A number of examples are instructive. Hagar, the pregnant Egyptian maidservant of Sarah and Abraham, demonstrated a radical trust in God for the life of Ishmael while she was in the desert following her mistreatment. Rahab, the harlot of Jericho, offered sanctuary to the Hebrew spies and chose loyalty to God above allegiance to her city-state. She thus saved her household and is recognized among Jesus' ancestors (Matt. 1:5).

Ruth likewise is named in Matthew's genealogy of Jesus, and she was the foreign widow who remained faithful to her mother-in-law Naomi. Ruth gleaned to survive while trusting in God's provision. The Hebrew midwives in Egypt (Ex. 1:15-22) saved the lives of male children and subverted Pharaoh's plans of destruction. They jeopardized their own lives to save the lives of newborn children. The widow at Zarephath (1 Kings 17) risked all and offered her last meal to Elijah while she and her son were at the point of death. Naaman's wife's Hebrew girl servant suggested who might offer healing to her master that was realized in seeking out Elisha (2 Kings 5). The lepers who camped outside the city gate of Samaria risked surrender to the enemy and discovered that the Aramean army was routed (2 Kings 7). They realized the selfishness of their initial response and shared the good news of their discovery with those remaining in the besieged city.

Such were the *anawim,* those who were marginal in society but open to new possibilities. Through their sacrificial acts they demonstrated their spirituality and their higher accountability to God. Along with the witnesses identified in Hebrews 11, they serve as models who taught by their way of faith, life, and love.

DISCIPLESHIP WITH JESUS CHRIST

Discipleship is essential to Christian spirituality and teaching. But discipleship is never self-centered or self-occupied in contrast with much contemporary interest in generic spirituality. Christian discipleship is always oriented to the way of Jesus and the community of His followers. The gift of teaching is a spiritual gift given for *the common good* (1 Cor. 12:7). The loss of perspective on *the common good* must be addressed by clerical and lay leaders who seek to nurture the spiritual lives of teachers. Clarity with regard to the what and why of Christian teaching must be a priority among those who serve in teaching ministries. This clarity is assured through exploring the foundational issues in Christian education which is required of each generation of Christians (Pazmiño, 1988). Beyond the common good that each local church must identify, appropriate, and live out, leaders can explore with teachers the particulars of discipleship.

Marianne Sawicki in her work helpful *The Gospel in History*, identifies four particulars of discipleship that relate to teaching: a personal encounter with Jesus; a call to which one responds; a mission to testify to others about Jesus; and a following of Jesus to death (Sawicki, 1988, pp. 60–62, 90). Each of these has implications for significantly nurturing the spiritual life of teachers.

First and foremost, *Christian teachers must have a personal faith encounter with Jesus and a commitment to follow Jesus Christ as Lord of their lives and teaching ministries.* This is basic, but requires the careful attention of those who recruit persons to serve as teachers. But more than this initial commitment, teachers are required to deepen and strengthen their ongoing relationship with Jesus. Spiritual leaders must attend to the nurture of the nurturers in the local church body. Teachers who do not regularly attend corporate worship services are at particular risk along with those who do not regularly nourish their own souls through personal Bible study, prayer, and devotion.

Secondly, *Christian teachers need to discern the nature of their call to teach and to develop their gifts of teaching as a part of that spiritual call.* A call to teach children, for example, requires distinct sensitivities and abilities from those required to teach youth or adults. The call to teach may also involve openness to work cooperatively on a teaching team that requires complementing the gifts of other teachers. The call to teach implies an openness to the evaluation of the content, process, and results of teaching in relation to the common good of the local ministry. I identify the specific areas for such an evaluation of teaching in the work *Principles and Practices of Christian Education* (Pazmiño, 1992, pp. 145–168). In all of these areas leaders nurture the spiritual lives of teachers by providing opportunities for self and group evaluations. Leaders also organize occasions for the appropriate celebration of what has been accomplished by the grace of God. Teachers need support and recognition for their efforts and encouragement for the continued outworking of their call. This is a vital part of the process.

Thirdly, *teachers need opportunities to be equipped or trained in fulfilling their mission to teach.* Various teaching skills can be improved through practice, and teachers can develop more creative and innovative styles if freedom is provided to test out new ideas and to explore options. Teachers need occasions to be in fellowship with other teachers and to realize that the problems they experience are also encountered by others. Teachers may also need to explore how their teaching can enable students to hear the Gospel afresh and to respond faithfully to the claims of Jesus Christ upon their lives. Various teacher training events must also include times to fellowship with the Master Teacher and to gain perspective in terms of the values and virtues of Christ's reign.

Fourthly, *discipleship in Christian teaching implies a willingness to follow Jesus to the death.* Dietrich Bonhoeffer in *The Cost of Discipleship* noted that when Christ calls a person, He bids one to come and die (Bonhoeffer, 1979, p. 99). Some teachers may view their ministry as a call to martyrdom in a challenging classroom, but the word *martyr* derives from the verb "to witness." Christian teachers are called to witness with not only their teachings about Jesus, but with their very lives about the life transforming power of the risen Lord. Following Jesus to the death requires that teachers be challenged with a lifelong denial of self so the life of Christ may be manifest in human form within the classrooms and other settings for Christian teaching. Leaders are to issue and model that challenge. Such a challenge can only be fulfilled by walking in and with the Holy Spirit.

WALKING WITH THE HOLY SPIRIT

Gonzalez notes that the basis for Christian spirituality is the Spirit, the Holy Spirit of God. One is spiritual because of the presence and indwelling of the Holy Spirit. A spiritual person, a spiritual teacher is one who has allowed the Spirit of the Lord to dwell in power (Gonzalez, 1990, p. 158). A spirituality without the Holy Spirit is a scandal in Christian faith and in Christian teaching. Christian spirituality is a way of deepening the experience of God's active presence through the work of the Holy Spirit in one's own life, in the life of the church, and in the history of the world. Christian spirituality is about opening oneself to the healing power of the Spirit which enables persons to become whole and reconciled with themselves, with God, and with the world. The world is God's creation and the object of God's love (John 3:16).

THE EXISTING SPIRITUALITY

An ecumenical study of spiritual formation conducted by the Programme on Theological Education of the World Council of Churches observed that all persons, all teachers and church leaders have some sort of spirituality.

> It may be bland, selfish, destructive or downright demonic, but every one of us has what Augustine would call an *ordo amoris* (order of loves). Our spirituality is not what we explicitly express, nor what we profess to believe, but how we *order our loves.* That ordering may be unarticulated, even quite unconscious, but the resultant spirituality pervades our whole life and involves our whole person. Our stewardship of time, energy, and substance reflects the way we live out and express the ordering of our loves. . . . There can be and indeed is what can be called a spirituality of consumerism, a spirituality of security, a spirituality of the avoidance of pain, or even a spirituality of destructive violence (World Council of Churches, 1987, p. 8).

148

A diversity of spiritualities exists and the important prior step in nurturing the spirituality of teachers is to be discerning of the existing spiritualities that pervade their lives, the lives of those who are leaders, and the life of the faith community itself.

By discerning existing spiritualities of teachers and other persons in a local church or ministry, a leader is better able to affirm and/or confront those loves that order the inner and outer faith life of teachers and students alike. A concern for the order of our loves and lives implies an interest in discipleship, discipline, and stewardship to which all Christians are called. For Christians the order of our loves is indicated in the biblical great commandment: to love the Lord our God with all of our hearts, souls, minds, and strength and to love our neighbor as ourselves (Mark 12:30-31).

While confronting the diverse false spiritualities and loves of our age, Christian leaders must recognize and celebrate the genuine expressions of Christian spirituality that are manifested in the lives of teachers, many of whom may be today's *anawim.* While living in an age of criticism and cynicism, spiritual leaders must consciously and consistently nurture a stance of affirmation among teachers. Constant criticism of others can limit them to their past, whereas appropriate affirmation can release them to the possibilities of present and future ministry. In relation to the teaching ministry, leaders must identify and share the particulars of Christian spirituality.

MARKS OF SPIRITUALITY

In relation to walking with the Holy Spirit, Christian leaders can both note and nurture the ten marks of Christian spirituality identified by the World Council study (World Council of Churches, 1987, 13–16) that can find expression in Christian teaching:

Reconciling and Integrative

A genuine spirituality is directed toward the wholeness of persons and communities. A danger exists in just focusing on content or persons to the exclusion of the wider community and society. Teachers should work for the common good, submerging private agendas and seeking for a unity across the diversity of spiritual life that persons experience in each Christian faith community.

Incarnational
A genuine spirituality addresses the here and now, where people live. In teaching this may require setting aside a plan when it is necessary to deal with pressing problems and issues. This does not succumb to the tyranny of the present, but represents an openness and flexibility to allow the Holy Spirit to work in unexpected ways through teaching.

Rooted in Scripture and Nourished by Prayer
Christian education classes and events can provide times to share prayer concerns and to actually pray. It is also possible in some worship settings to uphold in prayer particular teachers and their general concerns, without breaching confidentiality. This can be done in pastoral prayers along with regular prayer times during the week. The content of Scripture cannot be ignored as the key source for the Christian faith, especially in a time of biblical and theological illiteracy. Teachers are in need of encouragement in their personal and group practice of prayer and Bible study.

Costly and Self-giving
Christian spirituality confronts the reality of the cross of Christ in the world and in the life of many people who experience suffering and loss. We must share the challenges of discipleship with teachers even as we recognize their acts of self-giving. We must avoid teacher recruitment that dismisses the costs of teaching. The Christian faith embraces the scandal of particularity and vulnerability and this applies to the various ministries of teaching.

Life-giving and Liberative
Like birthing and parenting, spiritual formation provides space for life to grow. It also encourages teachers to advocate those concerns close to the heart of God. Christian teachers are to encourage choosing and affirming life as God's gift to humanity and the entire creation. Teachers are engaged in a spiritual

conflict with powers and principalities opposed to God. They are called upon to destroy those forces that destroy life by enabling students to name the destroyers and claim the very resources of God's Spirit for daily living.

Rooted in Community and Centered around the Eucharist, Communion, or Lord's Supper

The Eucharist is the banquet of God's reign and the center of worship. Teaching can be imaged as serving a feast at which all are welcome (Pazmiño, 1992, 120–122). In relation to the Eucharist which refers to thanksgiving, a key question to ask is: Do teachers attend corporate worship and participate around the Lord's table? An option may be to have a spiritual retreat for teachers, but their regular participation in worship is important for their spiritual nourishment. Teachers are in need of regular times for renewal, sabbath, and refreshment. Teachers need significant times for fellowship with the entire Christian community.

Expressed in Service and Witness

Spirituality involves a commitment to action, words, and deeds. Teaching is active service and serves as a witness to God's continued teaching in the Christian community. The danger in many church settings is burnout because there is not a balance with times of service and times of sabbath and receptivity to the ministry of others. Leaders can advocate specified terms of service that allow for teachers to be taught by others.

About Waiting for God's Surprising Initiatives

Teaching requires openness to God's mystery and surprises. Nurturing this receptivity may be fostered by asking the simple question of teachers: What is God doing in your life and teaching? This waiting is also nurtured through regular times of prayer that allow for silence and active listening to God.

About the Unfolding of the Loving Purposes of God Here on Earth

This mark of Christian spirituality is inspired by the prayer that God's will be done on earth as in heaven that some congregations regularly pray. It signals the need to link together the transcendent and the immanent dimensions of God through any ministry that includes teaching. The discernment of this connection requires the time and freedom to evaluate teaching.

Is Open to the Wider Community of Faith and Other Lands of Spirituality

This requires of Christians an openness to the wider household of God and to His general revelation through common grace. It is a perspective that avoids spiritual captivity to our own culture and the idols we too readily embrace. This openness avoids the arrogance of some Christians who refuse to see all truth as God's truth. In relation to Christian teachers, such an openness involves a risk along with a willingness to be stretched.

CONCLUSION

Nurturing of the ten marks identified as characterizing a Christian spirituality in relation to teaching requires that leaders themselves be filled with the Spirit and be open to grow with those called to be teachers. The ultimate purpose of nurturing the spiritual life of teachers must always be kept in focus, namely to glorify and enjoy God forever. This is the responsibility and joy of those who nurture teachers and who in turn are nurtured by them and God. The ministry of teaching is a high calling, and Christian leaders must nurture the spiritual lives of teachers so that the Gospel may be lived in and out today.

This chapter has explored the distinctives of Christian spirituality that need to be nurtured in the lives of teachers and all those in a faith community through the ministries of Christian education. The examples of the *anawim* who were willing to risk all and rely upon the provision of God in different situations were particularly noted. Nurturing the spiritual lives of teachers requires attention to the demands of Christian discipleship and to daily walking with the Holy Spirit. Such a walk requires an exploration of the existing spirituality in the faith community and the full expression of the various marks of Christian spirituality. Nurturing the spiritual lives of teachers holds the promise of their effective ministries in nurturing the spiritual lives of their students, fulfilling Paul's exhortation in 2 Timothy 2:2.

For Further Reading

Bonhoeffer, D. (1979). *The cost of discipleship* (rev. ed.). New York: Macmillan. Bonhoeffer explores the significance of Christian discipleship that can serve as a model for spiritual teaching.

Cully, I. (1984). *Education for spiritual growth.* San Francisco: Harper & Row. This work explores how spiritual life can be nurtured in individuals at each age level through religious education programming.

Gonzalez, J. (1990). *Mañana: Christian theology from a Hispanic perspective.* Nashville: Abingdon. The distinctive contributions of Hispanic spirituality and culture are explored in relation to Christian faith, life, and ministry.

Palmer, P. (1983). *To know as we are known: A spirituality of education.* San Francisco: Harper & Row. From the tradition of Quaker spirituality, Palmer explores teaching as creating a space which in obedience to truth can be practiced. He explores knowing as loving and the spiritual formation of teachers.

Pazmiño, R. (1988). *Foundational issues in Christian education: An introduction in evangelical perspective.* Grand Rapids: Baker. The text discusses Christian education with reference to the foundations upon which spiritual teaching can be built.

————. (1992). *Principles and practices of Christian education: An evangelical perspective.* Grand Rapids: Baker. A sequel to an earlier work, this text explores the specifics of teaching that can nurture Christian spirituality.

Sawicki, M. (1988). *The gospel in history: Portrait of a teaching church: The origins of Christian education.* New York: Paulist. This historical work explores the Gospel ministries of the word, care, and celebration as the foundation for teaching that seeks to be faithful to Jesus Christ and spiritually renewing.

World Council of Churches, Programme on Theological Education. (1987). *Spiritual formation in theological education: An invitation to participate.* Geneva, Switzerland: World Council of Churches. An ecumenical study that explores making theological education and ministerial preparation responsive to the stirrings of the Holy Spirit.

PRINCIPLES OF CHURCH RENEWAL*
Alan Schreck

God desires to keep His church vital. As we consider key principles of dynamic church life, we should recall that "dynamic" is from the Greek *dunamis* which means power. What is the source of power for the life of the church? The Holy Spirit—"the Lord and giver of life," as the Nicene Creed calls Him—is that source of the church's life and power, not only in our age but in every age. The Gospel of John (4:10; 7:38-39) speaks of the Holy Spirit as the "living water" who keeps the church alive; I like to think of the Holy Spirit as the church's "fountain of youth." Through the living water of the Spirit, the ancient church is ever young, vital, and powerful.

THE MEANING OF "RENEWAL"

When we speak about the renewal of the church, then, we are talking about a work of the Holy Spirit. If the Holy Spirit is not behind it, it is not authentic renewal. That elusive word "renewal" may have many meanings, but a simple definition is "the process of making something new, or like new, again." Christians do not need a new church. Jesus founded one church that, He promised, would withstand the gates of hell (Matt. 16:18). The new covenant between God and His people is definitive. It will never pass away. We will never need a

*© 1993. The Alliance for Faith & Renewal. Reprinted and adapted with permission from *Faith & Renewal* (Formerly *Pastoral Renewal*), P.O. Box 7354, Ann Arbor, MI 48107, U.S.A.

"new" new covenant. Therefore we do not need a *new* church. But we certainly do need a *renewed* church. We need the Holy Spirit to renew the church that Christ founded, that is, to make the church continually new.

The church was born at Pentecost with the first great outpouring of the Holy Spirit on all of Jesus' followers. To pray for renewal is to pray for the outpouring of the Holy Spirit—to pray that the church would have the same life and power today that it had when it was born. Peter Kreeft (1988) comments on the present-day church in his book, *Fundamentals of the Faith*.

> When Paul visits the church in Ephesus (Acts 19), he notices something missing—I think he would notice exactly the same thing in most churches and preach the same sermon—and he asks them, "Did you receive the Holy Spirit when you believed?" (Acts 19:2). Why would he ask that unless he saw a power shortage? Why did twelve fishermen convert the world, and why are half a billion Christians unable to repeat the feat? The Spirit makes the difference (p. 142).

We do not need a new church, but a new Pentecost—a new and continual outpouring of God's own Spirit on the church. That is the heart of authentic renewal.

RENEWAL: ALWAYS ESSENTIAL

From the history of the church we can learn a number of principles concerning the church's renewal in the Holy Spirit. The first and foremost is simply that renewal is always an essential part of the church's life. There is no perfect, sinless church. Every part of the body of Christ on earth is in need of continual renewal.

The good news is that God *is* continually renewing the church through the Holy Spirit. This is the story of the Old Testament. God made a covenant with His people, and then called them back, again and again, to faithfulness to that covenant. The Old Testament is an epic story of God's covenant-making, of the people's covenant-breaking, and of the constant renewal of the covenant by a faithful and merciful God. The Prophet Jeremiah foretells that God's solution to the weakness and infidelity of His chosen people is the establishment of a new covenant through which God would put His law in their minds and write it on their hearts (Jer. 31:31-34). The giving of the law of the old covenant to Moses on Mt. Sinai, accompanied by signs from heaven, foreshadows the sending of the "law" of the new covenant—the Holy Spirit—on Jesus' disciples like a mighty wind and with tongues of fire (Acts 2:1-4).

One might think that in the new covenant, sealed with Jesus' own blood and with the fullness of the Holy Spirit, there would no longer be a need for the continual renewal of the people of God. Many groups in Christian history have claimed to be the true heirs of a pristine church of the New Testament. They claim to be part of a church that is truly holy, by which they mean freed by God's grace from the evident sin and weakness that has disfigured other Christian groups throughout history.

The problem with this is that there never was an ideal, sinless church, even after the coming of Christ and Pentecost. The apostles, even after Pentecost, were not perfect, and neither were the churches they founded. St. Paul spends a large proportion of his letters dealing with problems and sin in the various local churches. The Book of Revelation includes seven letters to churches that were struggling to live the Gospel of Christ, calling them back to faithfulness where they had failed.

IS THERE A "PERFECT CHURCH"?

Perhaps the closest picture we have to an ideal church in the New Testament is the original church in Jerusalem, described in Acts 2–4. Through the power of Pentecost this church was continually " . . . praising God and enjoying the favor of all the people" (Acts 2:47). The same positive qualities were present in the churches of Ephesus and Antioch as well. However, a few chapters later, Acts reports some sobering events. Ananias and Sapphira were struck dead for lying to God (Acts 5:1-11). Schism threatened the church in Jerusalem in a dispute between the Hebrew and Hellenist Jewish Christians over the distribution of food to the widows (Acts 6:1-7). Later the Jerusalem Christians were involved in the great controversy over circumcision that threatened to divide the whole church (Acts 15). Thus even in the New Testament we find no "perfect" church, free of sin, crisis, or problems.

Like the church today, the church of the New Testament was in constant need of the reforming and renewing power of the Holy Spirit, and of the Spirit's guidance (often expressed through the church's elders) to resolve difficult problems, such as in Acts 15. Since there is no "perfect church" on earth, has Jesus' mission failed? No. Christians look forward to and pray for the day when Christ will return in glory and the church will be presented to Him as His bride, "without stain, or wrinkle, or any other blemish" (Eph. 5:27), ready for the wedding banquet of the Lamb (Rev. 21). Until then God prepares the church for the coming of Christ through continual renewal.

The Catholic tradition, which is my own, deeply appreciates how renewal is at the heart of the church's life and identity. This was expressed repeatedly at the Second Vatican Council (1963–65), in documents such as the "Decree on Ecumenism" and in the "Dogmatic Constitution of the Church" *(Lumen Gentium)*. The Catholic Church recognizes how easy it is to depart from living out the full Christian life, or to allow some essential elements of the Christian faith to be obscured or neglected in practice over the course of time. We rely on God, specifically the Holy Spirit, to constantly call us back from our sinfulness and shortsightedness to the full practice of the Christian faith in all its richness and beauty. If the Catholic Church did not believe in ongoing reformation and renewal, it would have disappeared long ago. But because of God's faithfulness to His covenant and the gift of the Holy Spirit, it is constantly being strengthened and renewed and has been able to thrive and grow for nearly 2,000 years.

RENEWAL: GOD'S GIFT AND OUR RESPONSE

Christians cannot take selfish pride in the longevity of the church, nor in its renewal, for they are both a gift of God. Renewal is primarily God's work, not ours. However, our response to God's grace is necessary, if the church is to be renewed. Our major task as Christians is to seek renewal within our own "households" — our particular part of Christ's body — confident that the Lord will pour out the grace of renewal on those who humbly and persistently seek it.

History teaches us that renewal usually comes through "saints" — women and men whose lives are radically dedicated to the Lord in prayer, humility, and obedience. "Men and women saints have always been fonts and origins of renewal in the most difficult circumstances throughout the Church's history. Today we have tremendous need of saints, for whom we must assiduously implore God" (Extraordinary Synod of Catholic Bishops, 1985, p. 47). This does not mean that those who respond to God's call are godly from the beginning. But through seeking to respond to God's grace, they are progressively purified and transformed into the image of Christ and are used by God to strengthen His body, the church.

All Christian traditions can point to certain individuals who have been instruments powerfully used by God for the renewal of the church. And part of the Good News of Jesus is that each Christian, including you and me, is called to be a saint, and to be used by God for the renewal of His church. The crucial question for each of us is: "Will we, and how fully will we, respond to God's grace and His call to be saints, to 'be holy as He is holy' (cf. Lev. 11:44-45; 19:2; 20:7; 1 Peter 1:15-16), so that we may be used by God to renew His church?"

How does renewal come about? Prayer must be at the heart of any authentic renewal movement. Only through prayer, humility, and obedience can the church hear God's call to renewal and respond to it. Besides being a precondition for renewal, prayer and holiness are also the most evident fruits of renewal. Authentic renewal may take many forms, but it always results in Christians following the Lord and His ways more faithfully and fervently.

DISCERNING AUTHENTIC AND INAUTHENTIC RENEWAL

Holiness, however, can be confused with rigorism or narrowly identified with particular religious practices or spiritual manifestations. Those involved in renewal may then attempt to impose certain behaviors on all other Christians as normative. Certainly there are practices and beliefs that are normative for the whole church, but these must be carefully discerned. The danger of treating particular norms and practices as if they were necessary and universal has recurred in renewal efforts throughout Christian history.

Take, for example, the Montanist movement that emerged in the second century. The priest Montanus, "father" of the movement, was disturbed by increasing laxity among Christians in prayer, fasting, and other disciplines, as well as by the decline of prophecy and other gifts. The followers of Montanus recognized their founder and two women, Maximilla and Priscilla, as possessing true prophetic gifts. Problems arose when the Montanists declared their prophecy and stricter ascetic practices — such as longer fasts and prohibition of remarriage after the death of a spouse — to be normative for the whole church. What could have been an authentic renewal movement was spoiled by their insistence that only those who were more strict and accepted Montanist prophecy were true, "spiritual" Christians.

In contrast, the monastic movement, which spread rapidly beginning in the fourth century, was also characterized by very strict fasting and other ascetic practices and manifested a variety of extraordinary spiritual gifts among its adherents. But instead of creating a schism, the movement greatly strengthened and enriched the whole church. Indeed, it produced some of the greatest saints and theologians of all time.

What made monasticism different from Montanism? While claiming only to be living normal Christian life in a radically committed way, the "monks" did not set up their particular calling as the norm for all Christians. This humility opened the way for other Christians to be inspired by the example of the monks and to be instructed by the wisdom the monks derived from prayer and holy living. Consequently, the monastic movement became a leaven of renewal for the entire church.

RENEWAL: TESTING, TRIAL, AND TRIUMPH

In the thirteeth century the church was in dire need of reform. This spawned many militantly anticlerical groups which insisted that the church return to a lifestyle of poverty and faithfulness to the Gospel. Some of these groups adopted a dualistic theology (matter is evil; only spirit is good) similar to that of the Gnostics and Manichees of previous centuries. Out of this situation emerged Francesco Bernadone, son of a wealthy cloth merchant, who heard the Lord's call to a life of Gospel simplicity and poverty, yet fully loyal to the Catholic Church in spite of its many struggles and weakness at the time.

Francis of Assisi was a "little poor man" who loved the incarnate Christ in all His creation and the crucified Christ in His suffering. By his example of following Christ, Francis began a stream of renewed Christian life that radically transformed the church of his time and still has great impact today through the religious order that he inspired, the Franciscans. Another "mendicant," or begging, order of that time, the Dominicans, founded by Dominic Guzman, also had great impact on the church through their radical Gospel way of life and by the great and saintly scholars which they produced, such as Thomas Aquinas.

Although these orders are now firmly established in the Catholic Church, they began as small renewal groups whose activities and life were sometimes suspect. The early Franciscans and Dominicans often were not well treated, either in the towns or in the new universities. Authentic renewal may take time to recognize, even by the church. The good fruit these groups bore resulted in their eventual acceptance, but not without trial. Because these groups were the result of an authentic grace of renewal, and because their members remained faithful to that grace with a Gospel spirit of love, humility, and obedience, they not only survived, but flourished within the church. We also see in their history the importance of church leaders recognizing authentic renewal movements and finding a place for them within the overall structure and life of the church.

PEAKS AND VALLEYS: CYCLES OF RENEWAL

The grace of renewal that brought about monastic communities and religious orders was not a grace that was once for all. After these groups became an established part of church life, they too were subject to decay and decline. It seems to be a principle of spiritual life that groups within the church, and even the church as a whole, will experience times of extraordinary growth and renewal, times of stability and preservation, and times of trial, purification, struggle, and decline. Each individual Christian experiences peaks and valleys; so too do groups within the church, and even, it appears, the whole body of Christ on earth.

When a person or group confronts a period of particularly difficult trial or struggle, a choice must be made. A person could decide to reduce his or her commitment, to take paths that lead away from faithfulness to God, or to stop following God entirely. A group could decide to abandon its mission or dissolve itself, or to reinterpret itself in ways that are out of harmony with its inner life. On the other hand, a person or group experiencing trial or struggle could cry out to God for renewal and resolve to seek wisdom and new strength from God. Great spiritual writers, such as John of the Cross, have noted that these "dark nights" of testing are potentially the most fruitful for spiritual growth and maturity.

Church history testifies that after the cross there is always the resurrection. Out of the ashes of humiliation and struggle, through faith and repentance, God's plan for renewal emerges. We witness this in Christian history as, for example, in historian Christopher Dawson's division of church history into six periods or "ages." In his analysis, each age begins with a period of growth or renewal, followed by some stabilization, and ends with a period of struggle or decline. But because God is faithful and committed to His people, at the point of the most severe difficulty or deterioration the Lord invariably raises up certain persons, groups, or movements who receive the grace of the Holy Spirit to bring about a new springtime of renewal. Often the renewal is painful and slow, but the grace is always there, for God is always faithful to His people.

SAINTS: POINTS OF LIGHT IN DARK TIMES

Even in times of overall decline or crisis in the church's life, there are always bright spots—points of light, to borrow a phrase—*saints* whom God raises up to give direction and hope. During the Avignon papacy, for example (when the popes left Rome and built a luxurious court in Avignon, France), Catherine of Siena brought forth God's word with clarity and power. Pope Gregory XI wisely heeded her prophetic warnings and returned to Rome. In the death camps of twentieth-century Nazi Germany, some Christians, like Maximilian Kolbe and Titus Brandsma, and outside the camps, Dietrich Bonhoeffer, were martyred for their faith.

When the Catholic Church was challenged to reform itself by the Protestant Reformation, God raised up a host of saints to promote renewal: Charles Borromeo, Teresa of Avila, John of the Cross, Ignatius Loyola, Francis Xavier, Philip Neri, Francis de Sales, Jeanne Francois de Chantal, Robert Bellarmine, Thomas More, Peter Canisius, Vincent de Paul. Clearly many saints were needed for the renewal of the Catholic Church during this difficult period. In any time when the church is undergoing trial and struggle, patience, faith, and sanctity are needed. With these God will be able to carry out His work of renewal.

IMPLICATIONS FOR THE CHURCH
AND RELIGIOUS EDUCATORS

Understanding the principles of church renewal can help us respond positively to the grace of renewal—the power of the Holy Spirit—that God continually offers to His church. In summary, the lessons from church history discussed in this chapter include: (1) God's faithfulness and His desire to continually renew His people; (2) our need to respond to His call and grace with faith, prayer, humility, and obedience; (3) the importance of not imposing the forms of a particular renewal as a norm for other Christians, who may not have that grace or call; (4) the need for the broader church to recognize authentic renewal movements and to integrate them into church life; (5) the inevitability of cycles of renewal, stability, and struggle that characterize the life of the church and individuals and groups within it; and, finally (6) the goal (and the source!) of all renewal being holiness—conformity to the teaching and example of Jesus Christ, our Savior, and sharing in the very life of God through the Holy Spirit.

For Further Reading

Chesterton, G.K. (1987). *St. Francis of Assisi.* Garden City, NY: Doubleday Image. A splendid brief portrayal of the greatest agent of church renewal of all time.

Dawson, C. (1960). *The historic reality of Christian culture.* New York: Harper and Bros. Outlines eras of renewal in Christian history, as well as brilliant insight into the development of Christian culture.

Flannery, A. (Ed.). (1975). *Vatican council II: The conciliar and post conciliar documents, vol. I.* Grand Rapids, MI: Eerdmans. The official documents guiding the renewal of the Catholic Church today. Contains many important principles of Christian renewal.

John Paul II. (1986). *Lord and giver of life: Encyclical letter on the Holy Spirit in the life of the church and the world.* Washington, DC: United States Catholic Conference. Includes Pope John Paul II's teaching on the role of the Holy Spirit in the renewal of the church.

Kreeft, P. (1988). *Fundamentals of the faith.* San Francisco: Ignatius. Lively and readable short essays giving an overview of basic Christian beliefs, including the work of the Holy Spirit.

Martin, F. (1990). *The life-changer.* Ann Arbor, MI: Servant. The subtitle says it all: "How you can experience freedom, power, and refreshment in the Holy Spirit."

McDonnell, K. & Montague, G. (Eds.). (1991). *Fanning the flame.* Collegeville, MN: Liturgical Press. A call to renewal in the Holy Spirit based on biblical evidence, early Christian writings, and observation of God's contemporary work of renewing the church. (This is a brief, nontechnical companion to a scholarly work by the same authors and publisher, entitled, *Christian initiation and baptism in the Holy Spirit: Evidence from the first eight centuries* (1991).

Merton, T. (1970). *The wisdom of the desert.* New York: New Directions. Cryptic but compelling sayings of the pioneers of the monastic movement, with a sterling introduction by Merton.

Schreck, A. (1990). *The Catholic challenge.* Ann Arbor, MI: Servant. How the Second Vatican Council Challenges and calls the Catholic Church, and all churches, to renewal by the power of God.

_____. (1987). *The compact history of the Catholic Church.* Ann Arbor, MI: Servant. Author's summary of Catholic history highlighting God's faithfulness in renewing the church in every age.

TEACHING SCRIPTURE INTAKE
Donald S. Whitney

Most churches are filled with devoted Bible-admirers, but not daily Bible-readers. Researcher George Barna reports that although three-quarters of Americans say they think it's important for people to read the Bible, only 12 percent do so daily (Barna, 1990, p. 118). His inquiries among professing believers reveal that only one in four (26 percent) evangelicals read the Scriptures every day. However, almost as many (22 percent) say they *never* read the Bible outside of church (Barna, 1991, p. 79).

The great question for Christian educators at this point is also the question for this chapter: How are we to get more of the adults in our churches to read and meditate on the Bible consistently? Leading Christians to read the Bible and to spend time thinking about what it says is not rocket science; it is fundamentally simple. It must be so because these practices are so *basic* to the Christian life.

THE NEED FOR SCRIPTURE INTAKE

Think of it this way: devotional intake of God's Word is essential for even the most minimal level of Christian spiritual health, regardless of a person's age, church, denomination, geographic location, or socioeconomic status. Though not without barriers, reading and meditating on Scripture is primary to normal Christianity; surely leading others to do it should not be so

164

complex that only highly-trained specialists could accomplish it. If that were the case, we'd never see church members with a sound, robust, transforming knowledge of the Bible (as we commonly do) unless their pastors or other Christian educators in the church knew the "mysterious intricacies" of getting people into the Word of God.

Don't misunderstand. I'm not saying that it is always easy to effect widespread and consistent Bible reading and meditation by members of your church. If it were effortless, the introductory statistics I mentioned would be much improved. But while this ministry may not be easy, it should not be complicated.

THE HOLY SPIRIT PROVIDES THE MOTIVATION

I'm also not saying that it is the charisma or professional expertise of the Christian educator that causes Bible reading and meditation to happen. The Holy Spirit provides the motivation for Christians to read the Bible and meditate on it. "For it is God who works in you," writes the Apostle Paul, "to will and to act according to his good purpose" (Phil. 2:13). Applied here, this means that the will to delve devotionally into divine revelation is supplied by the Holy Spirit. He is the One who gives the believer an affinity for what He Himself has written. He will often use means to do this, and that's where the ministry of Christian education is an important tool in the Lord's hands. But we must understand that while educators can fan the flame of desire for the Word of God, ultimately they cannot ignite it.

Instead of frustrating you, this should relieve and encourage you. God does not call you to do His job. He alone is the heart changer. "I will give you a new heart," the Lord says of His people in Ezekiel 36:26-27, "and put a new spirit in you; I will remove from you your heart of stone and give you a heart of flesh. And I will put my Spirit in you and move you to follow my decrees and be careful to keep my laws." This is true of all who have a new heart and God's Spirit within them. Only when a child of God is spiritually ill does he or she have no appetite for the Bread of the "word that comes from the mouth of God" (Matt. 4:4).

Recently, I was visited by a man in his mid-forties, a member of the church I'm privileged to pastor. Until his late-thirties, he had no interest in reading or thinking about the Bible. Through the faithful witness of a man who sold him a musical instrument, he eventually believed in Jesus Christ as his Lord and Savior. Right from the beginning of his new relationship with Christ he had a new heart hunger for God's Word. No one told him he must have it; he hungered simply because God had given him the new birth and a new heart. The Spirit of God, now dwelling within him, "moved" him toward the Word of God which resonated with the new life inside him. What God did in his heart is the ordinary work of the Spirit in conversion.

While this God-given appetite is "ordinary" (in the sense that it is commonly shared by Christians), its function is critical. As this desire is fed, the believer is strengthened spiritually and grows more sanctified, more like Christ. Jesus emphasized the importance of the intake of God's Word by God's children when He prayed this for them: "Sanctify them by the truth; your word is truth" (John 17:17).

How vital is the sanctification (a synonym for holiness) that comes by God's truth? We're told soberly, but plainly, "without holiness no one will see the Lord" (Heb. 12:14). And although the Holy Spirit will, by His nature and function, begin to create within the Christian a hunger for the holy truth and a holy life, we still must follow Jesus' example and teach believers truths such as these about God's Word and sanctification. As a result they will more clearly understand what the Lord has done within them and why, and how they are to respond to this work of God. Therefore a top priority for Christian educators must be to encourage those under their charge to read and meditate on the Word of truth which sanctifies them in preparation for seeing the Lord.

THE CHRISTIAN EDUCATOR PROVIDES RESOURCES AND REMINDERS

Given the fact that the Holy Spirit provides the motivation for Christians to read the Bible and to meditate on it, what is the ministry of the Christian educator in facilitating this process? One part of this ministry is to provide resources and reminders.

One of the most important resources to encourage the devotional reading of Scripture is a simple Bible reading plan. Throughout my childhood and youth Sunday School days, the back page of our quarterly always listed daily reading references for that three-month period. My teachers usually called attention to the plan, and some even asked class members each Sunday if we'd read those passages. This resource gave me direction and made it much easier for me to develop at an early age the lifelong discipline of daily Bible reading.

Bible reading plans are still found in the literature of many publishers of Christian education curricula. Since not everyone in your congregation uses, or is even exposed to your C.E. curriculum, you'll not want to rely on that resource alone. Many Bible publishers include daily reading guides in various editions (especially study editions) of the Bibles they print. But again, this resource will supply only a portion of those you're trying to reach.

You may choose to compile your own daily reading guide or reproduce one that is not copyrighted. In my pastoral experience I've found that most people enjoy best a plan that has them reading in more than one place each day. The variety militates against the difficulty some experience in prolonged sections of the Old Testament where the reading is not as easy as they find it in the New Testament. In other words, you'll probably get more people to read the Bible on a regular basis if you'll provide a systematic plan which does not start in Genesis and work in order to Revelation.

Of course, if people are adamant about reading "straight through," don't discourage them. I was amazed by an unconverted woman who announced her intention to read through the Bible by consecutive books. I appealed to my experience in an effort to get her to adopt another plan, but she was unmoved. When I heard that she found Leviticus and Numbers "mudlike," I knew she'd soon give up slogging through. When I saw her a year later, she astonished me with the report that she had finished the entire Bible once and was well into her second reading!

After years of usage, my favorite plan is to read in five places each time, starting with Genesis (the Law), Joshua (history), Job (poetry), Isaiah (the prophets), and the New Testament. Others prefer going to three places daily, beginning in Genesis, Job, and Matthew.

The regular distribution of a Bible reading plan serves as a needed *reminder* to people to stay faithful in their devotional intake of Scripture. Dissemination of the plan as a bulletin insert or through other means (especially in December and January) maintains its visibility to long-term members and helps to regularly promote it to new members. Our church fortifies this annual emphasis on a monthly basis. We type the daily readings for the forthcoming month (say August) on a bookmark-sized piece of paper, photocopy it, and use it as a bulletin insert on the last Sunday of the previous (in this case, July) month. On the back of the sheet are the readings for the following month (here, September) for those who have gotten ahead. Extra copies are placed on a literature table for absentees.

At any given time, some Bible readers in your church will be working their way through the entire Bible while others will be reading more or less haphazardly. For instance, I like to read through the Bible once each year, but I usually don't take all year to do so. During the rest of the year I will return for a closer look at selected books. The point is, resources and reminders are also needed for those regular Bible readers presently making a pilgrimage across the entire horizon of the Scriptures.

One of the most practical tools for those readers is a Bible reading record. The simplest option is to take a few minutes and make your own. On the left side of a piece of paper (you may need front and back if you choose 8½ by 5½ sheets) list the books of the Bible. To the right of each book put numbers for each chapter in that book. Genesis, then, would have the numerals 1 through 50 next to it. Beside First John would be 1 2 3 4 5 and adjacent to Second John just a 1. As a particular chapter is read, the number representing it is circled or crossed out.

There are four advantages to using this resource. First, it helps people keep track of their reading (past and present). Second, like a Bible reading plan, it gives direction, thus reducing the tendency for the Christian to simply let the Bible fall open at random for that day's reading. Third, the record of reading chapter after chapter, book after book, instills a sense of accomplishment in many previously discouraged Bible readers. Fourth, over time it can encourage those who thought they could never read through the entire Bible by showing them that they have nearly done so.

THE CHRISTIAN EDUCATOR PROVIDES
TEACHING AND TECHNIQUES

The ministry of a Christian educator, by definition, goes beyond supplying *resources* and *reminders* to providing *teaching* and *techniques.* What should be taught?

We should teach that Bible reading and meditation on God's Word are expected. When Jesus encountered those who claimed to be people of God, but who didn't know the Word of God as they should have, He often expressed His surprise by asking, "Have you not read . . . ?" (e.g., Matt. 12:3; 19:4) How are we to live, as Jesus did, "on every word that comes from the mouth of God" (Matt. 4:4) without reading the God-breathed words of Scripture? How can we "Let the word of Christ dwell in [us] richly" (Col. 3:16) if we do not even read it?

Meditation holds less of a sense of importance among most Christians even though the teaching regarding it is even more straightforward than with Bible reading. Let us take people often to the directives of Joshua 1:8 ("Do not let this Book of the Law depart from your mouth; meditate on it day and night.") and Psalm 1:1-3 ("Blessed is the man who does not walk in the counsel of the wicked or stand in the way of sinners or sit in the seat of mockers. But his delight is in the law of the Lord, and on his law he meditates day and night").

Of course, most of those in our churches who do not get into God's Word on a daily basis probably know, to a greater or lesser degree, that some means of Bible intake is expected of them. But the repetition of this teaching must always be a staple in the C.E. diet of our churches—even when we think it doesn't "work" well—because it is part of the whole counsel of Scripture. These mandates are part of our God-given curriculum, and even though many neglect them they are the means the Holy Spirit often uses to stimulate the proper response.

It is critical that we teach the importance of meditation *with* reading. Why is it that so often we finish our Bible reading and five minutes later can't remember a thing? It's because we read without thinking. I tell people it's better to read less—if necessary—in order to have time to meditate more. "The unfolding of your words gives light" says Psalm 119:130. While reading God's Word gives light too, reading is not real unfolding; meditation is.

Before teaching what meditation is, we also need to teach what it isn't. Many are frightened by the term meditation because until now they have only associated it with various types of Eastern mysticism. We should make it plain that while counterfeit meditation emphasizes *emptying the mind,* biblical meditation involves *filling it.* Christians aren't to attempt to "create their own reality" with meditation. Instead we're to think on things that are true (Phil. 4:8). The Bible specifies four objects of meditation: (1) God's Word (Josh. 1:8; Ps. 1:2); (2) God's Creation (Ps. 143:5); (3) God's providence (Ps. 77:12); and (4) God's character (Ps. 63:6; 145:5).

Teaching on meditation is more winsome when we emphasize its benefits. True success is promised to those who meditate on the Bible (Josh. 1:8). In Psalm 1:1-3 God pledges stability, fruitfulness, perseverance, and prosperity to those who think deeply about what He has written. Meditation also insures unusual wisdom and insight (Ps. 119:98-99).

Space doesn't allow for elaboration here, but along with the teaching of Scripture about meditation, the Christian educator needs to demonstrate meditation techniques as well. Even the basics of selecting a passage, verse, phrase, or word for reflection should be taught. In *Spiritual Disciplines for the Christian Life* I describe several simple methods of meditation, including repeating the words with emphasis on a different word each time, rewriting the text in your own words, listing applications, and praying through the passage (Whitney, 1991, pp. 43–51, 57–60).

I cannot write about meditation without mentioning its relationship to prayer. Bible intake and prayer are too often seen as two separate experiences. Meditation is the missing link between the two. If you can teach people to begin praying about what they are meditating on, you will increase their love of *both* Bible intake and prayer. A godly English Puritan named William Bridge said of meditation:

As it is the sister of reading, so it is the mother of prayer. Though a man's heart be much indisposed to prayer, yet, if he can but fall into a mediation of God, and the things of God, his heart will soon come off to prayer. . . . Begin with reading. . . . Go on with meditation; end in prayer. . . . Reading without meditation is unfruitful; meditation without reading is hurtful; to meditate and to read without prayer upon both, is without blessing (Bridge, 1989, pp. 132, 154).

THE CHRISTIAN EDUCATOR PROVIDES EXAMPLES AND ENTHUSIASM

We cannot lead people spiritually where we ourselves do not travel. Hypocrites are not followed. No Christian educator will be successful in developing Bible readers and meditators without consistently practicing these disciplines himself. Fulfilling this kind of ministry requires leadership via *examples* and *enthusiasm*.

Do you read your Bible daily? Have you read through the Bible? Do you meditate on what you read? Do you have the heartbeat of the psalmist who exclaimed, "Oh, how I love your law"? (Ps. 119:97)?

Modeling is crucial not only for our credibility, but also to show that it is possible and practical to read and meditate on Scripture. Because so many today have never read any volume as thick as the Bible, unless they know you do it, they may doubt if they can read through the entire book.

You also fortify their belief that the disciplines of Bible intake are doable when you chisel time for them out of your schedule as a daily priority. That's because "I just don't have time" is the most self-deceiving excuse non-Bible readers fling at us. Show them that commercial recordings of the Bible prove that the book can be completed in as little as seventy-one hours, thus a discipline of only fifteen minutes per day can result in reading through the Bible in a year's time; a mere five minutes daily takes you through in three years. Remind them that the average American spends enough time in front of the TV every *two* weeks to read the Bible from cover to cover. These facts, fused with your own testimony and *example,* will make your appeals both winsome and unassailable.

Speaking of testimonies, look for opportunities for church members to tell their own stories of *enthusiasm* for Bible reading and meditation. I was teaching a five-week series on the spiritual disciplines at a church and spent an entire session on meditation. I emphasized one particular method and asked the participants to try it during the week. The next Sunday the pastor's wife admitted that she had never been consistent in her daily devotions, but that during the past seven days she had meditated on a different verse of Scripture every day. She had astonished herself by daily spending an hour or more in meditation before she realized it, and then had to reluctantly tear herself away only because her duties absolutely demanded it. The difference, she maintained, was that now she knew how to meditate and to weave meditation and prayer into a seamless garment. Her enthusiasm for God's Word could not be contained and so was the interest in Bible reading and meditation that it sparked.

I've asked myself how I was influenced to read and think on the Word. I've already referred to my childhood models at the church (not to mention my father's example of daily Bible reading). But how did I come to my annual practice of reading through the entire Bible and my daily discipline of meditation? I started them because of two men, Jim and Bill. Both were "Christian educators" to me – one formally and one informally. Jim conveyed a *passion* about reading through the Bible; Bill was *enthusiastic* about meditation. Both taught me *by word* and *by example.* Both provided handy resources and reminders. Both showed me practical techniques. The Holy Spirit implanted the *desire* and the *power.* The result of their ministries to me will be eternal.

For Further Reading

Blanchard, J. (1984). *How to enjoy your Bible.* Colchester, England: Evangelical Press. Blanchard is a British evangelist and Bible teacher who has written a practical book that is helpful with methods and means. Deals some with evidence of the reliability of Scripture. Has a chapter evaluating different modern translations.

Fee, G. & Stuart, D. (1982). *How to read the Bible for all its worth.* Grand Rapids: Academie/Zondervan. The basic concern of this volume is with the understanding of the different types of literature that make up the Bible. Guidelines are given for the intelligent reading and studying of each genre of Scripture.

Foster, R. (1988). *Celebration of discipline* (2nd ed.). San Francisco: Harper and Row. The first great book this century on the general subject of the spiritual disciplines, including Bible study and meditation. Foster is a Quaker who quotes frequently from other Quakers, the early church fathers, Catholic and medieval mystics, and other writers generally unknown to most evangelicals.

Hughes, R. (1991). *Disciplines of a godly man.* Wheaton, IL: Crossway. Written by a leading evangelical pastor and Bible commentator. Although aimed at men, most of the book is valuable for anyone. See especially the chapters on "Discipline of Mind" and "Discipline of Devotion." Includes three Bible reading plans in an appendix.

Sproul, R.C. (1977). *Knowing Scripture.* Downers Grove, IL: InterVarsity. Sproul is one of America's best-known Christian writers, conference speakers, theologians, and Bible teachers. He has the ability to communicate the intricacies of theology in a practical and winsome way. This volume deals primarily with Bible study, but is a thorough and useful survey.

Thomas, G. (1980). *Reading the Bible.* Carlisle, PA: Banner of Truth. This thirty-two page booklet was written by a Baptist pastor from Wales who is one of the more prominent evangelicals in the U.K. It is an inexpensive work which deals exclusively with Bible reading and has a reading plan in the back.

Whitney, D. (1991). *Spiritual disciplines for the Christian life.* Colorado Springs: NavPress. Written by the author of this chapter. Based on 1 Timothy 4:7 with the thesis that the spiritual disciplines are the God-given means to grow in Christlikeness. See especially the two chapters on Bible intake (which include major sections on Bible reading and on meditation, as well as the chapter on prayer, which also discusses meditation at length.

FOURTEEN

FOLLOWING THE LORD'S PATTERN OF PRAYER

James C. Wilhoit

One thing about prayer needs to be made clear from the beginning—not all prayers are created equal. This does not mean that prayer is difficult or that God is fickle, delighting in one prayer and arbitrarily dismissing another. God desires our friendship and wants our prayers. However, like any dimension of a friendship—conversation, recreation, support, sharing—prayer should grow naturally out of the divine-human relationship.

The Bible itself is a wonderful, but often overlooked, guide for prayer. Scripture reminds us of God's priorities and lets us hear the prayers of those who knew the delight of effective and refreshing prayer. Praying and reading should flow together. Our prayer lists must come from both the "needs" of others as well as the passions of God expressed in Scripture.

USING THE LORD'S PRAYER
AS A RESOURCE FOR TEACHING PRAYER

When teaching prayer there is no better place to begin than with the model prayer given by Jesus. In less than seventy words He provides us with a complete pattern for our praying. Within the broad guidelines of this prayer lies the potential for raising any request or cry of the human heart to God. Effective and satisfying praying does not require the mastery of deep and difficult secrets. Taking Jesus' simple and straightforward teaching on prayer seriously and patterning our prayers after the principles found in the "Lord's Prayer" lays a foundation for true and effective prayer.

The "Lord's Prayer" is recorded in both Matthew and Luke. In Matthew it is part of the Sermon on the Mount and comes at the end of an attack by Jesus on religious display and self-glorification through showy prayers, public almsgiving, and attention-getting fasting. In Luke's Gospel a follower observes Jesus at prayer and asks, "Lord, teach us to pray" (11:1). In response, Jesus provides the Lord's Prayer as a pattern. It should come as no surprise that we have two different versions and settings for this prayer. Jesus probably gave this prayer in a number of settings and varied the exact content from time to time. He was more concerned about the pattern of this prayer than the exact wording, as indicated by His statement that this is *how* to pray, not *what* to pray.

Jesus' advice concerning what not to do in prayer is as timely today as it was in the first century (Matt. 6:1-8). He examines three popular expressions of Jewish piety: prayer, almsgiving, and fasting. In His criticism He shows how these had often become nothing more than institutionalized vehicles for religious display. Jesus makes it clear that religious acts done to impress others are of no spiritual benefit.

- Don't show off. In some circles you can win points by letting people know how much you pray. Such mixed motives can lead to prayers that offend God. Jesus suggests that: "When you pray, go into your room, close the door and pray to your Father" (Matt. 6:6). In other words, focus on prayer, not letting people know you pray.
- Don't judge the quality of your prayers just on length and eloquence. Avoid the sort of "vain repetitions" that marked pagan prayers. You are not to be like the hypocrites who put on a fanfare when they give gifts (6:2-4). Do your good works for God and not to be seen by others.
- Don't think of prayer as primarily asking and informing. You can't surprise God and certainly can't shock Him by your prayers. We pray to a loving God who "knows what you need before you ask him" (Matt. 6:8). "When it came to prayer, the pagans mistakenly believed that it was the squeaky wheel that would get the grease" (Garland, 1992, p. 216). They

thought they had to actively work to get God's attention. Imagine how staggering Jesus' simple "Our Father" would have seemed to those steeped in the practice of actively working to earn God's care.

God seeks the prayers of those who come offering prayers "in spirit and in truth" (John 4:23). To pray "in spirit" speaks of sincerity and single-mindedness. God's glory, not the praise of others, is the object of such praying. Praying "in truth" describes prayers that are based on "reality" grasped through the study of Scripture and the experience of God's grace. Such prayers seem natural because their foundation is the very character of God. We can add this reality to our prayers by growing in our knowledge of God and by praying the prayers of the Bible.

THE PRIORITIES OF THE LORD'S PRAYER

Our Father, which art in heaven, hallowed be thy name. Thy kingdom come. Thy will be done in earth, as it is in heaven. Give us this day our daily bread. And forgive us our debts as we forgive our debtors. And lead us not into temptation, but deliver us from evil: For thine is the kingdom, and the power, and the glory, for ever. Amen. (Matt. 6:9-13, KJV)

Woven into the very essence of this model prayer are priorities which challenge much of our praying. Jesus' priorities for prayer differ from our own, and this should come as no surprise since Jesus' priorities were God's. Compared with Jesus' singlemindedness, working for God's kingdom with all His heart, our devotion looks like a passing flirtation. Like the rest of the sermon, this prayer reflects the radical values of God's kingdom. Don't be discouraged when you see the difference between your prayer practices and the prayer priorities of Jesus. Rejoice that you have been given the insight and grace needed to change an area of your praying.

- It is God-centered. The first half of the prayer focuses on God. It seeks His glory and His will. It establishes our agenda for praying. In much praying, God's will is only mentioned in the apologetic footnote "If it be thy will." The emphasis of this prayer is on God: "Our Father . . . Thy name . . . Thy kingdom . . . Thy will. . . . "

- It involves the mind and the heart. All of our being is involved in prayer. True prayer can never be an activity in which the mouth runs on in eloquent petition while the mind wanders and the heart is indifferent. Prayer must engage all of our being; with heart, mouth, and actions we offer our prayers.

- It is community-focused. This is not a prayer filled with "gimmies" and self-centered pleas. This prayer is filled with the language of community. *"Our* Father . . . Give *us . . . our* daily bread . . . forgive *us our* debts . . . *we* forgive *our* debtors . . . lead us . . . deliver *us."* Prayer is a way of building up the church.

- It is balanced. True prayer consists of much more than just asking. It involves *adoration* ("Hallowed be thy name"), *intercession* ("Thy will be done"); *confession* ("Forgive us our debts"); *supplication* ("Give us this day our daily bread"); and deliverance ("Deliver us from evil").

THE PATTERN OF THE LORD'S PRAYER

We can recite the sixty-six words of the Lord's Prayer in less than fifteen seconds, but to really pray it you have to travel more slowly. Think of the various petitions in this prayer as the "Roman numerals" of an outline and your specific concerns as the "numbers and letters" that fall under these. As a teacher I find it very useful to reproduce the Lord's Prayer in outline form and encourage the students to use that as a basis of their praying. To help you build your own "Lord's Prayer Outline," a brief explanation of each petition and some suggestions concerning how to pray follow.

1. Remembering Who We Are and Who God Is: "Our Father Which Art in Heaven"

In this opening phrase we find both a God to love and a God to fear. This model prayer makes it clear from the very beginning who we are, members of God's family, and who God is, our loving, accepting, and holy Father who rules the world (which is what the shorthand phrase "in heaven" means). "Our Father, which art in heaven" is important because it sets the tone for the rest of the prayer.

Use the "Our" in "Our Father, which art in heaven" as a reminder to thank God that He made you part of His family. I like Larry Lea's suggestion to "Picture Calvary and thank God you can call Him Father by virtue of the blood of Jesus" (Lea, 1987, p. 189). In my mental picture I see the agony of the cross, the pain of being rejected by friends, and the sense of loss after seeing the work of a lifetime rejected. When I see more clearly the painful cost of Christ's work, I respond with thanks for what He did to include me in His family.

I also use the "Our" to remind me that I am part of a great community of faith which stretches through the centuries and around the world. I am strengthened when I realize that at the very moment I pray other believers around the world are praying to God and praising Him using this very same model prayer.

This petition should also remind us that we pray to a God who is both an accepting Father and the Ruler of heaven. It is important that we remember that we pray to a God who both desires our good and has the power to bring it about. Often our best efforts fail to bring about the good we so desperately desire: relationships crumble or the self-destructive habits of a friend continue. God operates with both perfect love and complete power. He does not sit and wring His hands at the events of the world.

Following the Pattern

Do not be too quick to pass over these words as mere "introduction." They set the tone for the whole prayer and make it the property of Christians. The early church safeguarded these words and prayed corporately only when Christians alone were present.

Remember: You can only say "Our Father, which art in heaven" if you are a functioning part of God's family, the church. You can only pray "Our Father, which art in heaven" if you have been born again from above and are a child of God. And you can only pray "Our Father, which art in heaven" if you live like God really is in charge of the universe.

"Our": This is a prayer for family members. Picture Calvary and thank God that through Jesus Christ's sacrifice you are part of God's family.

"Father": God's grace and active concern. Realize that He knows us and our needs. Lay aside your defenses. Run into His presence. But remember as well "in heaven": He is great and majestic. Remember that prayer is possible because of God's power and love.

2. Asking That God Be Honored: "Hallowed Be Thy Name"
This request, more than any other, sets this prayer off from most contemporary prayers. We laugh when we hear of the little boy in Sunday School whose recitation of the Lord's Prayer included the curious phrase "Harold be thy name." But most adults find this phrase more than a bit puzzling. We just don't spend a lot of time in contemporary society "hallowing" things.

These four words, "hallowed be thy name," reflect an important priority in biblical prayers that has virtually disappeared in contemporary praying. The prayers of the Bible reveal a deep concern for God's reputation/name. These men and women passionately cared about God's reputation and sought to see His name and honor vindicated through their prayers as can be seen in Daniel's model prayer of confession (Dan. 9:4-19). He is deeply grieved by the way the world scorns "Jerusalem and your people" and, hence, Israel's God, because of "our sins and disobedience." Daniel asks God to act and change this situation where the Jews lived in Exile and the surrounding nations mocked Yahweh's seeming inability to protect His people. Why does He want God to act? "For your own sake." True prayer is *fueled by a passion for God's reputation.* God delights to answer such prayers.

In the Old Testament period this emphasis on God's reputation brought with it an almost brash boldness. In their prayers this concern is often stated negatively: Lord, if You fail to do X the surrounding nations will think You can't act or don't care about us. For example, Moses prayed, "Why should the Egyptians say, 'It was with an evil intent that he [God] brought them

179

out, to kill them" (Ex. 32:12). Joshua prays with similar logic after the defeat at Ai (Josh. 7:6-9). After seeing the power of God at Jericho where the walls miraculously crumbled and victory was achieved spectacularly, this defeat at Ai confused Joshua. He fell on the ground—a shaken, embarrassed, and frightened general. Yet his biggest concern in the prayer is God's reputation. What did Israel's "turning their backs" in the battle do to God's name? We worry about our reputations, but do we have a similar concern about God's reputation? Joshua ends his prayer with a plea in the form of a question: "What then will you do for your own great name?"

The Babylonian captivity taught God's people that they are not exempt from divine judgment and, hence, potential divine disgrace before the nations. Yet the concern for God's reputation is not lost. Daniel's model prayer of confession shows a passionate concern for God's name and character. Certainly the little understood petition of the Lord's Prayer "hallowed be thy name" reminds us of the prominence a heartfelt concern for God's reputation should have in our prayers.

The experience of prayer in the Bible is often quite intense. With passion and honesty men and women pour out their hearts to God. Often they appeal to God's very character as a weapon in this struggle of prayer. They suggest that God should act in a given way because His honor, glory, grace, mercy, or trustworthiness demand such a response. The narrative accounts of these prayers leaves the distinct impression that God delights when His character is appealed to, but not presumed upon (Ex. 32:11-14; Num. 14:13-22; Deut. 9:26-29).

These appeals to God's character arise out of a knowledge of God that comes through His historically grounded divine revelation. The "pray-ers" of the Bible frequently allude to God's character or promises in their prayers. For example, Abraham based his prayer on God's character, "Will not the Judge of all the earth do right?" (Gen. 18:25) and Moses appeals to previous promises, "Remember your servants Abraham, Isaac and Israel, to whom you swore by your own self" (Ex. 32:13).

Following the Pattern
Our prayers should be built on a concern for God's reputation. God delights in hearing His people ask that He act to uphold

His reputation of justice, mercy, love, holiness, and kindness. The redeemed should passionately care about God's reputation and seek to see His name and character vindicated through their prayers. This concern for God's name lifts the prayers of the Bible from a self-oriented wish-fulfillment to a God-centered dialogue.

In this petition we ask that God's name — shorthand in the Bible for His very essence and character — be given the respect it deserves. Pray that:

1. God's name (His very character) will be given the honor it deserves by ourselves, the church, and the world. As a reminder of God's character, meditate on the Fourth Question and Answer of the *Westminster Shorter Catechism:* "What is God?" "God is a Spirit, infinite, eternal, and unchangeable, in his being, wisdom, power, holiness, justice, goodness, and truth."

2. Ask God to act to show forth His glory so that people will honor His name.

3. God's biblical names reveal His nature. Pray that you will truly come to know God by these names. Meditate on God's names. For example, *El-Shaddai* (God Almighty) is the name of God associated with the accounts of the patriarchs (Abraham, Isaac, Jacob) and speaks of God's power, majesty, and covenant/promise-keeping nature. God makes promises and is powerful enough to see that they are fulfilled. Praise God by hallowing (giving reverence to) His names.

3. Asking That His Will Be Fully Realized: "Thy Kingdom Come. Thy Will Be Done, in Earth As It Is in Heaven"

Notice again the priority given in the Lord's Prayer to God's agenda. First, in praying "hallowed be thy name," we ask that God receive the reverence/respect that His very character demands. Next, we ask that God's program of redemption be allowed to expand throughout all of the earth. "Thy kingdom come" and "thy will be done" are parallel phrases and mean essentially the same thing. In this petition we ask that God's reign — His righteous rule — be present on earth in the same way that it is in heaven. In heaven His reign is total, His will is eagerly done, and it is quickly executed without the limitations imposed by either self or Satan.

We see that prayer is more than simply adopting "God's perspective" on the issue at hand or reporting to Him our confidence that He is at work in the world. Prayer is not just a passive acceptance of the status quo, nor is it a belligerent, arrogant "storming the gates of heaven." Prayer is a subversive activity. We do not subvert God, but in true prayer we pray according to His will (that is what is meant by praying in "Jesus' name"), and He subverts us so that in the future we live and pray even more in accordance with His will.

Following the Pattern
Pray that God's righteous reign will extend to cover all the earth. Pray (by name) for those who labor to extend God's rule:

- Missionaries and evangelists
- Those challenging injustice with righteousness

Develop a strategy to pray for those areas declared to be God's will. I view my prayer concerns as fitting into a series of concentric circles. I begin by praying for those in the outermost ring first—I simply call it "the world"—and then move on to the church, my family, my personal concerns:
World: "For God so loved the world that he gave his one and only Son" (John 3:16).

- For national and international leaders: that your children may freely worship; for justice to be done. This must be a top priority in our prayer life. Just governments help the Gospel flourish (1 Tim. 2:1-2).
- For those who do not yet know God as their Father.
Church: "I will build my church and the gates of Hades will not overcome it" (Matt. 16:18).

- That Christian workers might be raised up (Luke 10:2).
- For unity and love in the church (John 13:34; 17:20-23).
- That your spiritual leaders will be wise, pure, and single-minded in their tasks (2 Tim. 2).
- That your church will "warn those who are idle, encourage the timid, help the weak, be patient with everyone" (2 Thes. 5:14).

4. Asking for Our Needs:
"Give Us This Day Our Daily Bread"

The prayers of the Bible abound with praise, thanksgiving, confession, benediction, dedication, and supplication. I have read suggestions that the "highest forms" of personal praying emphasize praise and downplay petition. The reality of life before God and certainly the experience of the biblical writers suggests that maxim is faulty. Supplication is the most prominent form of prayer in the Bible outside the Psalms. Also, in the some 600 prayers recorded in the Bible the chief motivation for praying is *self-perceived need*. We need not be embarrassed about coming before God with our needs.

Our supplications involve much more than words. They are, like prayer itself, first and foremost a way of living before God marked by a humble and loving dependency on Him. If there is a key to prayer it is not, as is so often said, faith, but *righteousness*.

Jesus' life is a powerful testimony to the effectiveness of prayers born out of a life lived in submission and love before the Father. His prayers did not merely bounce off the ceiling and limply fall back into His lap; they were a powerful force for good. They were effective because His life was marked by such integrity that His life of obedience and His praying said the same thing. "During the days of Jesus' life on earth, he offered up prayers and petitions . . . and he was heard because of his reverent submission" (Heb. 5:7). There is a deep and necessary connection between our praying and our living (James 5:16; Prov. 15:29).

The prayers recorded in the Bible are remarkably straightforward. As a general rule the "pray-ers" come before God with confidence and state their desires knowing that their prayers will be heard. There is little equivocation in their requests and they generally omit phrases like "if it be thy will."

Following the Pattern

"And what does the Lord require of you? To act justly and to love mercy and to walk humbly with your God" (Micah 6:8).

Pray that God's desires will be your desires and that God will provide your daily necessities. Here is a list of items concerning one's own life that should be prayed for. This is the area of your prayer outline that will be most unique.

- For those who mistreated me. Pray that you will not seek their downfall (Luke 6:28).
- That I will experience a fullness of the Spirit (Luke 11:13; Eph. 5:18)
- That my speech will honor You (Eph. 4:25) and that my love may abound (Phil. 1:9)
- That I will learn to cheerfully give and serve (2 Cor. 9:7)
- For my work and business dealings
- Ministry opportunities
- Needs of others: other Christians; family members; friends and associates; news items
- Other personal needs and wants

5. Asking for Our Needs:
   "And Forgive Us Our Debts,
   As We Forgive Our Debtors"

This petition isn't conditional. It doesn't say, "If you sin, forgive." Our sinning is assumed and the directness of this phrase reminds us of the universality of sin and the universal need for forgiveness. Jesus did not stop merely with having us ask God for forgiveness of our sins. ("Debts" is a term that covers all types of debt to God and others: moral, legal, family obligations, relational responsibilities.) He asks us to forgive those who have hurt us as well.

This petition requires us to do three things. First, we must pray that God will convict us of sin. Here is where Scripture and prayer work together so well. Often it is not at the moment of prayer that we are convicted, but later when we are reading the Word of God. Prayer and the Word are powerful when allowed to dwell together— don't let them be torn apart. Conviction does not mean "feeling guilty" about something. It means an awareness that something is wrong.

The Bible has much to say about guilt, but it focuses on legal or theological guilt. The Bible records no occurrence in which believers are urged to feel psychological guilt (i.e., sense of lowered self-esteem, feelings of divine rejection, depression, or feeling of being dirty) for their actions. It is Satan, not God, who is in the business of making us feel guilty. Remember that Jesus is our "Advocate" (1 John 2:1, NKJV) while it is Satan who is "the accuser of our brothers, who accuses them before our

God day and night" (Rev. 12:10). Our sins should lead to a "godly sorrow" which "brings repentance that leads to salvation and leaves no regret, but worldly sorrow brings death" (2 Cor. 7:10). The focus in psychological guilt is on yourself and the possible punishment. While "godly sorrow" has its focus on the future (Godly sorrow prompts us to ask, "How can I avoid doing that sin again?" not "What is going to happen to me?"), it also looks with sorrow and remorse on the person injured and when possible thinks about true restitution, not just something "to smooth over the problem."

Second, we must seek God's forgiveness for the offense or sinful pattern and ask for the power to walk rightly in the future. Third, we need to pray for those who have wronged us and ask that we will readily forgive them.

Following the Pattern

Think back over yesterday. Invite the Holy Spirit to convict you of your sins: "Search me, O God, and know my heart. . . . See if there is any offensive way in me, and lead me in the way everlasting" (Ps. 139:23-24). Confess corporate or national sins that blight our land. Own your sin, don't excuse it!

> *O merciful heart of God, in true penitence and contrition I would now open my heart to Thee. Let me keep nothing from Thee while I pray. Humbling as the truth about myself may be, let me yet take courage to speak it in Thy presence.*
>
> *I confess to the sin of laziness in this . . . and this. . . :*
> *I confess to the sin of vanity in this . . . and this . . . :*
> *I confess to this . . . and this . . . indulgence of the flesh:*
> *I confess to the habit of falsehood in this . . . and this . . . :*
> *I confess to this . . . and this . . . uncharitable word:*
> *I confess to this . . . and this . . . wrong direction my life had been taking:*
> *Almighty God, Spirit of purity and grace, in asking Thy forgiveness I cannot claim a right to be forgiven but only cast myself upon Thine unbounded love.*
> *I can plead no merit or desert:*
> *I can plead no extenuating circumstances:*

I cannot plead the force of temptations I encounter:
I cannot plead the persuasions of others who led me
astray:
I can only say, for the sake of Jesus Christ Thy Son,
My Lord. Amen
(Adapted from Baillie, 1949, p. 51)

Ask and claim God's present forgiveness for sins (1 John 1:9). Repent of those sins and seek to head in a new direction. Pray that you will naturally and joyously forgive others.

6. Asking for Our Needs:
"Lead Us Not Into Temptation,
But Deliver Us From Evil"

This petition frankly faces the reality of our situation. Through poetic language Jesus is telling us to pray that we be delivered from the clutches of the evil one. It is a request that openly acknowledges the inadequacy of our own resources. It is appropriate to place this request at the end of the prayer. After you have worshiped God, prayed that His reign would expand, asked for your needs, and sought His forgiveness, you know that you are coming to a very big God—one who can protect you. I had prayed countless prayers asking for protection, but it was not until I followed the model prayer of Jesus that I actually felt protection.

Following the Pattern

Teach me that such deliverance is now possible: Jesus gave His disciples "authority to tread . . . over all the power of the enemy" (Luke 10:19).

That my steps will be ordered by your Word: "How can a young man keep his way pure? By living according to your Word" (Ps. 119:9).

That I will be wise and discerning: "If you want to know what God wants you to do, ask him, and he will gladly tell you, for he is always ready to give a bountiful supply of wisdom to all who ask" (James 1:5, TLB).

That I will put on, through study and discipline, the whole armor of God (Eph. 6:10-18): "Finally, be strong in the Lord and in his mighty power. Put on the full armor of God. . . . For our struggle is not against flesh and blood, but . . . against the spiritual forces of evil. . . . Stand firm then, with the belt of truth buckled around your waist, with the breastplate of righteousness in place, with your feet fitted with the readiness that comes from the gospel of peace. . . . take up the shield of faith, with which you can extinguish all the flaming arrows of the evil one. Take the helmet of salvation and the sword of the Spirit, which is the word of God. And pray in the Spirit on all occasions" (Eph. 6:13-18).

That I will boldly confront the forces of darkness: "Submit yourselves therefore to God. Resist the devil and he will flee from you" (James 4:7).

Place a hedge of protection about me/us:

- Because I can declare You are "my refuge and my fortress, my God, in whom I trust" (Ps. 91:2). You have promised to protect me and command Your angels concerning me/us (Ps. 91:11).
- Because You are my shepherd (Ps. 23:1).
- Because You promised to strengthen and protect Your own from the evil one (1 Thes. 3:3).

7. Concluding with Praise

"For thine is the kingdom, and the power, and the glory, for ever. Amen." The model prayer of Jesus ends with doxology, and it is good for us to leave our praying on a note of praise. Praise is not the same as thanksgiving. We should leave thankful because we know God hears and responds in love, but more importantly we should leave in praise because we have encountered God. The time with God in prayer should prompt us to honor Him for who He is.

The Lord's Prayer has been used since the earliest days of the Christian church as a way of teaching believers to pray. It provides us with an outline for organizing our prayers and contains a marvelous summary of Christian doctrine. It is a tool for praying which each generation needs to rediscover its relevance to the deepest needs and longings of the human soul.

For Further Reading

Appleton, G. (Ed.). (1985). *The Oxford book of prayer.* New York: Oxford Univ. Press. A well-organized and comprehensive collection of prayer drawn from around the world and across the centuries organized, in part, around the petitions of the Lord's Prayer.

Barclay, W. (1968). *The beatitudes & the Lord's Prayer for everyman.* New York: Harper and Row. A very readable commentary on the Lord's Prayer.

Clements, R. (1985). *In spirit and in truth: Insights from biblical prayers.* Atlanta: John Knox. An examination of twenty-six prayers from both the Old and New Testaments.

Garland, D. (1992). The Lord's Prayer in the Gospel of Matthew. *Review and Expositor, 89* (Spring), 215–228. A very readable exposition on the Lord's Prayer with a good explanation of the contemporary prayer practices which Jesus criticizes.

Jeremias, J. (1967). *The prayers of Jesus.* Naperville, IL: A.R. Allenson. A classic critical study of Jesus' prayers.

Lea, L. (1987). *Could you not tarry one hour?* Altamonte Springs, FL: Creation House. This is the story of Larry Lea's coming to understand the place of prayer in his life and the life of his church. An appealing and useful book which is based loosely on the Lord's Prayer.

MacArthur, J. (1984). *Jesus' pattern of prayer.* Chicago: Moody. An expositional study of the Lord's Prayer. The systematic approach and clear presentation make it a useful place to begin one's study of the Lord's Prayer. The study draws heavily on earlier work and uses this one prayer as an opportunity to erect an entire theology of prayer.

Slack, K. (1973). *Praying the Lord's Prayer today.* Naperville, IL: SCM. A thoughtful book on how to use the Lord's Prayer as a model prayer.

Watson, T. (1960). *The Lord's Prayer.* Carlisle, PA: Banner of Truth. A great Puritan exposition on the Lord's Prayer section of the Westminster Catechism.

TEACHING PEOPLE TO PRAY
T.W. Hunt

The renewed interest in spiritual formation in colleges and seminaries has created unusual opportunities, but has been beset with problems peculiar to adjusting spiritual concepts to academic settings. These difficulties are heightened when the subject is prayer. Teaching prayer presupposes a certain theological and spiritual background in our students. We have to assume that our students have biblical information available to understand the contexts and basic purposes of prayer, even though we may be correcting some of these.

As teachers we are also hampered by the fact that we have no adequate measure of the spiritual qualities necessary for successful prayer, and prayer is above all, spiritual. At first glance it may seem that things we need most to know in order to pray are so formidable that we shirk from teaching the foundational principles which are basic to proper understanding of prayer. Nevertheless both Old and New Testament traditions assume that prayer can be taught.

BIBLICAL PATTERNS OF EDUCATION

The Hebrew background placed strong emphasis on the teaching of the Law. "These commands that I give you today are to be upon your hearts. Impress them on your children. Talk about them when you sit at home and when you walk along the road, when you lie down and when you get up. Tie them as symbols on your hands and bind them on your foreheads. Write them on the doorframes of your houses and on your gates" (Deut. 6:6-9). Teaching religious concepts was to pervade all of time and all of life. Since the giving of the Pentateuch, the Jewish people have vigorously counted religious education as part of their heritage.

Teaching is also an important part of the wisdom literature. The Hebrew ideal of Proverbs 22:6 has played a role in Christian tradition: "Train a child in the way he should go, and when he is old he will not turn from it." The Jewish emphasis was on the value of learning: "Instruct a wise man and he will be wiser still; teach a righteous man and he will add to his learning" (Prov. 9:9). The key to wisdom was through instruction. "Listen to advice and accept instruction, and in the end you will be wise" (Prov. 19:20).

This emphasis on the discipline of learning through teaching continued throughout the biblical revelation. In the promise that God would hear Israel's cry for help, the promise was that "your teachers will be hidden no more" (Isa. 30:20). The continued heritage of religious education was strongly established in the Christian tradition as Jesus ended His commission to make disciples . . . "teaching them to obey everything I have commanded you" (Matt. 28:20). And much of what He taught concerned prayer. In the early church, Paul taught the difference in the new and the old life, dealing with abstractions (Eph. 4:21-24). After Paul's pastoral instructions to his younger disciple, he enjoined Timothy, "Command and teach these things . . . devote yourself to the public reading of Scripture, to preaching and to teaching" (1 Tim. 4:11, 13). Teaching the intangibles of the new life in Christ not only was possible but apparently a pastoral duty.

Within the Hebrew context, learning was the heart cry of the spiritually hungry soul. The psalmist cried, "Praise be to you, O Lord, teach me your decrees" (Ps. 119:12). Despite the obstacles, the teacher of prayer should have the advantage of eager students. Curricula should be designed so students do not sign up for a course on prayer unless they are already eager to learn.

The poet cried to the Lord for learning, for God reveals Himself as a teacher. Isaiah quotes the Lord, "This is what the Lord says—your Redeemer, the Holy One of Israel: 'I am the

Lord your God who teaches you what is best for you, who directs you in the way you should go' " (Isa. 48:17). The psalmist asked, "Does he who teaches man lack knowledge?" (Ps. 94:10)

One of Jesus' principal roles was that of teacher, and one of the subjects He taught most frequently was prayer. "Teacher" was one of His titles (John 3:2); even His enemies called Him that (Luke 20:21). The purpose of His Galilean tours was to teach. "Jesus went throughout Galilee, teaching in their synagogues" (Matt. 4:23). The synagogue was itself a center of teaching. Toward the end of His life, His disciples knew that it was "his custom" to teach (Mark 10:1).

The New Testament enjoins us to teach. Paul instructed the Ephesians, "Bring [children] up in the training and instruction of the Lord" (Eph. 6:4), and because of Jesus' extensive teaching on prayer, this injunction certainly would include instruction in prayer. He directed the Colossians, "Let the word of Christ dwell in you richly as you teach and admonish one another with all wisdom" (Col. 3:16).

Within the context of the church, teaching was a mark of servanthood. The elder Paul advised the young Timothy, "The Lord's servant . . . must be kind to everyone, able to teach, not resentful. Those who oppose him he must gently instruct . . . " (2 Tim. 2:24-25). We have here a word about Paul's method of teaching, as well as the fact of teaching. As challenging and difficult as the teaching of spiritual concepts is, the Bible and all of Hebrew and Christian tradition clearly establishes that they can be taught.

WHAT TO TEACH

The first issue to settle is content. What shall we teach? In my own teaching of prayer over more than twenty years, I have found it easier to begin with the cognitive. Objective information is easy to test, and students start with material that is, at least, initially comprehensible. The Bible advises, "It is not good to have zeal without knowledge" (Prov. 19:2). After all, Paul said, "I will pray with my spirit, but I will also pray with the mind" (1 Cor. 14:15). Neglecting or rejecting knowledge was dangerous in the Hebrew tradition (Hosea 4:6). Isaiah claimed that the Lord said, "My people will go into exile for lack of understanding" (Isa. 5:13).

Cognitive Dimension
The student should start with the prayers of the Bible. I find that using specific examples arouses interest, and I prefer to share various biblical patterns before I get into the specific teaching of the Bible on prayer. I begin with the bases for requests that Bible characters used in various circumstances: God's honor was involved in Ezra's prayer request in Ezra 8:21-23; Nehemiah appealed to the attributes of God in Nehemiah 1:5-6; Hezekiah invoked the sovereignty of God in 2 Kings 19:15, 19. Students can be taught God's character through the meanings of His various names and can be encouraged to use these names at times in prayer. Examples such as these establish a God-centered framework for the rest of our teaching. The student begins by knowing that prayer originates in God and serves His purposes before it serves ours.

Other objective content we can teach is the various types of prayer. I prefer to teach first those kinds of prayer which relate us to the *person* of God — confession, worship, praise, and thanksgiving. For confession, of course, we have the matchless example of Psalm 51. David's acceptance and admission of his own personal failure stands in contrast and submission to his picture of God's faithfulness and mercy. For worship or adoration, we have the psalms (for example, Ps. 100:2).

In my own teaching, I distinguish between worship, which is adoration, and praise. We must love and adore God before we can praise Him properly. Praise is the elevating of God's attributes or His actions. Again, dozens of psalms fit this category (Pss. 8; 27; 65, and many others). Thanksgiving is not an event but an attitude (1 Chron. 23:30; Eph. 5:20). The experienced teacher of prayer will multiply these examples hundreds of times over. My own list grows with each passing year.

Just as these prayers relate to the person of God, *asking* prayer relates to the work of God. For me, it has proved easier to convey asking properly if I distinguish between petition for oneself and intercession for others. Numerous biblical examples facilitate this teaching. Petitions, for example, can be those of Jacob (Gen. 32:9-12), Gideon (Jud. 6:36-40), Solomon (1 Kings 3:9), Jabez (1 Chron. 4:10), Job (Job 42:7-10), Paul (Eph. 1:15-21; 3:14-21), and supremely, Jesus (John 17). Again, experience and study will enlarge these lists.

Another dimension of cognitive learning which can communicate easily in the early stages is the content of prayer. Many of the examples given so far point to the primacy of God's purposes over human intent. The kinds of requests that Bible "pray-ers" asked for are also instructive. Missions can occupy much of our prayer content (Acts 13:3; Eph. 6:19-20; Col. 4:2-4; 2 Thes. 3:1) (Hunt and Walker, 1988).

Along with anchoring our students in the biblical framework and the examples, we can share the Bible injunctions, promises, and limitations on prayer. The most important concepts we must share are those of Jesus (Matt. 6:5-15; 7:7-12; Luke 11:1-13; 18:1-14; John 14:13-14; 15:7, 16; 16:23-27). Jesus taught more than any other person in the Bible about prayer. Paul's teaching on prayer and that of the other New Testament letters supplements that of Jesus (Rom. 8:15, 26-27; Eph. 6:18-20; Phil. 4:6; Col. 4:2-4; 1 Thes. 5:17-18; 1 Tim. 2:1-4; Heb. 4:15-16; 10:19-22; 11; James 1:5-8; 5:13-18; 1 Peter 3:7; 1 John 5:14-15; and others).

Affective Dimension

In addition to the cognitive, we must somehow communicate the affective. Worship itself implies that we love God. We cannot pray for others effectively if we do not love them with divine love. As difficult as it is to require or to teach the affective, the cognitive encourages the affective. The worship prayers of David stimulate and foster an attitude of devotion to the Lord. We find twenty-five intercessory prayers in Paul's writings that provide us with real encouragement to love our churches and disciples as he loved his (e.g., Eph. 1:15-21; 3:14-21; Phil. 1:2-11; Col. 1:3-14; Phile. 4-6, and so forth). While we cannot measure the affective dimensions of prayer, we can usually recognize them. We do try to communicate the affective without testing it.

In addition to the affective, we must teach certain spiritual qualities which are immeasurable. The most important of these is faith. Our greatest assets are the biblical examples and biblical teaching. Jesus communicated faith by telling about its possibilities (Matt. 21:21-22). Genuine prayer also requires humility. Most veteran teachers of spiritual formation can draw from their experiences of examples of powerful "pray-ers" who accomplished much through their intercession, but were unknown publicly. God uses the humble.

Submission to God is another important quality. Only submission can say, "Your kingdom come" (Matt. 6:10). Again, the biblical examples are our best instrument (e.g., Luke 1:38; John 18:11). To communicate the importance of spiritual qualities, I compare the difficulty that "natural man" has in understanding spiritual truth with the impossibility of literal translation from one language to another (1 Cor. 2:14). Obviously I have to choose my languages and my examples carefully! If we are serious about teaching prayer, we will have to foster qualities which we cannot test. Good teaching involves communication, impartation, and encouragement.

THE QUALITIES OF AN EFFECTIVE TEACHER

Several qualities mark a good teacher of prayer. One is authority. After Jesus' teaching in the Sermon on the Mount, "the crowds were amazed at his teaching, because he taught as one who had authority" (Matt. 7:28-29). Authority develops in us as we are certain we are teaching truth. Deriving our teaching from the biblical content underlines our authority. Authority also is reinforced by knowledge (Heb. 5:11-14). The teacher of prayer must be a student of prayer. Above all, he or she must be a practitioner. "You who teach others, do you not teach yourself?" (Rom. 2:21) Jesus taught by giving an example (John 13:7).

What methods of teaching communicate the basics of prayer? Jesus used discursive teaching (as in the Sermon on the Mount) and that has been the most frequently used method ever since. Discursive teaching is more effective if combined with the visual. I use large numbers of charts and diagrams on the overhead projector and chalkboard. A second technique is the storying method. Missionaries are discovering this method as a powerful tool in transmitting the Gospel. Jesus used it extensively, especially in teaching prayer (Mark 4:2; Luke 11:5-7; 18:2-8, 10-14). Even though we teach in literate cultures, most students think visually, and a graphic story reaps great dividends. Dialogue teaching is effective and demands considerable alertness and familiarity with the materials. The students can also be taught to pray Scripture (e.g., the Psalms).

The most effective teaching is modeling. A student of prayer needs to hear his or her professor practice effective prayer and should have some evidence that he or she exercises habitual prayer. For the twenty-four years that I taught in a theological seminary, I began every semester by having each of my students fill out a three-by-five card on the greatest prayer needs of their lives. Each day I would privately pray through all the cards for the classes I was to teach that day. It provided a quick means of getting to know the students and helped cultivate a dynamic relationship with most of them. Also, as they saw answers to their prayers, these communicated the intangible of faith. I believe they "caught" more than I "taught" in the formal classroom setting.

Their subsequent ministries have repeatedly demonstrated that they entered and pursued their careers with a functioning relationship to the Lord. Along with the cards, we should use an abundance of personal illustrations. These, of course, will develop if we are practicing prayer over a period of time. Also, biographies of the famous prayers of history are effective in imparting the intangibles (Madame Guyon, David Brainerd, Praying Hyde, George Muller, Hudson Taylor).

Prayer assignments are difficult. We cannot "assign" the practice and development of faith, love, or humility. Within cognitive areas, we can assign Bible passages and test comprehension. We can assign and test study material from textbooks. Large numbers of Scriptures should be memorized (one per week or one per class), and we can test these. The students should keep a prayer journal, complete with prayer lists and a diary of their prayer habits with successes and failures. I have checked to see if a student kept a prayer journal, but normally I did not ask to examine it. Under the right circumstances, however, a student may be willing to share his or her most private thoughts with a sympathetic teacher. Most assignments should involve measurable objectives.

The Master Teacher, of course, was Jesus Himself. He used many methods. In the Sermon on the Mount, His method was discursive and conceptual (Matt. 6:5-18). At times, as we have seen, it was parabolic. He suited His instruction to the occasion. Significantly, the disciples asked Him to teach them prayer after they observed His practice (Luke 11:1). His model became their motivation. The Model Prayer (Luke 11:2-4 or Matt. 6:9-13) is a point of departure for many insights into the basics of prayer and our relationship to God. He also taught by promise (John 14:13-14).

Our greatest assurance is the continuing help of the Holy Spirit. In Nehemiah's important prayer, recounting the history of God's leadership of Israel, he said, "You gave your good Spirit to instruct them" (Neh. 9:20). He is, after all, the ultimate teacher of our materials. The psalmist correctly coupled God's teaching with the Spirit: "Teach me to do your will, for you are my God; may your good Spirit lead me on level ground" (Ps. 143:10). Since the teaching of prayer involves so many abstractions difficult to limit to our normal academic bounds, we may rest assured that the Spirit of God can accomplish what seems impossible to us.

I have avoided the subject of Christian mysticism, not because it is unimportant but because it involves the most private of all prayer experiences. Teaching is a public activity, and to some extent, we can hardly successfully capture in measurable terms that which was originally so private. Nevertheless, we can expose our students to some of the biographical material of mystics such as Hugo of St. Victor, Teresa of Avila, St. John of the Cross, and Therese de Lisieux. Students should certainly be exposed to contemplative prayer, as well as, for example, centering prayer.

In the final analysis, the conclusive test of our teaching will be the ultimate private continuing practice of our students. For this reason, we can never expect immediate satisfaction. We may have to give grades at the end of the course, and these do indicate important accomplishments. Growth in prayer requires years. We can really only plant seeds. The years tell us what we have actually achieved. The seedlings sometimes become giant trees, and then we know that our struggle was worth the effort.

For Further Reading

Baillie, J. (1949). *A diary of private prayer*. New York: Scribners. A collection of thoughtful prayers for morning and evening which can easily be personalized.

Bloom, A. (1970). *Beginning to pray*. New York: Paulist. Covers the basic issues of what prayer is and what it means to pray. Written by a Russian Orthodox archbishop for "people who have never prayed before," it has become a modern spiritual classic. Useful for people at all levels of spiritual development.

Bounds, E.M. (1982). *Power through prayer*. Springdale, PA: Whitaker House. A brief classic by a pastor who was personally committed to prayer and whose writings reflect his concern that pastors see prayer as their first calling. This book focuses special attention on the "preacher and prayer."

Bryant, D. (1988). *Concerts of prayer* (rev. ed.). Ventura, CA: Regal. A description of a powerful movement of group prayer directed toward world evangelization.

Christenson, E. (1975). *What happens when women pray*. Wheaton, IL: Victor. A guide on developing a praying church which grows out of the author's experience through her church and seminar work on prayer. While it is based on the stories of her work with women, its principles go beyond what the title implies.

Clements, R. (1985). *In spirit and in truth: Insights from biblical prayers*. Atlanta: John Knox. An examination of twenty-six prayers from both the Old and New Testaments.

Foster, R. (1992). *Prayer: Finding the heart's true home*. San Francisco: HarperSan Francisco. A comprehensive survey of prayer growing out of the author's personal practice of prayer and his theologial/biblical reflections on prayer and the nature of God.

Hallesby, O. (1975). *Prayer* (C.J. Carlsen, Trans.). Minneapolis: Augsburg. A simple and attractive treatment of prayer that places emphasis on the character qualities, humility, and simplicity needed for effective prayer. Aimed at the maturing Christian who desires a more effective and meaningful prayer life.

Hunter, W. (1986). *The God who hears*. Downers Grove, IL: InterVarsity. This is a God-centered discussion of prayer. It gives a good presentation of both the essence of prayer and the character of God. Deals with commonly asked questions about prayer's purpose, effectiveness, and necessity.

Hybels, B. (1988). *Too busy not to pray*. Downers Grove, IL: InterVarsity. A practical guide to establishing a prayer life. It emphasizes the need for one's prayer life to include both intercession and listening.

Muck, T. (1985). *Liberating the leader's prayer life*. Carol Stream, IL: Word/Christianity Today. Written for church leaders, this volume seeks to help leaders see the impediments that stand in the way of an effective prayer life. Written in a journalistic style with an abundance of references to interviews and current trends.

White, J. (1978). *Daring to draw near: People in prayer.* Downers Grove, IL: InterVarsity. An insightful book on prayer which uses the prayers of ten Bible characters as the basis of this discussion concerning the practice of prayer.

SIXTEEN
THE IMITATION OF CHRIST:
MEANS AND END OF SPIRITUAL FORMATION
Robert P. Meye

In Romans 8:29 the Apostle Paul projects the glorious destiny of the children of God: The sons and daughters of God are "predestined to be conformed to the image of his Son" (RSV). The entirety of Paul's ministry is shaped by the apostolic call to lead believers to this glorious end. Thus, Paul's preaching, teaching, and exhortation—with his entire being—are placed in the service of Christian formation, that is, formation in Jesus Christ.

In service of that high goal, Paul proclaims Christ at every opportunity and by all means. One basic means of placing Christ before the believers is embodied in his apostolic exhortation to *the imitation of Christ.* Out of his own whole-souled imitation of Christ, Paul is also bold to call believers to the imitation of himself, imitator of Christ. Coordinated with the call to the imitation of Christ, Paul points to the example of Christ—and also to himself as an example of one who follows that example.

Indeed, and this is the thesis of the present essay, in Paul, as in the New Testament generally, *the imitation of Christ is both a fundamental means and the glorious goal of Christian formation.*

THE IMITATION OF CHRIST AND THE IMAGE OF CHRIST

Consider a question and an explanatory note. How is the *image of Christ* related to the *imitation of Christ?* Isn't it one thing to

199

say (with Paul) that the divine goal for believers is conformation to the image of Christ, but another to point to the imitation of Christ as the goal of Christian formation? Two explanatory notes, one linguistic and one theological, are in order. First, it is important to observe the linguistic unity binding together the Latin words from which our English words "image" (imago, noun) and "imitation" (imitare, verb) are derived. The latter term (imitare) is derived from the former (imago); the two words have a common root and a common orientation. The action (to imitate) corresponds to the goal of the action (the image).

Second, in the Pauline perspective in particular—and the New Testament perspective generally—there is not an absolute dividing line between the status of one's life in Christ in the present and in the future. The people of God in history are already "in Christ"; they are described by the Apostle Paul as a redeemed and holy people even though their full redemption and perfection (sanctification) are yet future. Thus, the imitation of Christ in the present time is but prelude to final transformation into the glorious image of Christ. Again, for the Apostle Paul the imitation of Christ is both a fundamental means and the glorious end of Christian formation into the image of Christ.

Although the number of instances of the language of imitation in the Pauline vocabulary is limited—in contrast to well-known terms or expressions such as "faith," or "love," or "in Christ"—the appearance of the language of imitation at critical points in the Pauline argument shows the importance for Paul of the imitation of Christ. This observation is supported by an abundance of passages throughout Paul's writings in which the apostle clearly points believers toward Christ or himself or others as in some way exemplary of the way of faith. *In Paul, faith (in Christ) is necessarily expressed in the imitation of Christ.*

The use of the explicit language of imitation and example, and wider use of implicit language and patterns of imitation, are visible beyond Paul throughout the New Testament. Most importantly—as will be developed—this pattern has its foundations in Jesus Christ, above all, as we shall see below, in the call to discipleship. There are notable instances of explicit language of imitation and example in, among others, the Gospel of John,

Hebrews, and 1 Peter. But these and the remaining New Testament documents also have a rich variety of ways and means of pointing toward exemplary persons and exemplary ways of calling believers toward the imitation of Christ.

A review of some of the Pauline passages and other texts using the language of imitation and example is in order at this point. Some elementary observations will be attached to these various writings.

Some Basic New Testament Data and Principles

Several forms in the Greek New Testament are best translated with the language of imitation. Some basic terms and their New Testament locations are listed here for convenience:

- The verb *mimeomai,* "imitate" (2 Thes. 3:7, 9; Heb. 13:7; 3 John 11)
- The noun *mimetes,* "imitator" (1 Cor. 4:16; 11:1; Eph. 5:1; 1 Thes. 1:6; 2:14; Heb. 6:12; 1 Peter 3:13)

To these we may add related words such as the following:

- The noun *typos,* "example," "model," "pattern" (1 Cor. 10:6, 11; Phil. 3:17; 1 Thes. 1:7; 2 Thes. 3:9; 1 Tim. 4:12; Titus 2:7; 1 Peter 5:3)
- The noun *hypodeigma,* "example" (John 13:15; Heb. 4:11; 8:5; James 5:10)

The first part of Paul's letter to the Christians at Thessalonica provides a helpful look at his own appeal to the pattern of imitation and example:

- 1 Thessalonians 1:6-7: "You became *imitators* of us and of the Lord: in spite of severe suffering, you welcomed the message with the joy given by the Holy Spirit. And so you became a *model* to all the believers in Macedonia and Achaia."
- 1 Thessalonians 2:14: "For you, brothers, became *imitators* of God's churches in Judea, which are in Christ Jesus: You suffered from your own countrymen the same things those churches suffered from the Jews."

In their setting these passages give rise to several important (if mostly obvious) observations regarding the imitation of Christ.

1. Imitation involves an imitating *subject* and an imitated *object*—in this case, personal subjects and objects.

2. The imitated object is an *example* for the imitator.

3. As in the case of the texts before us, imitation can apparently be (a) a most important *action* which (b) betrays one's most central *orientation.* The first thing that Paul does is to commend the Thessalonians for their imitation of himself, whose own exemplary life among them is underlined at length in the second chapter of the letter.

4. The primary personal objects of imitation are Jesus Christ, the Lord of the church, and Paul the Apostle of Christ. But the examples which draw persons toward conformity to the image of Christ are not limited to Jesus Christ Himself and His servant Paul. Of the Thessalonian believers Paul observes that even as they have followed the example of Paul (and of Christ), they themselves have also become an example to others. Paul envisions a "chain" of examples. Just as the apostle delivered to others the oral tradition which he received, even so in his life and the life of the churches, an example received from a church is passed along to yet other churches. (In 1 Thessalonians 2 Paul underlines the importance of congruence between word and example.)

5. Imitation touches both *outward conduct and inward disposition.* There has been considerable discussion regarding the scope of imitation: is it a matter of attitude, or does it also involve attention to detail, to specific conduct? Both Paul's references to his Lord, and his own personal narrative, regularly touch both the springs of conduct and conduct itself. Given Paul's own detailed report of his own sufferings, which he understands to be "in Christ," it is impossible to suppose that his references to the obedience and suffering of Jesus have only a "general disposition" in mind.

Other New Testament passages give added dimension to our understanding of the imitation of Christ:

- 1 Corinthians 4:16: "Therefore, I urge you to *imitate* me."
- 1 Corinthians 11:1: "Follow my *example,* as I follow the *example* of Christ."

THE IMITATION OF CHRIST: MEANS AND END OF SPIRITUAL FORMATION

- John 13:15: "I have set you an *example* that you should do as I have done for you."
- Acts 20:35: "In everything I did, I *showed* you that by this kind of hard work we must help the weak, remembering the words the Lord Jesus himself said: 'It is more blessed to give than to receive.' "

6. The imitation of Christ, or of Paul, is not simply a pattern which a believer *might* or might not adopt. The imitation of Christ, and the imitation of Christ through Paul, is an essential aspect of the call to the obedience of faith located at the very center of the Apostle Paul's mission (Rom. 1:5; 16:26).

7. The place of "the imitation of Christ" is underlined in the fact that Paul, the imitator of Christ, and Christ before him, consciously place themselves before disciples/believers as an example to be imitated. In so doing, they "give themselves" to others in the service of their mission.

Other passages provide yet additional perspective on imitation in the New Testament:

- Romans 4:12: "And he is also the father of the circumcised who not only are circumcised but who walk *in the footsteps* of the faith that our father Abraham had before he was circumcised."
- 1 Corinthians 10:11: "These things happened to them as *examples* and were written down as warnings for us, on whom the fulfillment of the ages has come."

8. Imitation can look to a broader pattern of existence. In this text, as in Romans 4 generally, Paul uses as an example the broad pattern of Abraham's faith as displayed in the Scriptures.

9. Even as there are good examples to be followed, so there are also bad examples to be avoided. The generous use of bad examples in the Scriptures not only directs a warning to believers, but is a reminder to the believing observer of the text that there is a lesson to be learned from the very example which is to be avoided.

Reservations Regarding the Imitation of Christ
We have not yet noted reservations sometimes held by Christian scholars and theologians regarding the imitation of Christ.

Some of these need to be kept in mind (albeit for differing reasons): (1) It is often noted that Martin Luther, looking out on the ecclesiastical scene of his own time, worried about the drift into "works righteousness," which he attached to some efforts toward the imitation of Christ. Those worries have continued to the present moment. (2) Again, doubt is expressed by some scholars regarding the interest of the Apostle Paul in "the historical Jesus" and, consequently, doubt regarding Paul's interest in the details of Christ's life as being of essential importance for believers, and subject to imitation by them. Here, imitation is rather connected to the self-humbling of the transcendent Lord (as in Phil. 2:5ff). The imitation of Christ is seen as related not to details of conduct, but to the attitude of the Son of God who humbles Himself and gives Himself in suffering and death for others. (3) And especially in respect to detail, scholars often worry out loud about "mere" imitation, that is, that imitation may focus on mere details, not on the larger reality controlling specific actions.

The New Testament Encourages Alternative Interpretations of Itself

(1) In respect to the worry about "works righteousness" (as in Luther), it must be said that the imitation of Christ is firmly rooted in canonical Scriptures of the New Testament and appears there in the imperative mode. The imitation of Christ is an apostolic command, and the command is implicit in Jesus' call to disciples to follow Him. St. Augustine was surely correct in equating following Jesus and imitating Jesus. The imitation of Christ may well offer the temptation to "works righteousness"; but the Apostle Paul, and his Lord before him, declared that there is no quarter of life—including religious life—which is free from this temptation. For Paul, this temptation is part and parcel of the sinfulness of sin (Rom. 7). But the the sinful abuse of a practice should not be allowed to negate the practice.

(2) The debate regarding Paul's interest in the "life of Jesus" has gone on for a long time and cannot be resolved in a few sentences. However, it must be said that the apostle who celebrated God's "sending his own Son in the likeness of sinful man" (Rom. 8:3) so that "through the obedience of one man

the many will be made righteous" (Rom. 5:19), and who persecuted the followers of Jesus, was an apostle for whom the concrete life of Jesus Christ is surely essential to faith. Both the life
and the suffering and death—and the exaltation—of Jesus are
essential reference points in the faith of Paul.

The force of the texts already noted do not allow a separation between deeds and dispositions. Neither Paul nor the
other New Testament authors would know how to separate
dispositions from deeds. Deeds are a fruit of the heart, and
deeds have their own good or evil fruit in the dispositions or
character of the human being.

(3) In respect to the fear regarding "mere imitation," the
best counsel is to follow the lead of the New Testament, in
which imitation and example are used boldly, without qualifica-
tion. (One might say that in the New Testament, Jesus Christ is
the great qualifier of all imitation!) Interestingly, one does not
encounter comparable reservation in commentary relative to
such New Testament themes as faith, righteousness, or obedience. But there are also kinds of "faith" and "righteousness"
and "obedience" which are clearly unacceptable within the
New Testament's own perspective.

Concerning Imitation in Human Formation
It is amazing that Protestant theological scholarship generally
has been so insensitive to the role of imitation in human life.
Roman Catholic scholarship, although it has a closer kinship
with Protestant scholarship in recent decades, has had a much
larger place for the imitation of Christ. *All biblical interpreters
need to recognize the fact there is perhaps no more important
factor in human formation than the combination of example
and imitation.* Psychologists, sociologists, educators, and an-
thropologists have long since emphasized the central and vital
importance of imitation throughout human existence.[1] A deeper understanding of the comprehensive role of imitation in all
of human life could open the door to a more positive approach
to the doctrine of the imitation of Christ. The infant begins life
in imitation of parents and significant others. That pattern continues right on through earliest childhood, adolescence, the
teen years, and young adulthood. The pattern is found in every
social class in all cultures. And the imitative pattern encom-

passes both the elemental aspects of human existence, such as talking and walking, and extends on into the most complex areas of human conduct and character. Evidently, *to be human is to be an imitator.*

To be sure, *there are dangers in imitation, even as there can be danger in eating or talking or even loving*—all activities of fundamental importance to human existence. One may imitate the wrong things, or the wrong people. Imitation may remain in an unconscious and/or immature track, rather than growing into an increasingly self-conscious and mature pattern or one may not mature in one's self, and unthinkingly follow a pattern of conduct which is not one's own. But, again and again, the optimal way to realize a good goal will incorporate some pattern of imitation of the incarnated good—above all, faith would say, the imitation of God (see Eph. 5:1), the very source of the Good.

The Imitation of Christ in the Gospel Narratives

It is important to recognize how imitation happens. How does the imitator become formed in the way(s) of the example? How is one formed in the image of Christ? The formative process begins as the Example, Jesus Christ, binds Himself to those who are to imitate Him. Jesus calls disciples to follow Him, wherever He goes. Jesus constitutes the disciples as His circle, His companions, His family. In this circle, He is the compelling presence, the significant Other who wills to shape the disciple's life in all its parts—and looks for the disciples to share that will.

This is either the explicit or the implicit thrust of each of the four Gospel narratives. Just as the parent is the "significant other" whom the infant must imitate, even so Jesus is that "Other" whom the disciples must imitate. Jesus is the manifestation of the kingdom of God. Jesus is the Holy One. Jesus is the window to God. Jesus is the way to God. There is no other One to whom they can go. Even though Jesus does not typically use the explicit language of imitation and example, the disciples are, in Jesus' call to follow Him, placed in the way of being imitators of Jesus.

The language of discipleship in the Gospel narratives is transformed into the language of imitation in the epistles. The Gospels narrate the way of discipleship before Easter but with the intention of instructing believers in the risen Christ in the way of imitation of Christ. The life of faith after Easter — the way of imitation — is an extension of the life of discipleship before Easter. To follow Jesus is to be an imitator of Christ; to be an imitator of Christ is to live as a follower of Jesus.

The Way of Human Imitation — A Model

It is important, if we are to understand the imitation of Christ, to ponder the way in which imitation takes place in human life. We can be helped by recourse to a simple example of imitation; although there can be unending variations in patterns of imitation, there are some persistent patterns in all imitation.

The relationship between a ski instructor and a novice skier, in which framework the pupil is "formed" as a skier, helpfully illustrates the way of imitation. Skiing may be envisioned here as "a way of life" — a way of life (more or less) perfected in the instructor. Once the novice has chosen (in this case) to learn from the *Meister,* that is, once the relationship of example and imitator is established, there are a number of dynamics which are persistently evident in the formative relationship.[2]

(1) The basic instruction takes place on the slopes, not in a "classroom," in recognition of the fact that imitation of a "lived example" is a primary means of learning — especially in projects involving the whole person.

(2) The instructor simultaneously provides an example to be imitated and verbal instruction explicating the example. Example and instruction illuminate each other. Learning is maximized through the dynamic relationship which exists between example and instruction.

(3) As instruction proceeds, the instructor models and teaches skiing by addressing the whole and the parts of the art of skiing. After all, skiing consists of both elements, the whole and the parts, and skiing cannot be well learned apart from persistent unitary attention to both.

(4) It is especially important to observe that *there is always an overflow from the parts to the whole and from the whole to the parts.* As the instructor shows the student how to handle the downhill ski on a turn, he or she invites attention to the way in which the uphill ski, and then the whole body, is to be addressed. *Authentic learning in the project of imitation involves the symbiotic overflow in imitation from the whole to*

the parts and the parts to the whole. Excellence in skiing (authentic imitation of the example or image of perfect skiing) first takes place as part and whole function as one. Skiing *in part* offers only a bad example! At the same time, there is no skiing at all that does not consist of component parts of the activity all working together.

(5) As learning proceeds—just when the student had imagined that things were going well—the instructor places yet other important aspects of the art of skiing before the pupil, challenging the will and ability of the pupil all over again. There is ever new ground to gain in perfecting the art of skiing. The good example (of the instructor) lures the imitator forward toward an increasing mastery of the project.

(6) We note finally, although the illustration could be productive of other points, that learning and maturing in the art of skiing is only possible because someone preceded the student in the way of skiing and now serves as an example and a teacher. Even more, the example of the master skier, coupled with the example's constant encouragement, work together to perfect the novice in a daunting venture.

Christian formation is much more than a matter of skiing, but the two processes have in common the formation of human beings in a complex process. Each suffers without an example to be imitated. Each needs an example in action and interpretation of the example. Each is a complex of many parts and a larger whole. Each is ever subject to maturation in the imitative project. Each needs encouraging enablement and enabling encouragement. But the point here is not to multiply parallels between the ways of imitation "in Christ" and the ways of imitation in skiing. Rather, *we are called to remember that imitation is one of the most natural and significant elements in human formation; and as it conforms human beings to the image of Jesus Christ, the pattern of imitation is "the most natural thing in the world" for those in Christ.*

MAJOR PRINCIPLES OF IMITATION

Imitation generally, and the imitation of Christ in particular, are many splendored projects. Thus, much remains to be said regarding the imitation of Christ as a fundamental means and the glorious end of Christian formation. The following notes are especially worthy of attention:

(1) The Christian community is one with the world in the practice of imitation as a primary means of formation. *The great difference between the example and imitation in human formation and in Christian formation is, of course, to be found in the great Object and Subject of Christian imitation.* Christ's incarnate life, His redemptive death, His risen glory and exalted place at the right hand of God, His directing and illuminating and empowering presence in the Spirit, His steadfast love and mercy, His eternal wisdom — all this is "invested" in the project of *Christian* formation.

(2) In a world and in a church with a diversity of models and examples clamoring for attention, the doctrine of the imitation of Christ tacitly declares that *Jesus of Nazareth is the normative model for human life today.* Even as there is salvation through Christ alone, even so the way in salvation is exemplified by the Savior. The way of faith is the way of imitating the Savior. Only so can the good work begun in the believer be completed for the day of Jesus Christ.

(3) The tension between the solid place of the New Testament call to the imitation of Christ and distortions in practicing it or undue reservations in affirming it could easily render the community of faith insensitive to a great fact: the call to the imitation of Christ is, above all else, Good News. Jesus Christ came proclaiming the Gospel of the kingdom and called disciples to follow Him — in the way of imitation. In his letters to the young churches Paul ever celebrated the great Gospel of Jesus Christ and called the faithful to the imitation of Christ. *The call to the imitation of Christ is one with the Gospel of Jesus Christ, and is a reflection of that Gospel, that is, of that Good News.* The call to the imitation of Christ must be ever celebrated as a gracious invitation and a graced event.

(4) The mystery of imitation of Christ is that in this project of imitation the finite and imperfect (the believer) seeks — and is called — to imitate the infinite and the perfect (Jesus Christ). This is the glorious calling, the "high calling" in Christ Jesus. But the effort falls short. In spite of the distance between the pilgrim and the Image which is her destiny she is called to

continue the pilgrimage, in spite of falling. *Thus, the way of imitation can only be the way of repentance and confession of sin.* And it can only take place with enablement from God the Father, God the Son, and God the Holy Spirit.

(5) We have observed that imitation of persons (and in the imitation of Christ we are called to the imitation of a *Person)* is a project which somehow involves the whole person. The obedience of imitating Jesus Christ calls the church and the believer to attend to the entire sweep of the canonical witness to Jesus Christ. One often observes, whether in theology or in popular Christianity, a certain separation between (say) the Gospels and the epistles, or between narrative and teaching.

But Jesus Christ is the *incarnate* Word of God. To know Christ we need to see Him and to follow Him in the entirety of His mission — in His word, deeds, and attitude. *The call to imitation has the virtue of calling faith to attend to the whole Christ.* The church, in its preaching and teaching, and worship and witness, in all its life, needs to be devoted to the whole Christ and attentive to the whole canon. Only so is Jesus Christ truly the object of imitation and only so will the imitation project be at once faithful and fruitful.

(6) The imitation of Christ is a project embracing and calling upon the entire community of faith. The Spirit who illumines the way of imitation has gifted the body of Christ with the discernment, exhortation, and encouragement of which the Spirit knows the imitator ever has need. Not least in support of this way is the lively example, as seen in the Christians at Thessalonica, provided in and through the community of the Spirit.

Within the community of the Spirit, a host of practices and exercises all transport the believer toward formation in the image of Christ. Not only example and teaching, but preaching, worship, the liturgy, the sacraments, hymnody, evangelism, Christian service, all these having been formed from and *through* Christ, contain essential dimensions forming the individual and the community in Christ. *Just as the human family has an indispensable role in human formation, so the community of the Spirit has an essential role in Christian formation.*

(7) All this lays a heavy imperative upon the faithful teacher, indeed upon all believers. The real danger in respect to the

imitation of Christ is that the pattern of imitation be broken, that the believer turn aside from living in the pattern of the Great Example. The glorious possibility is that the faithful teacher—and, again, all believers—may faithfully imitate and thus provide a "mirror image" of Jesus Christ. The imitation of Christ is at once a most demanding task and a most glorious privilege in Christian formation.

Such is the great mystery of the Christian life and Christian formation. In Christ, God was pleased to make His dwelling among and with humankind. Through the Spirit of Christ that indwelling continues. God's dwelling *with* and dwelling *in* humankind offers at once the glorious example and the glorious means of conformation to the Son of God. The indwelling Spirit of Christ both traces the way of the Lord for the disciple and empowers the disciple in that pattern of imitation in which the believer is formed in Christ.

Notes

1. The following authors offer a cross-section of significant learning and reflection in the process of imitation in human formation: A. Bandura & R.H. Walters (1963), *Social learning and personality development.* New York: Holt, Rinehart and Winston; A. Bandura (1969), *Principles of behavior modification.* New York: Holt, Rinehart and Winston; O. Mowrer (1950), *Learning theory and personality dynamics.* New York: Ronald Press; O. Mowrer (1960), *Learning theory and the symbolic process.* New York: Wiley; B. McLaughlin (1971), *Learning and social behavior.* New York: Free Press; N. Miller & J. Dollard (1967), *Social learning and imitation.* New Haven: Yale Univ. Press; J. Piaget (1962), *Play, dreams, and imitation in childhood.* New York: Norton; J. Piaget & B. Inhelder (1969), *The psychology of the child.* New York: Basic Books.

2. Mowrer (1950), in a footnote laden with meaning, observes that "imitation may thus be said to be the non-verbal equivalent of studying."

For Further Reading

A. Bandura, & R. Walters. (1963). *Social learning and personality development.* New York: Holt, Rinehart and Winston. The depth and breadth of imitation in shaping human attitudes and conduct are explored and convincingly stated from the vantage point of psychiatry.

Bonhoeffer, D. (1959). *The cost of discipleship.* London: SCM. Bonhoeffer's well-known statement on (the cost of) discipleship is important adjunctive reading to serious reflection on the imitation of Christ.

Griffiths, M. (1985). *The example of Jesus.* Downers Grove, IL: InterVarsity. This is a most helpful, semipopular treatment of the example of Jesus by a church leader with a fine sense of what needs to be said on this subject.

Malatesta, E. (1974). *Imitating Christ.* St. Meinrad, IN: Abbey. This volume offers a translation of the very important series of essays on the imitation of Christ which appeared in the well-known French Catholic dictionary on spirituality, *Dictionnaire de Spiritualité.*

Rahner, K. (1983). *The love of Jesus and the love of neighbor.* New York: Crossroad. This eminent Roman Catholic theologian's essay on "Our Relationship to Jesus" is a pearl of great price! He not only offers an unforgettable essay on the love of Christ and the love of God, but opens the door in us to a deepening of that love.

Reid, J. (1963). *Our life in Christ.* Philadelphia: Westminster. A stimulating treatment of the larger theme of life in Christ which embraces the question of imitation of Christ along the way.

Schnackenburg, R. (1968). *Christian existence in the New Testament.* Notre Dame, IN: Univ. of Notre Dame Press. Schnackenburg helpfully and convincingly emphasizes the equation of following Jesus and the imitation of Christ.

Schoen, D. (1987). *Educating the reflective practitioner.* San Francisco: Jossey-Bass. This contemporary treatment of education is most illuminating in explicating the function of imitation in learning.

Schrage, W. (1988). *The ethics of the New Testament.* Philadelphia: Fortress. This outstanding work on the ethics of the New Testament (translated from the German original) is an important adjunct to thinking through the implications of imitation in New Testament perspective.

Schweizer, E. (1960). *Lordship and discipleship.* London: SCM. Schweizer's work has long been a standard reference work for thinking through discipleship in the New Testament.

Segovia, F. (Ed.). (1985). *Discipleship in the New Testament.* Philadelphia: Fortress. This collection of essays on discipleship contains some very important recent reflections and a bibliography on the imitation of Christ.

Tinsley, E. (1972). *The imitation of God in Christ.* London: SCM. Tinsley's major study on imitation has long been a standard reference work on the subject. The study ranges through the biblical literature and provides excellent pointed studies of various New Testament texts and themes important for understanding the imitation of Christ.

PERSONAL HEALING AND SPIRITUAL FORMATION
Leanne Payne

"My dear children, for whom I am again in the pains of childbirth until Christ is formed in you" (Gal. 4:19).

How is it that we *become persons,* that we find our one true self in Christ? How is it that Christ is formed in us? How is it that God (the eternal) shines through us (the finite)? The Uncreated through His creatures? How do we educate and minister in His name and power? How do we walk in the Spirit as St. Paul admonishes and move in the Spirit's gifts, what Leslie Weatherhead called the "dynamic spiritual energy which the church of the first century knew"? The answer has always to do with His sovereign Presence over us, with us, within us: Incarnational Reality.

In Him we become fully human. In Him we begin to do His works. This involves *incarnation;* by this I mean a descent of the Spirit into our deepest being and lives. In Christ, the will, intellect, imagination, feeling, and sensory being are hallowed and enlivened. We begin to fully live, to participate in the eternal, the immutable, the indestructible. We receive healing; we are formed spiritually.

We live in a day, however, when few — even among those who call themselves Christian — truly believe in Christ's Real Presence in and with us. This reality, however, is what sets Christian education apart from its secular counterparts; it is its absolute distinctive.

TEACHERS AS SACRAMENTAL VESSELS

"No generation can bequeath to its successor what it has not got.
You may frame the syllabus as you please.
But when you have planned and reported ad nauseam,
if we are skeptical we shall teach only skepticism to our pupils,
if fools only folly, if vulgar only vulgarity,
if saints sanctity, if heroes heroism.
Education is only the most fully conscious of the channels
whereby each generation influences the next.
It is not a closed system.
Nothing which was not in the teachers
can flow from them into the pupils
(Lewis, 1970b, p. 116).

The Christian reality, beyond all else we would pass on, is more caught than taught. God with us, and the spiritual power and energy which attends this greatest of all Realities, is not something we can pass on to others if we do not ourselves know and walk in it. The effective Christian is one who learns to acknowledge the Presence of God and invite all the needy into that Healing Presence. Such a Christian holds, as a fragile vessel, the powerful grace that is always descending from God, and its fragrance, like the costliest perfume, is wafted upon the breath of the Spirit for the benefit of others. This grace includes, of course, wisdom and knowledge from Him who is called the Living Word. He, the Living Knowledge, the Living Source of all that ever was, shall be, or now is, imparts His mind and Life to us.

The teacher who sees personal healing and spiritual formation occurring in the classroom walks in a knowledge of the presence of this Holy God. Such a teacher passes on the knowledge and dispositions needed to live in God's presence. The life we are called to proclaim is a supernatural, not a "natural" one, and we ourselves are living epistles—if indeed we illustrate and pass on the awesome truth we teach. Otherwise, in our very persons and in the atmosphere of our classrooms, we belie the truth we teach. We pass on skepticism. Sin and unbelief are "natural," even in a sense "genetic" to fallen humankind; only in the presence and power of that greater Life do we live out the Christian Reality.

HEALING IN THE PRESENCE

In the Presence of God, the real "I" in each one of us as individuals is revealed. False selves fall from us as the true are called forward and named. Only in His Light are the disparate parts of myself from which I am estranged found, touched, and integrated into the "I" that God created me to be. With this in mind, we quickly see that personal healing and spiritual formation are connected. As Christ is formed in us, our wounds are ministered to, even "anointed" as sources of healing power for others. Ruth Pitter, the English poet, wrote: "Alleluia, all my gashes cry." My very gashes, whether caused by my own sin or that of another, cry "Alleluia" once Christ touches them. Health as well as maturity, for myself and for others, is the result.

This healing is released when we raise Christ's Cross for all to see, and then tell the truth about what it means. We (the Pastoral Care Ministries Team and I) never cease being awed at the miracle that happens when we invite needy ones to look up with the eyes of their hearts and see Christ dying on the Cross in order to take into Himself their sins, their pain, their sorrow, even their limitations. We speak words to this effect: "It was His vocation to become that very darkness, that awful thing, that is even now destroying you. Look up to Him, and see your sin, your darkness, even your barriers to becoming all you were created to be, flowing into His wounds as you confess them."

We help them do this. The body prays too, as C.S. Lewis reminds us, so we help them lift their hands and faces up to God as this cleansing is going on (Lewis, 1963, p. 17). The eyes of their hearts are still set on Him, and together we watch as God does His gracious work in their needy souls.

We invite the covetous and the envious, the proud and the hopeless, the faithless and the joyless, the loveless and the murderer, the thief and the liar, the adulterer and the fornicator, the homosexual offender or sexually perverted of any kind: we invite all to do this, and we see the broken healed and transformed by His grace. We see those who are supposed to be past helping, get help—perhaps, especially those.

We invite the abused, and all who suffer from mental and emotional darkness to do this same thing with their pain and their fearful memories. Looking to Christ-on-the-Cross they see the One who willingly became the Victim, and they are invited and helped to forgive even their worst enemies. Soon they find it doesn't do (that it is even harmful) to think of themselves as victims. In a fallen and tormented world, they are now in the Victor. He is in them.

Continually we ask God for the tongue of a poet with which to paint pictures of His redemption, and of what it looks like as it is translated into the spiritual and psychological "cells" of their being, and yes, even their physical cells. It turns out that virtuous as well as vicious habits connected with character formation change (among other things) the very structure of the brain. The soul's terrain that God has in mind for us turns out to be a "soulscape" green with a becoming that impacts our total being. It is heaven's own turf to which we beckon seeking souls away from their wilderness of sin, anxiety, hopelessness, and compulsive behavior.

We who do the ministering are struck with the marvelous simplicity of it all, the way the Lord not only heals the soul but works with those of us who collaborate with Him. It is even as St. Mark reported: "Then the disciples went out and preached everywhere and the Lord worked with them and confirmed His word by the signs that accompanied it" (16:20).

Christ heals and completes His people as we humbly invoke His Presence and, simply as we can, tell once again the story of the Cross, the way Christ died to take our sin, our woundedness into Himself. We call all to repent and to the kind of radical obedience to Christ that results in full integration of the personality and of a freedom none but those who experience it can understand. The Lord of Life then, ever eager to heal, confirms His word with signs following, namely, with healing and spiritual formation for all who turn and look fully to Him.

THE DILEMMA OF THE MODERN PERSON

"To a phenomenal degree, appearance has replaced reality"
(Mackay, 1969, p. 13).

The greatest need we have today is for healing of the dreadful split between head and heart that runs so deep in us as moderns (see chapter 10, "The Terrible Schism in the Heart of Man," in *The Healing Presence*), one that has resulted in what I have come to call "the disease of introspection" (Payne, 1989, pp. 133–137). The soul needing healing or help in the areas of spiritual formation most often does not get it because he is locked into the spirit of the age—a rationalism that has replaced the good of reason and usurped the heart's intuitive ways of knowing and receiving from God. This " 'knowledge-by-acquaintance' *(connaitre),* " a " 'tasting,' of Love Himself" that "the humblest of us, in a state of Grace," can know, is lost to us (Lewis, 1960, p. 174). C.S. Lewis has said: "It is religion itself—prayer and sacrament and repentance and adoration—which is here in the long run, our sole avenue to the real" (Lewis, 1970a, p. 46). This "avenue to the real" has been largely replaced by looking inward, a concentration on the self, and one's subjective feelings—all at the expense of objective reality. The "disease of introspection" substitutes for the acknowledgment of all that is real outside the self (Payne, 1989, pp. 139–165). (See *The Healing Presence,* chapters 11 and 12, "The True Imagination," and "Introspection versus True Imagination.")

Our counseling offices, whether in Christian education, the church, or in the more therapeutic disciplines, are filled with those suffering from this intolerable split. To experience closure of this chasm within our beings is to find the most incredible healing. Until we do, ministers and teachers as well as the needy are in the throes of endless abstraction. We think, think, think—but increasingly of nothing of substance. The shadow or "appearance" of Christian reality then substitutes for the Real.

Though this split affects every level of society, it is nowhere more apparent than in the university and nowhere more harmful than when part of Christian education. It is the split that Kierkegaard cried out about when he said we've forgotten how *to exist, to be*—that we can only think and talk about being.

The church has understood and preached that

> Christ came,
> Christ died,
> and Christ will come again,

but generally speaking it has not learned consistently to proclaim His *real presence* with us in the now and the "divine energy" with which we are to move in this Presence: "How tremendous is this power available to us who believe in God. That power is the same divine energy which was demonstrated in Christ when he raised him from the dead" (Eph. 1:19-20, PH).

THE NEED TO EMPHASIZE CHRIST'S REAL PRESENCE

This concept and reality is as foreign to much of the church's mind-set as to that of the secular, the unconverted person, and even the outspoken arch-materialist. To begin to "walk by the Spirit" (Gal. 5:16, RSV) as St. Paul tells us and "walk in the light, as he is in the light" as John reminds us (1 John 1:7), we must first be healed of this mind-set.

Ours has been, for the last several hundred years, an increasingly heady religion, one in which we substitute conceptual knowledge *about* God for the walk with Him. This is the kind of "headiness" that causes us to lose the good of reason, while making rationalists of us (Payne, 1989, pp. 80–87).

It also makes weary activists of us, for the schism is between the power to act and the power to be *(acting* and *being)*. It is between the more conscious, scientific, rational powers and faculties of the mind and those of the more "subconscious" intuitive, imaginative, feeling, willing ways of response to all that *is*. The denial of the latter leaves us open to unremitting activism and rationalism.

This rift, though it started in an earlier century, hardened in the seventeenth century with what is called Cartesian Dualism. Rene Descartes' dictum: "I think, therefore, I am," defined the soul, reducing it to intellect. In this way of thinking, the soul is split off from its spiritual, emotional, intuitive, imaginative properties, all those faculties with which we see God, commune with Him, and with our fellows.

Our gravest problem, today, as Christian educators, is essentially twofold. We have lost the Judeo-Christian worldview, and with it, the knowledge of the soul. We do not understand its feeling, imaginative, intuitive, and symbolic properties. We have adopted undiscerning views of the soul, such as those held by the secular (materialist or spiritualist) psychologies of the day.

We, in effect, no longer accept the soul's existence as part of the Unseen Real — at least not according to the Judeo-Christian model. As Christians then, we have essentially lost the greater part of our souls. We can no longer celebrate a soul capable of symbolizing, feeling, imagining, and intuiting a Real that is greater than our unassisted intellect. The soul is more than capable of hearing and responding to God after the fashion we see in the Scriptures.

SPIRITUAL FORMATION AND HEALING
ARE RELATED TO MENDED RELATIONSHIPS

Christ empowered and commanded His followers to heal because He knew that all people, in their exterior relationships and within themselves, are broken and separated. In order to gain wholeness and the opportunity to mature as persons, we must acknowledge and deeply repent of the separations in our lives. The primary separation is between the self and God, out of which issue the separations between the self and other selves, the self and nature, and the self and one's "deep heart."

The healing of this latter separation brings into harmony the intellect and the heart, that is, the cognitive and intuitive capacities and ways of knowing; and these "two minds" are thereby enabled to balance and complete each other. The will, the emotions, the intuitive and imaginative faculties are cleansed and receive the very life of God.

With this healing, the self is freed to come into the Presence of the Unseen Real — the Presence of God Himself — where we "become partakers of the divine nature" (2 Peter 1:4). It is in this way that we become persons. True personality is rooted in relationship: first of all in God, the Uncreated, then with everything He has created.

IMAGERY AND SYMBOL

Psychological and emotional healings through prayer have to do with a miraculous resymbolizing of the human heart, one that restores to it the scriptural, incarnational view of reality.

The Scriptures are at once the repository and the great guardian of the Christian world picture—that is, what I call the incarnational symbolic system. It is our paradigm for life or our picture of true reality. A sound understanding of the Scriptures therefore evokes true imagery within the heart, just as it grants a sound theology to the mind. For example, the way humankind in general or the individual heart images God is judged to be adequate or inadequate, true or false, as it lines up with the way the Scriptures image God. The images that come to us from within (our own heart) and from without (the cultural and competing symbolic systems of the day) are therefore always to be filtered through and measured by the Scriptures.

This is crucial because imagery, symbol, revelation, and experience can be and are interpreted by the human systems—those devised in separation and even in opposition to God and His revelation of Himself to us in and through Christ and the Scriptures. The importance of this cannot be overemphasized because we are mythic beings: we live by and in our symbols. Humans are animals who *symbolize,* who *talk.* (To talk is to symbolize; language itself is symbol.) Thus, humankind is set apart from the rest of the natural creation.

When a sound symbolic system (an integrated way of seeing reality) is missing, a lesser one takes its place. When great and good symbolic images of God, the cosmos, fatherhood, motherhood, masculine, feminine, and so on are rejected or simply absent from the psyche, then lesser images (and even entire symbolic systems) develop to take their place. While the wisdom of this world ignores the Incarnation and the Cross, we Christians are foolish enough to proclaim a virgin-born Christ nailed to a cross. And in doing that we see the floodgates opened and God's wisdom and saving, healing power released into the lives of all who look to Him. But not before true images of this redemption are restored to the soul.

ALIEN SYMBOLS

With the Christian's loss of the Judeo-Christian symbolic system, new systems rich with alien symbolic imagery have flooded in. The symbolism of the occult, and various Eastern, pagan, pantheistic, and gnostic (e.g., feminist, Jungian, New Age) systems too often informs the minds and hearts of many churchgoers.

Should we be inclined to test the worldview by which we live, we would do well to look at the ways and the methods by which we expect change in both our classrooms and counseling offices. How do we image this change? Are there yet inner images connected to Christian baptism that immediately come to the fore—such as those that picture the action of taking one's place in Jesus Christ's death and rising and of a vital, ongoing becoming in a real and not an abstract Christ? Of the old self, as a filthy cloak of self-centeredness and evil deeds falling from us, and the putting on of the new—a holiness beyond ourselves? Of a full Eucharistic celebration with our brothers and sisters that continues the work of baptism and further mediates to us God's Presence? Or were the images a bit more humanistic, or mechanical—more allied finally to, for example, "behavior mod" or other forms of conditioning for the "right" behavior?

The full structure of scriptural reality forms a symbolic system within the Christian mind that restores to it the incarnational (Judeo-Christian) worldview, and at the same time discerns and displaces the inner images that are materialistic or spiritualistic (e.g., Freudian, Jungian, gnostic, feminist, etc.). These latter systems embody symbolic images of *becoming* that have nothing to do with the Cross and the Incarnation. These images have increasingly insinuated themselves into the Christian's view of self and reality, and they show up in our educational theories and methods.

PRACTICING THE PRESENCE

I know of no better way to overcome the rift between head and heart than teaching the practice of the presence of God—the acknowledgment that He is with us in the present moment. God has a special relationship with His people; we are a people of His Presence. The sooner we start to call to mind that He lives with and in us, and remains in and with us, the sooner we learn to listen and obey Him.

By way of beginning to practice the Presence, I ask all (including the neediest) to lay hands on their breasts and repeat after me:

> We acknowledge, Lord, that You are in the Father
> and that we are in You,
> and that You are in us.

Those who have been empty all their lives, begin to be filled. They begin to feel solid. They begin to know they have a center—a divine Center where Christ dwells—and that they are strongly rooted to the earth—that they have a place in it. The most wounded often learn the quickest for they are most painfully aware of their emptiness. A radical obedience to Christ ensues, and a radical kind of freedom is won. The most wounded turn out to be the strongest leaders. For all of us, the acknowledgment of the Real Presence with and in us is not only crucial to our regaining a Christian worldview, it is, in fact, a matter of the soul's life or death. It is what believing in Christ, in His incarnation, and His Cross is all about; it is what Christian reality is.

Some of the most important prayers we pray are for the healing of memories (that is, the in-depth forgiveness of sin); for deliverance from fear; for healing of the disease of introspection (the painful thinking that ensues from the split between head and heart); for healing of the will; the imaginative and intuitive faculties; the feeling being. And we pray for God the Source of all Being to set into the most crucially wounded a sense of being, where there was before only the terror of nonbeing.

The way we've learned to pray for healing of the soul turns out to be the way of spiritual formation. It is actually the foundational Christian work, the work of a true and full Christian baptism. Once the baptismal work is set in, the soul never stops growing. It is not afraid to know and become. The great virtue of knowledge is closely related to the greatest virtue—that of love. We cannot love what we do not know. Christian education, with access to Him who is Living Knowledge, is limitless with possibilities.

INTUITING THE UNSEEN REAL:
KNOWING GOD FOR CERTAIN

We have here affirmed "seeing with the eyes of the heart." This is not to put forth a practice of "imaging," or of assigning undue value to our idle fancies. When we ask needy souls to look up and see Christ crucified, dying to take into and upon Himself their sin and need, we assist them, as it were, from the head to the heart—from the realm of abstraction about God to the God who is really there. To look up, see, and listen to God with the eyes and ears of our hearts is in keeping with the way we are created, while at the same time it is in strong opposition to the materialistic worldview we labor under today. It is in keeping with the way we as creatures apprehend the Unseen Real:

I keep asking that the God of our Lord Jesus Christ, the glorious Father, may give you the Spirit of wisdom and revelation, so that you may know him better. I pray also that the eyes of your heart may be enlightened in order that you may know the hope to which he has called you, the riches of his glorious inheritance in the saints, and his incomparably great power for us who believe (Eph. 1:17-18).

Wisdom, revelation, and hope come to us as we fix our eyes on Jesus. There is the real presence of God at work in and with us, and the heart graced with faith, sees and apprehends it. Faith, and the faith-filled heart, sees and hears God and has a much greater capacity for intuiting the unseen real than we seem able to effectively acknowledge and live out as the church today.

For Further Reading

Byrd, R.C. (1988). Positive therapeutic effects of intercessory prayer in a coronary care unit population. *Southern Medical Journal, 81*(7), 826–829. An empirical investigation of the effects of prayer on coronary patients.

Laubach, F. & Lawrence, Br. (1973) *Practicing His presence.* Goleta, CA: Christian Books. This work combines the writings of two Christians who devoted their lives to the service of others and disciplining themselves to constantly be aware of God's presence.

Lewis, C.S. (1962). *Letters to Malcolm: Chiefly on prayer.* New York: Harcourt, Brace. A classic exploration of prayer. This is not a systematic treatment of prayer, but the reflections of a person of prayer on the difficulties, methods, joys, and problems of prayer. An easy-to-read source of insights into prayer.

Mackay, J. (1969). *Christian reality and appearance.* Richmond, VA: John Knox. A masterful treatment concerning what is the essence of Christianity and how we often are seduced into honoring counterfeits of this reality.

Payne, L. (1989). *The healing presence.* Wheaton, IL: Crossway. A practical guide concerning how one can cultivate an awareness of God's presence and receive healing through this relationship.

_____. (1988). *Real presence: The Christian worldview of C.S. Lewis as incarnational reality* (2nd ed.). Wheaton, IL: Crossway. Shows how God is the most real being in the universe and what that means for our daily lives.

_____. (1991). *Restoring the Christian soul through prayer.* Wheaton, IL: Crossway. A helpful treatment of some spiritual problems which hinder so many. Clear suggestion on how to overcome self-hatred and bitterness are given.

Vaswig, W.L. (1977). *I prayed, He answered.* Minneapolis: Augsburg. A pastor discovers the power of prayer when his son is healed following an emotional break.

EIGHTEEN
THE SPIRIT IS WILLING: THE BODY AS A TOOL FOR SPIRITUAL GROWTH
Dallas Willard

"Spiritual formation" is the process through which those who love and trust Jesus Christ effectively take on His character. When this process is what it should be, they increasingly live their lives as He would if He were in their place. Their outward conformity to His example and His instructions rises toward fullness as their inward sources of action take on the same character as His. They come more and more to share His vision, love, hope, feelings, and habits.

This process of "conformation to Christ," as we might more appropriately call it, is constantly supported by grace and otherwise would be impossible. But it is not therefore passive. Grace is opposed to *earning,* not to effort. In fact, nothing inspires and enhances effort like the experience of grace.

Yet it is today necessary to assert boldly and often that *becoming Christlike never occurs without intense and well-informed action on our part.* This in turn cannot be reliably sustained outside of a like-minded fellowship. Our churches will be centers of spiritual formation only as they understand Christlikeness and communicate it to individuals, through teaching and example, in a convincing and supportive fashion.

THE BODY AND THE SPIRITUAL LIFE

Probably the least understood aspect of progress in Christlikeness is *the role of the body in the spiritual life.*

Almost all of us are acutely aware of how the incessant clamorings of our bodies defeat our intentions to "be spiritual." The Apostle Paul explains that "the sinful nature [flesh] desires what is contrary to the Spirit, and the Spirit what is contrary to the sinful nature. They are in conflict with each other, so that you do not do what you want" (Gal. 5:17). And Jesus' words, "The spirit is willing but the body is weak" (Matt. 26:41), are generally accepted as a *final* verdict on what human life must be like until we escape the body through death.

On the other hand, if the body is simply *beyond* redemption, then ordinary life is too. Many Christians seem prepared to accept this—at least in practice. But then "spiritual formation" really becomes impossible. That would be a defeat of major proportions for Christ's cause and could never be reconciled with the call to godly *living* that both permeates the Bible from end to end and resonates with the deep-seated human need to live as one ought.

We are glad, then, to find scriptural teachings about the body and its flesh running directly contrary to the "hopeless" view. Jesus is the primary witness to the unity of flesh and spirit before God. Long before His entry into history, however, the psalmist spoke of his body longing for God (Ps. 63:1), of his "heart and flesh cry[ing] out for the living God" (84:2), and called upon all flesh to "praise his holy name for ever" (145:21).

The Prophet Joel foresaw the time when God's spirit would be poured out upon all flesh (Joel 2:28-29). That prophecy began to be fulfilled on the Day of Pentecost (Acts 2:16-21). Thus the picture of the body and flesh found in the writings of Paul stands in the sharpest of contrasts with the "hopeless" view of the body. The body is presented as a temple inhabited by the Holy Spirit. It is not meant to be used in sinning, but is meant for the Lord, "and the Lord for the body" (1 Cor. 6:13).

Through the power of God which raised Christ from the dead, Paul tells us, "your bodies are members of Christ himself" (1 Cor. 6:15). Our bodies do not even belong to us, but have been bought by Christ, who gives them a life "from above" and opens the way for us "to honor God with [our] body" (1 Cor. 6:13-20). Thus we can "offer our bodies as living sacrifices, holy and pleasing to God," this being "our spiritual act of worship" (Rom. 12:1).

HUMAN NATURE

In order to understand the role of the body—both negative and positive—in the spiritual life, and in life generally, we must take a deeper view of the nature of human personality, character, and action.

Each of us grows up in surroundings that train us to speak, think, feel, and act like others around us. "Monkey see, monkey do," goes the proverb. This is the mechanism by which human personality is formed, and it is largely for the good. But it also embeds in us habits of evil that permeate all human life. Humanly standard patterns of responding to "the cravings of sinful man, the lust of his eyes and the boasting of what he has and does," which the Apostle John said make up "the world" (1 John 2:16), seize upon little children through their participation in the lives of those around them. Sinful practices become their habits, *then* their choice, and finally their character.

The very language they learn to speak incorporates desecration of God and neighbor. They come to identify themselves and be identified by others through these practices. What is wrong and destructive is done without thinking about it. The wrong thing to do seems quite "natural," while the right thing to do becomes forced and unnatural at best—especially if done because it is right. You can observe this in almost any ten-year-old child acting freely with her peers or living in the family setting.

The New Testament texts normally use the word "flesh" to refer to the human body formed in the ways of evil and against God. Not that the human body as such, or even desires as such, are evil. They are God's good creations, and capable of serving and glorifying Him, as we have seen already. But when shaped in a life context of family, neighborhood, school, and work that is godless or anti-God, they constitute a pervasive structure of evil. Desire then becomes the "sinful passions . . . at work in our bodies" (Rom. 7:5). Our very bodies are poised to sin, only awaiting the occasion. As God said to Cain in the ancient story, "Sin is crouching at your door; it desires to have you, but you must master it" (Gen. 4:7). The situation becomes so bad that Paul says "nothing good lives in me, that is, in my sinful nature" (Rom. 7:18).

When we come to new life in Christ, our bodies and their deformed desire system do not automatically shift to the side of Christ, but continue to oppose Him. Occasionally a remarkable change may occur, such as total relief from an addiction. But this is very infrequent, and it is *never* true that the habits of sin generally are displaced from our bodily parts and personality by the new birth.

James reminds us that "each one is tempted when by his own evil desire, he is dragged away and enticed. Then, after desire has conceived, it gives birth to sin; and sin, when it is full-grown, gives birth to death" (James 1:14-15). Peter urges us, "as aliens and strangers in the world, to abstain from sinful desires, which war against your soul" (1 Peter 2:11). Paul tells us that if we live in terms of the flesh we will die: "But if by the spirit you put to death the misdeeds of the body, you will live" (Rom. 8:13). Elsewhere he cites his own example as one who "beat[s] my body to make it my slave, so that after I have preached to others, I myself will not be disqualified" (1 Cor. 9:27). And all of these are statements to Christians of long standing.

CHRISTLIKENESS MUST BE PLANNED FOR

Admittedly, this sounds strange in today's religious context. It is a simple fact that nowadays the task of becoming Christlike is rarely taken as a serious objective to be thoughtfully planned for and the reality of our embodied personality dealt with accordingly. I have inquired before many church and parachurch groups regarding their plan for putting to death or *mortifying* "whatever belongs to your earthly nature" or flesh (e.g., Col. 3:5). I have never had a positive response to this question. Indeed, mortifying or putting things to death doesn't seem to be the kind of thing today's Christians would be caught doing. Yet there it stands, at the center of the New Testament teachings.

When Jesus taught about discipleship, on the other hand, He made it very clear that one could not be the servant of the body and its demands and also succeed in His course of training. This is the meaning of what He said about denying ourselves, taking up our cross, and "losing our life" for His sake and the Gospel's (Matt. 10:39; 16:24-26), and about "forsaking all" to follow Him (Luke 14:25-35). It is the same theme that is struck by Paul: "Those who belong to Christ Jesus have crucified the sinful nature [flesh] with its passions and desires" (Gal. 5:24). He puts in contrast those who make a god of their belly (Rom. 16:18; Phil. 3:19), the "belly" being the bodily center of desire.

Of course one cannot overcome the hardened patterns of desires by force of will alone. Rather, it is as we by faith place our bodily being in subordination to Christ that we experience a new presence in our members, moving them toward the good things of God and allowing the old bodily forces to recede into the background of life where they belong. Thus, it truly is "by the spirit" that we "put to death the misdeeds of the body." The natural desires, and my body itself, remain with me, of course, but now as servants of God and of my will to serve Him, not as my masters.

Our part in this transformation, in addition to constant faith and hope in Christ, is purposeful, strategic use of our bodies in ways which will retrain them, replacing "the motions of sin in our members" with the motions of Christ. This is how we take up our cross daily. It is how we submit our bodies a living sacrifice, how we "offer the parts of our body to Him as instruments of righteousness" (Rom. 6:13).

WHEN DIRECT EFFORT FAILS

Sometimes, of course, submission to God means just to do what pleases Him. Ultimately that is always our aim. But frequently we are unable to do this by *direct* effort. Often when we come to do the right thing we have *already* done the wrong thing, because that is what was sitting in our body "at the ready." Intention alone cannot suffice in most situations where we find ourselves. We must be "in shape." If not, "trying" will normally be too late, or totally absent. Instead, our intention and effort must be carried into effect by *training* which leaves our body poised to do what Christ would do well before the occasion arises. Such training is supplied by *the disciplines for life in the Spirit.*

Now a *discipline* is an activity in our power, which we pursue in order to become able to do what we cannot do by direct effort. Disciplines are required in every area of life, including the spiritual. Therefore Jesus directed and led His disciples into disciplines for the spiritual life: fasting, prayer, solitude, silence, service, study, fellowship, and so forth.

For example, Jesus told His closest friends that they would run like scared rabbits when His enemies came to capture Him. They emphatically and sincerely denied it. But the body has a life of its own which far outreaches what we know of ourselves. The readinesses actually in their bodies would not support their intention. Jesus, of course, knew this.

When He took Peter, James, and John into the Garden of Gethsemane to aid Him in His struggle, they fell asleep. He awoke them and told them how they could succeed with their good intentions, which He never questioned. How were they going to die for Him if they couldn't even stay awake with Him for an hour? So He said: "Watch and pray so that you will not fall into temptation. The spirit is willing, but the body is weak" (Matt. 26:41). He tried to help them understand how their bodies were influencing them and what they could do to keep it in line with their spirits. "Watching," or staying alert to what was happening, and praying with Him, was something they could have done. Surely participation with Jesus in the awesome events of the Garden *would* have fortified them against failure to stand with Him later. As it turned out, what was in their bodies and souls—fear of death and shame—remained unchallenged and their "temptation" did overwhelm them.

Quite generally, now, the teachings of Jesus are viewed as so "hard" only because our embodied personalities are formed *against* them. Take, for example, His teaching in Matthew 5:22 that we should not speak insultingly of or to others, calling them "fools" (i.e., "twerps," or worse). I have known many "faithful Christians" who use vile and contemptuous language on others that do not perform just right in a traffic, work, or even a home setting. They say "That's just me," or "I can't help it."

Similarly, we can note the lustful stare that Jesus speaks of in Matthew 5:28, or the striking back by word or fist later on in this chapter, or the practicing of religion for human applause with which He deals in the next chapter. No law of nature forces the "easy" and disobedient response in these situations. It is just a habit embedded in our bodies and, of course, habits always produce powerful rationalizations for themselves.

Now suppose that we decided to learn how to do what Jesus says we should do in these cases. Suppose, for example, we wanted to train ourselves to bless and pray for anyone who does something in traffic that endangers or displeases us. Instead of calling one a fool or a stupid jerk or worse, we are going to use words of blessing and let our hearts go out in generous good will toward others. Could we do it? Of course we could, if we took appropriate steps. It is not the law of gravity that makes us assassinate the humanity of others.

HOW WE CAN CHANGE

And *how* would we do it? First, we begin by acknowledging the good of what we were going to do and asking God's assistance. Second, we begin to practice controlling our tongue. Not by trying not to insult people *when* they shake us up. No, we begin further back from the target situation. Possibly we step out of the realm of words by not speaking for a twenty-four-hour period—even by dwelling in silence with the TV and radio off. This probably will require that we go into solitude for the period of time.

Note that all of this is something we do with our bodies. We relocate and reorient our body in our world. We learn a new relation to our body—specifically, ears and tongues. This pervasively impacts our minds, hearts, and souls, as it gives opportunity to explore our world in silence and find our proper place in it. This in turn allows us to gain insight into why we use the accustomed foul and insulting language.

Of course, it is because it gives us a sense of power over the "jerk." It lies on a continuum with shooting him. That insight then opens up better ways of viewing what is actually going on in traffic or elsewhere—indeed in life. Suddenly we see what pathetic behavior "exploding" is and find attractive alternatives to it. We can even begin to develop the habit of blessing now, for we see the goodness of it and know that we are capable of silence, where we find God present. The words of James become very meaningful: "Everyone should be quick to listen, slow to speak and slow to become angry" (1:19).

We enter into *each* of the teachings of Jesus by choosing different behaviors that are relevant, finding the space — making the arrangements — in our lives to put them into action, and "re-visioning" the situation in the new behavioral space including God. The interaction between new uses of the body and inward re-positioning toward the context is essential. Learning to do what He taught is not just a "mental shift" without assistance from a modified use of the body, for behavior and life are not mental.

The lustful look also is bodily behavior and based on bodily behavior. We choose to be in position and posture to engage in it. Millions of people say they cannot stop it, just like those who rationalize their verbal assaults on others. But it is, in fact, only a habit of self-indulgence. It can easily be broken when that is earnestly wanted. You do not have to look at the bodily parts of others, and you can train your thoughts away from lusting if you cultivate chaste habits of thought and attitudes. Appropriate disciplines of study, meditation, and service, for example, can break the action of looking to lust, as many have established by experience. Here too the use and training of the body is the place where faith meets grace to achieve conformity to Christ.

What we find, then, is that the body is the place of our direct power. It is the little "power pack" that God has assigned to us as the field of our freedom and development. Our lives depend upon our direction and management of them. But the body can acquire a "life of its own" — tendencies to behave without regard to our conscious intentions. In our fallen world this life is prepossessed by evil, so that we do not have to *think* to do what is wrong, but *must* think and plan and practice — and receive grace — if we are to succeed in doing what is right.

But Christ shows us how to bring the body from opposition to support of the new life He gives us, "the Spirit" now in us. He calls us to share His *practices* in sustaining His own relationship to the Father. Indeed, these practices — of solitude, silence, study, service, prayer, worship — are now the places where we arrange to meet regularly with Him and His Father to be His students or disciples in kingdom living.

Some may think it strange that such practices, the disciplines for life in the spirit, are all bodily behaviors. But it cannot be otherwise. Learning Christlikeness is not passive. It is active engagement with and in God. And we act with our bodies. Moreover, this bodily engagement is what lays the foundation in our bodily members for readinesses for holiness, and increasingly removes the readinesses to sin—"So that now as always Christ will be exalted in my body, whether by life or by death. For to me, to live is Christ and to die is gain" (Phil. 1:20-21).

For Further Reading

Foster, R. (1988). *Celebration of discipline.* (Rev. ed.). San Francisco: Harper and Row. A contemporary classic on the disciplines for the spiritual life.

McGuire, M. (1990). Religion and the Body: Rematerializing the human body in the social sciences of religion. *Journal for the Scientific Study of Religion, 29,* 283–296. An excellent entree into philosophical and academic interpretations of the body's role in personality, with bibliography.

Taylor, J. (1992). *Holy living and holy dying,* "Classics of Western Spirituality" series. New York: Paulist. Many other editions. Practical directions on the use of the body for spiritual growth by a great Christian of the sixteenth century.

Willard, D. (1988). *The spirit of the disciplines.* New York: Harper and Row. Especially chapters 1 through 7, which deal with basic points in a theology and soteriology of the body.

NINETEEN

SPIRITUAL FORMATION IN CHILDREN
Robert Clark

In recent years theologians, educators, and parents have shown greater interest in the subject of spiritual formation. The purpose of Christian life is for us to know God personally and become more like Jesus Christ, a complex process. We must also learn to work with God through the Holy Spirit to discover how we can help children develop spiritually in total personality structure.

Spiritual formation begins before a child is born and the results continue throughout the life span. The psalmist said:

> For you created my inmost being; you knit me together in my mother's womb. I praise you because I am fearfully and wonderfully made; your works are wonderful, I know that full well. . . . Your eyes saw my unformed body. All the days ordained for me were written in your book before one of them came to be. (Ps. 139:13-14, 16)

The Apostle John declared, "Dear friends, now we are children of God, and what we will be has not yet been made known. But we know that when he appears, we shall be like him, for we shall see him as he is" (1 John 3:2).

As a human being created in God's image from conception, each person is shaped by the Creator, by relationships with others, by environment and society. Parents and others responsible for nurturing children cannot begin too soon preparing them spiritually for life!

The Apostle Paul, convinced of the need for spiritual formation, charged Timothy to "continue in what you have learned and have become convinced of, because you know those from whom you learned it, and how from infancy you have known the holy Scriptures, which are able to make you wise for salvation through faith in Christ Jesus" (2 Tim. 3:14).

WHAT SPIRITUAL FORMATION IS

Even though the concept of spiritual formation has existed since the creation of humankind, and has been expressed in a variety of ways, we often use different terms to express the same idea. Terminology such as nurture and admonition, spiritual development, sanctification, faith development, leading individuals to Christ, and character formation have reference to the same concept—that of empowering individuals to find Christ as Savior and grow in His likeness. Spiritual formation is a step by step and stage by stage process through which a child is guided, encouraged, nurtured, admonished, and disciplined to embrace Christ as Savior and be discipled to develop as a Christian through the work and power of the Holy Spirit.

Spiritual formation integrates total personality development. The physical, intellectual, emotional, and social aspects must be merged with the spiritual as we guide a child in faith development. Each area of personality interacts with the others as the child lives with family and other caregivers. As a child passes through each developmental stage in the life span, his or her personality needs must be met in various ways. Gorman (1990, p. 65) summarizes formation succinctly.

> Formation involves more than "learning" as usually conceived of in our educational institutions. Formation suggests the impact of that learning on a life so that the matrix of perspective, behavior, values, and personhood are changed, reshaped with new contours and intentions. This realignment, restructuring, and reforming of a dynamic being comes with internalization and integration.

Because spiritual formation is highly individualized and no

two individuals can be taught or will develop in exactly the same way, we use a variety of methods in laying foundations to help a child come to know Christ and grow spiritually.

SCRIPTURAL BASIS FOR SPIRITUAL FORMATION

The purpose of Scripture is to teach us God's plan of redemption and how we can become more like Christ our Savior during life's journey.

Many references in Old and New Testaments consist of commands to families regarding spiritual formation. Deuteronomy 6:6-7 is the prime example of parental responsibility in teaching and modeling spiritual truth: "These commandments that I give you today are to be upon your hearts. Impress them on your children. Talk about them when you sit at home and when you walk along the road, when you lie down and when you get up." In Deuteronomy 31:12 Moses commanded Israel to "assemble the people— men, women and children . . . so they can listen and learn to fear the Lord your God and follow carefully all the words of this law."

In the Garden of Eden God gave Adam and Eve the responsibility of caring for His creation and rearing their children according to His plan. In Genesis 4 the story of Cain and Abel implies there was a right way to train children as evidenced in the offerings each son brought to the Lord. God had regard for Abel and his offering, but rejected Cain's offering. The rejection of Cain's offering brought great pain to the family when Cain rebelled and killed his brother.

Throughout the Old Testament God expected the patriarchs to evidence spiritual formation in their lives and family responsibilities. They were to teach God's law and commandments and lead their families according to God's plan. When they obeyed this spiritual responsibility, families and the nation of Israel prospered and were successful spiritually. When they disobeyed God's commandments, they suffered for their sin and became spiritually destitute.

In the New Testament, Christ emphasized the significance of children and set an example of taking time to be with them and praying for them (Mark 10:13-16). Paul admonished parents in the churches at Ephesus and Colosse to nurture and discipline their children. Not a single reference in the New Testament places the responsibility with the church. In both the Old and New Testaments, God has given parents the divine responsibility to "bring them up in the training and instruction of the Lord" (Eph. 6:4), and this training is to be initiated by the father!

PERSONALITY DEVELOPMENT IN SPIRITUAL FORMATION

The Lord Jesus grew in every area of personality according to Luke 2:52, and children today should be given the same opportunity to develop fully as individuals with the greatest emphasis on spiritual formation.

Physical Development
Growth patterns in physical development affect abilities intellectually, socially, and spiritually. Arnold Gesell and his colleagues studied hundreds of children over a period of time and compared them to determine at which ages they were able to perform such actions as walking, running, cutting with scissors, and drawing. They determined the ages of "average" children from their findings. Gesell and his associates have provided some significant data as guidelines for maturation, though the studies have been questioned since the researchers did not explain "why" these changes occur (Craig, 1989, pp. 142-143).

Intellectual Development
Piaget has made an outstanding contribution in the intellectual development of children. In his studies of children, Piaget saw intellectual development in four discrete and qualitatively different stages. Infants from birth through the first year are in the *sensorimotor* stage. They have very keen senses and react to their environment. They use action schemes—looking, grasping, and mouthing—to discover the world about them. From ages two through seven, children are in the *pre-operational* stage when they judge things by appearance. They begin to use symbols such as language. They are overly concrete, illogical, and egocentric in their thinking. From seven through eleven,

children enter the *concrete operations* stage and begin to think logically but are still concrete in their thinking. They can classify things and deal with a hierarchy of classifications. Around twelve years of age, adolescents enter the stage of *formal operations* and can begin to handle abstract concepts (Craig, 1989, pp. 36–37).

Psychosocial Development

Erik Erikson suggested four stages through which children progress in their psychosocial development. In infancy, children learn *trust vs. mistrust.* During the ages of two through three years, young children learn *autonomy vs. shame and self-doubt.* They discover their own bodies and how to control them. In stage three, at ages four and five, they begin to explore beyond themselves. They develop *initiative vs. guilt.* Initiative is learned through constructive experiences or relationships. They can also feel guilty for many of their own actions if they are severely criticized or punished.

In the fourth stage of development, children from six through eleven pass through the stage of *industry vs. inferiority.* They become industrious through numerous skills and competencies, or they can feel inferior if they do not measure up in self-concept or in the expectations of their peers and others (Craig, 1989, p. 42).

Spiritual Development

Spiritual formation (faith development) can and should be integrated into all these maturational and developmental stages. Since an individual is a total person, integration of each area of personality must take place. Fowler has suggested three stages of faith development in a brief summary:

> *Primal faith* (Infancy): A prelanguage disposition of trust forms in the mutuality of one's relationships with parents and others to offset the anxiety that results from separation which occurs during infant development.

> *Intuitive-projective faith* (Early Childhood): Imagination, stimulated by stories, gestures, and symbols, and not yet controlled by logical thinking, combines with perception

and feeling to create long-lasting images that represent both the protective and threatening powers surrounding one's life.

Mythic-literal faith. (Childhood and beyond): The developing ability to think logically helps one order the world with categories of causality, space, and time; to enter into the perspective of others; and to capture life meaning in stories (Fowler, 1991, pp. 24–25).

Fowler's stages tie in significantly with Piaget's intellectual stages. As a child's intellectual capacities develop, he is able to begin to understand biblical concepts and theology. *How* we teach children is as important as *what* we teach them! Certainly parents and teachers need to be aware of literal and concrete thinking in intellectual processes and not assume understanding takes place because spiritual truth has been "dumped on the child."

Social and Emotional Development

In the social and emotional areas of life, trust in human and divine relationships begins in early infancy. As an infant learns to trust or mistrust parents and other caregivers through bonding, separation from caregivers, autonomy and other early relationships, a trust relationship can be developed spiritually. The child will begin to trust in a broader circle of relationships (such as Sunday School and day-care teachers). Eventually, that trust relationship can go beyond human relationships for her to trust in the Lord. These trust relationships are "caught" as well as "taught" through positive modeling and nurturing.

PARENTAL RESPONSIBILITY IN SPIRITUAL FORMATION

Effective Modeling

The home is the best place for a child to develop faith. The environment is a natural setting in day-to-day living for modeling the Christian faith. One of the greatest responsibilities parents have is to be good models to their children. No other means of child training pays such great dividends as modeling.

Parents need to know Jesus Christ as Savior-Lord, develop a personal relationship with Him, have strong faith, and practice biblical principles.

They need to be growing spiritually so their children can see how they trust the Lord daily in difficult and adverse circumstances as well as in pleasant and joyful times. By life example children can see their parents practicing what they know. Many times later in life, children may not remember what their parents said, but they will remember their example.

Train Up a Child

In Proverbs 22:6 we read parents are to "train a child in the way he should go, and when he is old he will not turn from it." The "way he should go" may be interpreted to mean principles in God's Word, through the developmental stages of life or by the way God has created and shaped the child in his own personality style. Since spiritual formation is a lifelong process, a child may mature and leave home, but what he was taught will remain for a lifetime.

Positive and negative behaviors, attitudes, and knowledge continue to affect children throughout life. Some experiences may need to be overcome, especially if they are detrimental to future development. No parent is perfect in child rearing and will make blunders. However, the Lord honors parental faithfulness as parents lay foundations for life. God will reward them for being consistent and persistent as Isaiah wrote: "For it is: Do and do, do and do, rule on rule, rule on rule; a little here, a little there" (Isa. 28:10).

Goal of Christian Parenting: Empowering

As family counselors and teachers, the Balswicks suggest the goal of Christian parenting is to empower their children to maturity. This empowering is significant in spiritual formation. They define empowering as "the process of instilling confidence, of strengthening and building children up to become more powerful and competent. The most effective empowerers are those individuals who have themselves been empowered by the unconditional love of God and the Holy Spirit" (Balswick, 1991, p. 103).

Parents accomplish this goal of empowering through four

styles. The first is *telling*. This takes place in early childhood when the parents tell their children what needs to be done, where, when, and how. This style exercises a high level of control with low socioemotional support.

The second parenting style is *teaching*. Teaching involves moderately high levels of control and socioemotional support. In teaching, communication can be two-way through dialogue and discussion. Communication in this style is more parent-centered.

The third parenting style is *participating* as parents become player-coaches who engage in activities more directly with their children. The children are instructed, but their parents do more modeling. Children are encouraged to do things in their own ways and be their own persons. They learn through trial and error with support and consolation from parents.

The last parenting style is *delegating*. This style more likely fits highly mature children, able to take responsibility and perform tasks on their own. Parental control and socioemotional support are reduced. Reciprocity is shared and indicates a mature relationship exists. Parents let go and encourage their children to make decisions. They show respect and belief in their children. At this level parents become close friends with their children.

Balswicks (1991, pp. 105–107) suggest the four parenting styles develop into a continuum and reflect the child's increasing maturity. Growth takes place on the part of the parents as well as the children. The most competent children are produced through a combination of high parental support and high inductive control. In the maturation process, parents and children should empower each other.

PROVIDING OPPORTUNITIES FOR SPIRITUAL FORMATION

Spiritual formation can take many shapes and forms. As parents, teachers, and others work with children, they have various opportunities to lay foundations creatively through a multitude of methods and materials. Paul reminded Timothy that from infancy he knew the Holy Scriptures. His mother and grandmother were faithful in teaching the Scriptures to him (2 Tim.

1:5). The Bible does not indicate how he was taught, but the teaching probably took place in informal settings through modeling, observation, readiness, questions, discussions, and experience rather than structured classroom-type activities. Because of the difference in age-group and attention spans, the need for physical activity, involvement and experiencing, every child will develop at his own pace.

Spiritual formation is not an easy task. Gorman (1990, pp. 67–70) suggests an intentional design of opportunities to progress in internalizing and integrating new aspects of faith. The factors include: *articulation* (the "what" or dimensions of which we speak and which we seek); *imagination* (what we can become, the assurance of what we hope for, the certainty of formation and maturity yet unseen); *praxis* (opportunity to experience formation-building encounters and choices); *community* (the network of relatedness and support for security in risking transformation); *formation guide* (the role as guide in becoming an enabler in another's character development); and the *Holy Spirit* (the eventual refiner and producer of spiritual formation in the individual).

Leading Children to Christ
The most significant step in spiritual formation is receiving Jesus Christ as Savior. There is no specific age at which this step is accomplished. Cognitive development, one's view of God's holiness contrasted with the child's recognition of her own sinfulness, the clarity of the presentation of the plan of salvation, and the working of the Holy Spirit all contribute to an intelligent and life-changing acceptance of Christ as Savior.

This step of personal commitment is essential for spiritual development to take place (see chapter 3). In presenting the gift of salvation, we should emphasize that God has a wonderful plan for humanity. He is making a beautiful home in heaven for those who believe in Him and acknowledege Jesus as their Savior.

Teaching Spiritual Truth and Doctrine
Basic facts and principles from the Scriptures need to be taught from infancy. As the child grows, these truths can be expanded and developed more deeply as the child is ready for them.

Repetition with variety along with questioning lead to understanding. The great doctrines of the Christian faith need to be explained simply, clearly, and concretely. The child must live the Word as well as understand it intellectually.

Topics to Be Taught

In order to grow in Christ, children must be taught what prayer is and how to pray. They need to learn what it means to be a member of God's family and what God expects from us as His children. The family needs to participate in a local church through regular attendance, involvement, and service. Children should understand the meaning of the sacraments or ordinances — both baptism and the Lord's Supper, what God's Word teaches about them, and why and how we can participate in them meaningfully to glorify God. They also need to understand that baptism does not save, but represents the new life a person has in Christ. Children also need to learn how to share their faith.

Children must understand the significance of communion, what God's Word teaches about it, why and how we can participate in the ordinance meaningfully to glorify God.

Principles from God's Word on loving God and others, obedience, trust, forgiveness, patience, kindness, communication, values, and hope are topics we must teach in the contexts of the home and church to help children develop spiritually.

Spiritual Instruction (Confirmation) Classes

Some churches offer confirmation classes for children in order to admit them to full membership in a church. The method of instruction typically involves the use of a catechism (a series of questions and answers based on church doctrine), usually memorized and recited. Teaching doctrine helps children have a better grasp of what their church believes. One danger of this method of instruction is that questions and answers may be memorized intellectually, without an affective change in the heart or life.

Parent Equipping

The church has a responsibility to supplement what parents do in teaching and training their children. Parents need to be equipped with parenting skills to do a more effective job. Courses on spiritual formation, child development and training, modeling, stewardship, discipline, family worship, and recreation can provide help for parents as they teach their own children.

Teacher Training

The church needs to provide teachers equipped to teach children effectively. Teachers should be trained in the development of children, spiritual formation, discipline, and how they can work with the home in building positive relationships. The Sunday School (the main teaching arm of the church) needs to provide systematic instruction in the Word of God at all age levels. Long-range curriculum planning can insure a sound biblical and educational base, coordination, continuity, sequence, articulation, and wise choice in selection and use of materials.

Methods, Materials, and Activities

Scriptural truth can be taught through a large variety of methods such as stories, memorization, dramatic activities, audiovisual media, games, field trips, and other creative activities. Materials may be found in Christian bookstores, church and public libraries, craft stores, and things around the home. Activities must be selected according to the cognitive and spiritual levels of the child. An environment responsive to the child's skills and stimulation, timed slightly ahead of the child's developmental level, will accelerate a normal child's progress (Craig, 1989, p. 172). Spiritual formation must be integrated with the child's personality and developmental needs.

CONCLUSION

Williford suggests two important ideas for parents in spiritual formation. He emphasizes parents must live and strive for goals of spiritual formation in their own lives and set aside quality time in their busy schedules to build effective and lasting relationships with their children (Williford, 1990, p. 588).

We can do much to aid children in spiritual formation. However, we must realize we are involved in a Divine process.

Lasting results can be accomplished only with the help of the Holy Spirit and prayer. God uses parents, teachers, and others as His instruments, but change in character is a supernatural work. Eternal results are seen only as we yield ourselves to the Lord and allow Him to work through us in this awesome responsibility.

For Further Reading

Anthony, M. (Ed.). (1992). *Foundations of ministry: An introduction to Christian education for a new generation*. Wheaton, IL: BridgePoint/Victor. An in-depth study of the foundations for ministry in Christian education; integrates biblical truths with the latest insights from the social sciences and contemporary thought; a well-organized and practical information on spiritual formation.

Balswick, J.O., & Balswick, J.K. (1991). *The family: A Christian perspective on the contemporary home*. Grand Rapids: Baker. An excellent and biblically based book on the contemporary family with its stages, functions, and problems; it is skillfully written and has helpful insights on spiritual formation in the family.

Barron, R., Brubaker, J.O., & Clark, R. (1989). *Understanding people* (3rd ed.). Wheaton, IL: Evangelical Training Assoc. A practical guide through the life span with a study of the characteristics and needs of each age group; it offers suggestions on how to meet total personality needs with the major focus on spiritual development.

Clark, R.E., Brubaker, J. & Zuck, R.B. (Eds.). 1986. *Childhood education in the church*. Chicago: Moody. A comprehensive volume on ministering to children in the church and family, with a wide variety of practical topics contributed by childhood specialists. It offers many helpful insights on spiritual formation.

Clark, R.E., Johnson, L. & Sloat, A.K. (Eds.). (1991). *Christian education: Foundations for the future*. Chicago: Moody. A foundational and comprehensive text based on biblical principles and current research in the social sciences for contemporary and future Christian education ministry, filled with practical insights and applications for spiritual formation.

Craig, G. *Human development*. (5th ed.). (1989). Englewood Cliffs, NJ: Prentice-Hall. An excellent text on life-span development with an in-depth study of each age group, based on comprehensive research from the social sciences with appropriate applications at each age level.

Drushal, M.E. (1991). *On tablets of human hearts*. Grand Rapids: Zondervan. A well-documented and helpful resource in providing a quality Christian education for children. Drushal combines educational theory and biblical principles with practical applications.

Fowler, J.W. (1991). *Stages of faith and religious development.* New York: Crossroads. An in-depth study of faith development and the stages through which individuals go to arrrive at spiritual maturation. Fowler interrelates faith development to the theories of human development of Erik Erikson, Jean Piaget, and Lawrence Kohlberg.

SPIRITUAL FORMATION OF ADOLESCENTS
James Bryan Smith

One morning at around 4 A.M. I was up feeding my four-month-old son. Half-awake, he clutched his bottle and began eating. I looked at him and said spontaneously, "I love you, Jacob." He glanced at me with a smile. I thought to myself, and then said out loud to him, "I wish you could understand how much I love you, but you can't understand that yet, can you?"

As he continued staring up at me it suddenly occurred to me: he can understand how much I love him, he does know that he is loved. He may not have the capacity to use words to understand or describe it, but he knows it. He sees it in my face, he feels it in my hugs, he experiences it in my presence. He just does not have the words.

ADOLESCENTS *ARE* BEING FORMED SPIRITUALLY

When I first started working with young people I underestimated their ability to relate to God. Because they lacked the vocabulary and the cognitive development which I thought were necessary, I assumed they were unable to embark on a real spiritual journey. As a youth leader I spent most of my early days merely doing religious baby-sitting. My main objectives were to keep the kids off of the streets, teach them some of the ABCs of the faith, and hope they turned out okay.

Time and experience changed my thinking. I began to realize that just as my infant son is capable of knowing my love, so an adolescent is capable of knowing and relating to God. Jesus went even further by saying that the greatest in the kingdom is a child (Matt. 18:1-3). This simple awareness radically changed my work with young people. In fact, I came to the conclusion that all people—children, adolescents, young adults, adults, and older adults—are in the process of spiritual formation. By virtue of being alive we are all being formed spiritually. As you read these words, the spiritual lives of adolescents are being formed, in good ways and in bad.

WHAT IS CHRISTIAN SPIRITUAL FORMATION?

Part of the process of spiritual formation involves developing a sense of our true identity. Our *spirits* are *formed* as we take in information about who we really are and as we begin living our lives on the basis of that identity. The deepest truth about any person is his or her identity. "Who am I?" is not only the question we all ask, but it is particularly the cry of the adolescent. Christian spiritual formation is coming to the right answer to this question and then living our lives on the basis of that proper identity.

The non-Christian has no resources except the surrounding world to define identity. Thus, parents, teachers, friends, and significant others form a kind of mirror which reflects one's self-image. It reveals one's looks, intelligence, skills, and value. This mirror produces a limited and distorted image of our true selves, and one which is in stark contrast to the identity discovered in Christ. Later in this chapter we will look at how significant this mirror becomes to the adolescent, and consequently, why Christian spiritual formation is so important for young people.

OUR IDENTITY IN CHRIST

The Christian finds identity in Jesus Christ. The Christian faith informs us that we are children of God, that He loves us despite our unloveliness, and that He chooses to save us instead of condemn us. But more than that, the Christian faith tells us that we are, by virtue of accepting our acceptance in Christ, made new (2 Cor. 5:17). The old has passed and the new has come. And what is the new? Christ living His life in us (Col. 1:27).

The Christian finds identity in the life, death, and resurrection of Jesus Christ. We say with Paul, "I have been crucified with Christ; and it is no longer I who live, but it is *Christ* who *lives in me.* And the life I now live in the flesh I live by faith in the Son of God, who loved me and gave himself for me" (Gal. 2:19-20, NRSV, emphasis mine). Christian spiritual formation is arriving at this awareness of our true identity and letting Christ live His life in and through us.

A Christian is one who has been transformed by the life, death, and resurrection of Christ. Like a caterpillar becoming a butterfly, we are transformed in the twinkling of an eye. Christ's resurrection is not merely a proof of His deity, it is the means of our transformation. Having been baptized into Christ's death, we are united with Him in His resurrection and therefore enabled to walk in newness of life (Rom. 6:1-14). By a single sacrifice Christ has made us perfect forever (Heb. 10:14). How is this so? Because He is living His life in us. He did not come merely to provide a means for us to get to heaven, He came to live in us. Just as the Father lived His life in Jesus — and so enabled Him to do all that He did, so that life is now manifest in us. Apart from God we can do nothing (John 15:5).

GROWING IN GRACE

Spiritual formation is a process of growing in God's grace. By grace I mean not only God's unmerited favor or simply the forgiveness of our sins, but the new life found in Christ Jesus. Christian spiritual formation occurs when we live out this truth. But it does not stop here. We do not simply *know* about grace, we *grow* in grace (2 Peter 3:18). In chapter 18, Dallas Willard defined spiritual formation as "the process through which those who love and trust Jesus Christ effectively take on His character." (Willard, see p. 225). The process of growing in grace is adopting this identity as our own — this truth about how we relate to Christ or who we are in Christ — and responding to the world from that foundation.

Hebrews 10:14 describes not only our *objective* identity as those who have been made perfect by Christ's once for all sacrifice, but it also describes our *subjective* identity as well: "By one sacrifice he has made perfect forever *those who are being made holy*" (emphasis mine). We are in the process of being sanctified, or being made holy (Bridges, 1991, p. 102). Effectively taking on Christ's character is the process of being made holy in behavior by the One who has already made us holy in standing.

Why is this approach to spiritual formation so important? First, it establishes the truth of who we are, and we cannot grow in our relationship with God with a false identity.

Second, we cannot genuinely love God until we understand all that He has done for us. We may serve or obey God out of fear or a sense of duty, but it is His love and kindness that will lead us to love Him in return.

Third, we will lack the right motives for practicing spiritual disciplines and may easily slip into a deadly legalism. The spiritual disciplines are, by their nature, susceptible to misuse. It is easy to practice the disciplines as a way to improve our standing with God or to earn His love. Knowing that we cannot improve our standing (we have been made holy, unblemished, and beyond reproach; cf. Col. 1:21-22), nor earn more of His love, frees us from the performance trap. We can rest in what Christ has done and allow Him to complete the good work He began in us. The key is our identity. As we shall see, at no stage in life is this more necessary than in adolescence.

THE INNER WORLD OF THE ADOLESCENT

Many of the problems experienced by adolescents stem from the lack of a solid identity. Uncertain of who they are, locked in rapidly changing physical bodies, and confused by the changing opinions of others, adolescents live in a turbulent inner world. The signs of their stress are apparent: substance abuse (a leading cause of death among teenagers), sexual promiscuity (which has tripled in the last two decades), and suicide (5,000 each year) (Tishler, 1981, p. 23).

If Erik Erikson (1986) is right, *the primary task of the teen-*

age years is to construct a sense of personal identity. Lacking a sense of identity, the adolescent is tossed to and fro, susceptible to the influence of others, and prone to stress, which often manifests itself in destructive behavior. The solution many adolescent psychologists put forth involves creating "space" for the young person to discover true identity. They suggest a *moratorium,* a time and a place where adolescents can engage in the serious work of constructing a sense of who they are. But where will we find such a place? And if we find it, how will we help them discover who they truly are? It is at this point that secular psychology falls short.

HOW AN ADOLESCENT SELF EMERGES

There are two primary ways young people develop a sense of who they are: *imitation* or *integration.* Imitation is the process of adapting to one's surroundings by patching together the beliefs and behaviors of others. Adolescents try to develop a sense of who they are by attempting to look, act, think, and sound like someone else.

On the other hand, integration is the process of testing, separating, and discriminating between several types of beliefs and behaviors until one discovers that which is genuine and real. This process involves intentionally weighing the merits and drawbacks of many different viewpoints and perspectives. It involves interaction with others, personal reflection, and the freedom to explore.

Young people who take the road of imitation end up with a patchwork sense of self that is fragile and ultimately unsatisfying. For example, the adolescent who defines himself as a "jock" or a "hood" has an identity based on externals (e.g., clothing, activities, language). When faced with a trying circumstance his hollow self-image breaks down. Constantly restless, adolescent imitators live with a great deal of turmoil.

HELPING THEM TAKE THE ROAD LESS TRAVELED

The better highway, and the road less traveled, is that of integration. A young person who takes this seemingly more arduous path actually works less in the long run. A strong sense of self is formed, making it difficult to break down, whether pressured by peers or trying circumstances. This person is more likely to be able to postpone gratification in order to reach higher goals. The direction for her life comes from within (Elkind, 1984, p. 9).

What will this mean in the life of the church? While many in the church will argue that encouraging the exploration and the testing of ideas may be harmful, and instead want to narrow the adolescent's field of experience, I would argue that spiritual formation can only occur in the midst of struggle. Examination stimulates growth. We must not create young imitators, sending them off to college, work, or marriage as hollow believers who can only mimic truths that are not their own. They must learn to own their beliefs.

REJECTING GOD, OR REJECTING AN INSTITUTION?

This may involve—dare I say—even leaving the institutional church. It is common for adolescents to reject the traditional church and its ministries. They have reached an age at which, for the first time, they are able to distinguish between *institutional* (formal and social religion) and *personal* religion (which is private) (Elkind, 1984, p. 42). What they are rejecting is not God, but the adult approach to God. In actuality, adolescents (who are extremely private) will often turn to God in a very personal way. God can become their closest friend, their refuge in times of trouble, their Shepherd who guides and comforts them.

The rejection of the institutional church may actually be an opportunity for spiritual growth and nurture. Up until now, the beliefs of the young person were held *tenuously,* but not owned. Most of the time young adults return to their parents' tradition, but this sabbatical from institutional religion that so many adolescents take is frightening to parents and disheartening to youth leaders. The solution is not to force or coerce young people into the typical structures the church has always used, but rather, to nurture and encourage their personal relationship with God.

WHAT DO YOU THINK ABOUT ME?

More than any other period in our lives, adolescence is a time of preoccupation with what others think about us. Elkind (1984, p. 33) believes adolescents live with an *imaginary audience*. This imaginary audience becomes a mirror in which they seek to develop their self-image.

Adolescents both want and need mirrors (Fowler, 1981, p. 151). But the mirrors must be good. They need the eyes and ears of trusted people who can help them develop a proper identity. Like the carnival mirrors that are bent out of shape, thus reflecting a distorted image, the surrounding world projects a distorted image to adolescents. The church has the ability *to restore a true and accurate self-image.* Distortion can hold many in bondage; the truth can set them free.

Spiritual formation, as I have stated, is simply a process of coming to the truth of who we are and living out of that truth. The only truly accurate mirror is Scripture. As we look into the Bible we see our incredible value, our true nature, our inability to live independently, our complete redemption, and our regeneration in Christ who dwells within us. Spiritual formation is learning to listen to the Spirit bear witness with our spirits that we are children of God (Rom. 8:15). This identity, this self-image, can exert a powerful ordering on a young life (Fowler, 1981, p. 154).

THE NUMBER ONE CRY OF ADOLESCENTS

Knowing what adolescents are *concerned* about is essential if we are to aid them in the process of spiritual formation. Their concerns are not to be ignored or taken lightly, but rather, are the very stuff of spiritual formation. In order to do this we need to be aware of their inner yearnings. What we see on the outside may not be a reflection of what is on the inside.

The number one cry of adolescents is that of self-hatred. It is the most commonly voiced and the most intensely felt cry. One out of four are much troubled by feelings of self-hatred (Strommen, 1988). Merton Strommen believes that the core of the problem has to do with obtaining God's acceptance. His classic surveys indicate that adolescents are capable of understanding God's *forgiveness*, but are very reluctant to understand His *acceptance.*

Why are adolescents so prone to this problem? Their self-awareness is new, and consequently, their self-image has only recently emerged. It is untested and untried. Thus, they constantly measure themselves against others as a means of establishing their worth. This is ultimately a losing game because there is always someone prettier, more handsome, smarter, or funnier. This is why it is not uncommon to see an attractive girl think she is ugly.

It is also a deadly trap. Low self-image impairs a person's ability to develop social relationships; the inability to develop relationships increases the low self-image and on and on. "I'm no good; no one wants to be my friend," leads to, "No one is my friend, so I must be no good." The issue of our identity is essential, and adolescence is the age when we birth our self-image. Thus, there is no better time to develop a proper self-image — one based on God's view of who we are, not on the world's distorted reflection.

A PRACTICAL STRATEGY

What can be done? Two things can help. First, help the young person to know and understand his or her identity in Christ. This can best be done by developing a one-on-one discipling relationship with individuals; however, this sort of approach can also be done in small group settings. Through teaching and individual exploration, adolescents can focus on the complete work of Christ (redemption) and the power of His Spirit in us and can develop a solid self-image based on the Scriptures and not on the changing opinions of the world around them.

I am talking about teaching them Christian doctrine. Theology and doctrine, Strommen believes, are not of interest to adolescents (Strommen, 1988). I disagree. What is uninteresting to the adolescent is the traditional way of teaching theology and doctrine, that is, lecture-style teaching that lays out concepts and ideas that are removed from everyday experience. We need to use creativity, hands-on activities, and stimulating interaction in our teaching methods. What we must not do is change the content of the material. The content of the Christian message is precisely what the adolescent is seeking.

Second, help them to continue growing in that relationship through specific activities that enhance relationship with God. I am referring particularly to the classical spiritual disciplines of prayer, reading, studying, and meditating on the Scriptures, fellowship with other believers, worship, solitude, and so on (Foster, 1988). These have been called the *means of grace.* Through them we increase our understanding of who we are, we increase our awareness of God's presence in our lives (in joy and sorrow), and we increase our ability to become weak so that God might become strong in us (2 Cor. 12:9).

Statistics show that very few adolescents feed their self-images from Christian sources. Even young people involved in youth programs are seldom encouraged to develop an active relationship with God. Only one half of all church youth pray regularly; nearly two thirds never read the Bible; only one in five will attend church next week (Strommen, 1988). Keep in mind that these are statistics of *church* youth, not nonmembers!

Is the solution to force them into more church activities? No, instead we must learn to listen to them and respond to their cries. Adolescents struggle with alienation. In one large denomination, 63 percent of the youth polled expressed a sense of alienation from God, and half of them said their sense of alienation was acute. Of all the church youth Strommen polled, 43 percent expressed a strong desire to have a deep faith relationship with God (Strommen, 1988).

STAN THE BUTTERFLY

Stan came to my office one day completely shaken. I had never met him, but he told me almost immediately that he was contemplating suicide. Choking out the words that he was "worthless" and "just in people's way." After an hour it was obvious that his deepest problem was self-hatred.

Although a handsome, bright, and athletic young man, Stan was so steeped in self-hatred that he could barely look up while he talked. I directed him to a good and trusted professional counselor who spent time with Stan for the next six months. Though he became stabilized, his problems did not cease.

One day he came to hear me teach. I was speaking on the amazing love of God, the complete work of Christ, and the fact that true peace and happiness come from a right relationship with God through Jesus Christ. Stan stopped by my office a few days later and said, "You explained that God loves us unconditionally and that we can find what we are missing if we have a relationship with God through Jesus Christ. How do you do that?"

After an hour of hearing the truths of the faith in plain language, he was ready to pray, asking God to come into his life. Right away he began attending our campus fellowship regularly. I had been teaching on the indwelling Christ and the power of His life in us. I used the caterpillar-become-butterfly illustration at one point. After it was over Stan marched up to me, and with a big, bright smile said, "I am a butterfly!"

Over the next several months he became more and more active in his spiritual life. We had given him a Bible because he was now hungering to read it and learn more about God. He became more social and more alive each day. He would often visit me to ask questions about the Bible, or get books that would help him along the way. His newfound identity had changed everything about him.

THE CRY FOR SPIRITUAL FORMATION

Stan's story is not unique. Our world and, even more particularly, our churches are filled with adolescents in pain. We hear the deafening adolescent cry to be entertained and are prone to place all our energy and emphasis on meeting this request. However, in doing so we fail to listen to the depths of the cry which expresses a need to be in communion with God. It is the cry for spiritual formation. As teachers and educators, the cry provides an opportunity that we dare not neglect. The holy habits and divine disciplines that can be inculcated in the adolescent formation process provide the potential for developing a disciple for life!

Further Readings

Bridges, J. (1991). *Transforming grace.* Colorado Springs: Navpress. Bridges explains how the grace of God can transform one's identity, freeing us from the trap of having to earn God's favor, and teaching us how to live confidently in God's unfailing love.

Csikszentmihalyi, M. and Larson, R. (1984). *Being adolescent: Conflict and growth in the teenage years.* New York: Basic Books. The authors monitored the activities of adolescents and at intervals had them record their feelings. This book paints an excellent picture of the inner and outer world of today's young people.

Elkind, D. (1984). *All grown up and no place to go.* Reading, MA: Addison-Wesley. The author shows how today's teens are expected to confront an adult world prematurely and without adequate preparation. It is a book every parent and youth worker should read.

Foster, R. (1988). *Celebration of discipline* (Rev. ed.). San Francisco: Harper & Row. A landmark book in that it reawakened modern Christians to the classic spiritual disciplines. A very inviting book that inspires one to throw open the windows and bask in God's transforming presence.

Fowler, J. (1981). *Stages of faith: The psychology of human development and the quest for meaning.* San Francisco: Harper & Row. Fowler explains the different ways we come to know and understand God at different ages and stages of life.

George, B. (1989). *Classic Christianity.* Eugene, OR: Harvest House. One of the most clearly written books on the transforming power of God's grace, making the crucifixion and resurrection understandable and meaningful in ordinary life. No book better explains the freedom and new life we have in Christ.

Strommen, M. (1988). *Five cries of youth* (Rev. ed.). San Francisco: Harper & Row. Strommen polled thousands of church youth, seeking their thoughts and feelings. The result is a helpful description of the inner cries of today's young people.

Willard, D. (1988). *The spirit of the disciplines.* New York: Harper & Row. Willard helps us understand how the disciplines work to form us spiritually. His explanation of the three stages of personal redemption (chap. 7, pp. 114–118) is especially helpful.

SPIRITUAL FORMATION IN OLDER ADULTS
Beth E. Brown

As America rides the crest of an "age wave," the church is less than prepared for the impact of its thunderous crash upon culture. Gerontologists and futurists are committed to interpreting the social, lifestyle, and business implications of this age wave. So must Christian educators study the impact of an aging America on spiritual formation and the life of the church.

In New Testament times, only one person in ten lived to be fifty years old. At the turn of this century, only one half of the population survived to see fifty. Today, two thirds of all Americans will live well into their eighties. Many demographers predict that the median age in the United States, which was 32.9 in 1990, will eventually reach fifty!

The oldest of the Baby Boomers are soon to turn fifty (1996); and as they age they are expected to redefine later life, presenting images of aging vastly different from those of their parents and grandparents. They will not only live longer than earlier generations, but they will live with greater physical health and vitality, working more years, and retiring several times or not at all (Dychtwald, 1990). The task of the church is to redefine spiritual vitality for those committed to loving and serving Christ, as their faith matures in the later years of life.

Understanding spiritual formation in older adults should be of keen interest to Christians of all ages. Gerontological futurist Ken Dychtwald is convinced that "if during youth and middle age we could instill in our lives a sense of how to create a meaningful, rich, and active old age, we could have a higher likelihood of actually achieving it" (Dychtwald, 1990, p. xvii). How much more worthwhile for Christians to envision mature spiritual vitality and move toward this maturity while they are young.

Yet, Americans, stifled and blinded by rampant gerontophobia, are incredibly reluctant to explore new images of aging. Ageism abounds in a culture that values "new" things and discards the "old." Ageism is defined as "that cluster of attitudes and practices that leads us to discriminate against old people" (Bianchi, 1982, p. 135). This discrimination harms older adults and must be confronted by those who seek to live justly as demanded by a holistic understanding of the Gospel.

Ageism in the church today manifests itself in building construction, program scheduling, and worship experiences that are blind to the particular needs of the disproportionate number of seniors in the congregation. To combat this ageism, the church must articulate a biblical theology of aging, learning to celebrate and encourage spiritual vitality within its older members.

SPIRITUAL FORMATION IN OLDER ADULTS IS ROOTED IN BIBLICAL TRUTH

In addition to embracing the God of Scripture and the great hope of salvation through Jesus Christ, older Christians will only discover spiritual vitality for themselves as they adopt a countercultural and thoroughly biblical understanding of aging. Biblical images of aging paint a realistic, yet hopeful, picture of the winter of life. A biblical theology of aging not only condemns ageism, but empowers seniors for continued service.

In the Bible, long life is viewed as a gift given by God (Ps. 91:16), not a sentence to be endured. Physical aging is part of God's plan and God grants most people the gift of seventy years on earth (Ps. 90:10). Gray hair, rather than something to hide with artificial color, is described as a "crown of splendor" (Prov. 16:31). God instructed those in the community of faith to "rise in the presence of the aged and show respect for the elderly" (Lev. 19:32), a strong admonition to the young who would choose to ignore older members. God is not only faithful to the young but promises: "Even to your old age and gray hairs I am he, I am he who will sustain you. I have made you and I will carry you; I will sustain you and I will rescue you" (Isa. 46:4).

SPIRITUAL FORMATION IN OLDER ADULTS BUILDS ON THE PAST

People do not become more religious just because they grow old. But those who have focused on knowing God in younger years are likely to give focus to their faith journey in later years. Spiritual formation in older adults is an ongoing process and a continuation of experiences and insights acquired in earlier stages of life. The nonnormative variables of human development accentuate the uniqueness of senior adults. Therefore, the diversity of faith development among older adults precludes a precise description of spirituality in later life.

Using a Fowler model of faith development, one can underscore the cumulative role of multiple crises experienced over life by most older adults that propel them into a deeper understanding of faith and certainty of God's faithfulness. Seniors have likely affirmed the stories of faith (mythic), participated in a faith community (conventional), defined their personal faith (individuative), and even come to rest in God's sovereignty when life's disappointments made no sense (conjunctive). Perhaps this is one of the mysterious joys of long life, having "had to suffer grief in all kinds of trials" that faith "may be proved genuine, and may result in praise, glory, and honor when Jesus Christ is revealed" (1 Peter 1:6-7).

Reminiscence, an important spiritual discipline in later life, is more than recalling past events and people. Rather, older adults should reflect on the past in order to see God's presence in prior events and relationships. Kierkegaard said, "Life is lived forward but understood backward." Memories help older adults know who they have been, who they are, and who they are becoming. As Fischer notes, "We do not merely have these memories; we are these memories" (1985, p. 34).

Spiritual healing can come through reminiscence. Paul Maves (1986, p. 138), a minister who is himself in his seventies, writes:

Perhaps one of the hardest tasks of all is to allow the healing of bitter memories accumulated over the years. These include rejections endured, abandonments lived through, trust betrayed, love turned to hate, dreams disappointed, injustice suffered, and good intentions misunderstood. These poison the system, corrode our integrity, and alienate us from others. We need to get rid of the garbage of unresolved conflict, unfinished grief work, and leftover anger.

Integrative reminiscence helps enrich one's sense of self-worth and reconcile one's past (Wong & Watt, 1991). As spiritually vital older adults engage in life review, they can celebrate God's grace. They can receive God's forgiveness, forgive themselves and others, affirm God's presence in their past, and find hope for God's eternal presence in this life and the next.

SPIRITUAL FORMATION IN OLDER ADULTS REQUIRES THE ACCEPTANCE OF LOSS

"Spirituality for aging will remain shallow unless we dwell in some depth on the special and threatening problems of old age" (Bianchi, 1982, p. 131). We must face the numerous losses of old age and not disguise them with dreams of leisure activities. Some of the losses which confront older people are:

1. *Time.* Time is running out and becomes a precious resource. Older people realize that they may not be able to accomplish all that they had hoped.

2. *Strength and Health.* The body is wearing out and youthful beauty, as Milton wrote in *Paradise Lost,* turns to "withered, weak, and gray." In addition, many must learn to live with chronic illnesses, such as arthritis.

3. *Finances.* The materially advantaged are more readily accepted into society, but the elderly poor face abandonment.

4. *Vocation.* Most older adults are no longer able to accomplish all that they once could.

5. *Space.* Many elderly are less mobile and some are confined to home.

261

6. *Friends and Family.* Death comes to all. "We grieve not only for our losses, but for the ultimate loss of self. Spouse and friends are part of who we are, and when they are gone, we feel pared down; part of us is missing" (Fischer, 1985, p. 117).

The natural tendency to avoid pain tempts old and young alike to deny these losses, however "the road to spiritual depth does not skirt major problems, but enters into them with full recognition. The way out is not around, but through the pain of loss" (Bianchi, 1982, p. 138).

Theological reflection on suffering and loss can help older adults turn losses into gain, "to learn how the stripping process which often accompanies aging can be a gradual entrance into freedom and new life, how, in fact, aging can be winter grace" (Fischer, 1985, p. 4). What are the gains that accompany and emerge from life's losses?

7. *Wisdom.* Experience can help to clarify life's priorities, empowering people to do what is right. Seniors can experience a renewed understanding that each day of life is an expression of God's grace. Each day is a gift from God to be celebrated, to be fully lived! While the writer of Ecclesiastes is very frank about the losses of old age, he still advises that "people ought to enjoy every day of their lives, no matter how long they live" (Ecc. 11:8, NCV).

8. *Freedom from Daily Deadlines and the Pressure to Achieve.* The winter of life can be a quiet season offering time for reflection and the unhurried practice of the spiritual disciplines. The wife of a retired pastor recently remarked about the luxury of added time together that she and her husband now enjoy. They linger after breakfast to pray unhurried prayers for family, friends, church, and needs around the world.

9. *Continued Learning and Creativity.* Opportunities to learn do not cease at retirement. The loss of vocational identity may precipitate a renewed interest in education as retirees travel and take time to broaden their knowledge. Elderhostels flourish worldwide, as senior adults travel to university campuses to study from a fascinating and varied curriculum. Denver Seminary founded SeniorSchool in 1990 to afford senior adults the opportunity for continued theological education. Community centers offer prolific seminars and classes to capture the interests of seniors.

10. *Opportunity for Service.* Winter can also be a season of care and compassion. Many senior adults volunteer their resources to serve their churches, local communities, and beyond.

11. *Reaffirmed Self-worth.* Belonging to God and being created in God's image enables Christians in later life to counter society's messages of the diminished value of seniors. Older Christians rejoice in the truth that they are forever God's children and joint-heirs with Christ.

12. *Hope.* Christians inherit eternal life. They are able to come to terms with death by their hope in the resurrection of Jesus Christ.

Summary

In summary, the losses of later life can serve to order life's priorities and may slow the pace of life enough for serious reflection on those priorities. For example, a relationship with God and with significant others may finally supersede preoccupation with material possessions and financial security. And the loss of former routine may become a catalyst for new learning and service. Whatever losses may accompany aging, older Christians can rest in God's undiminished love for them and in His promise of eternal life.

SPIRITUAL FORMATION IN OLDER ADULTS IS INDIVIDUAL

If older adults are to continue growing spiritually, they must reassess their identity by asking themselves: "Who am I now in the winter of my life? Having come to terms with my past, how am I to live out the remaining years of my life in a way that will glorify God?" Reading God's Word and communing with God, older believers continue to discern who they are in relationship to the Almighty and how they are to live. Now they are called to apply God's truth to the context of old age.

Later life is never meant to be a season of stagnation, while one simply waits for death. Living as a Christian offers older believers an ongoing development in love, trust, and character as they continue to grow in Christlikeness. They must resist comparing themselves to the "super-old" but, while facing their personal limitations, give themselves completely to God.

They can know that in their weaknesses, God's grace is truly sufficient and His power is made perfect (2 Cor. 12:9).

Too often the relationship between soul and body is overlooked in the study of formation. The spiritual life is more apt to flourish in older adults who give personal attention to their physical well-being. Measures of nutrition and physical health are highly correlated with measures of emotional and spiritual well-being. In many cases, spiritual depression will dissipate as older adults begin to eat a healthy diet, have regular medical exams, monitor medications carefully, and exercise regularly. Christian educators who minister with the elderly should counsel holistically, considering physical well-being as integral to spiritual well-being.

SPIRITUAL FORMATION IN OLDER ADULTS IS CORPORATE

Participation in the faith community is vital to spiritual formation. The church plays an essential role in the spiritual well-being of the older adult. According to Charles Fahey, director of the Third Age Center at Fordham University, "Perhaps the most extensive and significant role of the local congregation is providing the older person with a sense of belonging and stability in a rapidly changing world" (Fahey, 1985). Through the enormous change that accompanies aging, faith offers continuity and the local church becomes the visible expression of that continuity.

In community, older adults both give and receive nurture. A symbiotic relationship should exist between the young and old. Rather than polarizing those in the faith community by age, the church should teach and live out interdependence. The Apostle Paul underscores that every part of the body of Christ is necessary as all work together for the benefit of the whole. No part of the body can tell another, "I don't need you!" and those parts that some would describe as weaker are indispensable (1 Cor. 12:21-22). Yet, sadly, the young too often see the old as weak and easily dispensed with. The church should be the place where the young bring their strength, enthusiasm, and idealism, and join forces with the old who offer their wisdom. All the generations live out Christ's love by learning to both give and receive.

Religious ritual binds the young and old together, deepening their commitment to Christ and to each other. The observance of the Lord's Supper helps believers, personally and corporately, to remember Christ's redemptive work and to celebrate His present and future kingdom. Rituals go beyond cognition; they offer experiential learning, linking both affect and thought. Beyond the celebration of the Lord's Supper or baptism, older adults could be formed by community through rituals specific to their stages of life. Rituals with Christian friends can deepen the experience of God in such life events as retirements, birthdays, housewarmings (or apartment warmings), as well as at funerals where the faith community remembers a life lived well and shares both corporate grief and hope.

Many Americans have come to understand retirement as an event which marks the end of work and service on behalf of others and initiates a new life of leisure and self-indulgence. Using the oft-repeated phrase, "I've had my turn to serve; now it's someone else's turn," many Christian adults turn to a primarily self-serving agenda. God, however, describes the righteous older adult in very different language. The righteous, who are firmly planted in God's truth, will "still bear fruit in old age, they will stay fresh and green, proclaiming, 'The Lord is my Rock' " (Ps. 92:14-15). Older Christians have an ongoing responsibility to bear fruit and serve. In stressing "being" over "doing," the church can miss this point. Typically, the church gives a distorted message of social responsibility which says, "you've had your time of service; now you can just be. Do what you want to be good to yourself." Thus, the elderly are encouraged to disengage from the community and the exercise of their spiritual gifts.

Christians are called to a life of service until death. In service, believers of all ages find joy—the blessing of giving to others (Acts 20:35). Many older people experience pervasive loneliness. Fischer (1985, pp. 23–24) posits that older people often see loneliness as the absence of activity: "The emotional isolation experienced by many old people is a kind of boredom born of indifference. They have nothing worthwhile to do, no goals or plans." The body of Christ offers the antidote for this malady, offering older members the opportunity to join in its mission to serve Christ and extend His kingdom into the lives of the spiritually, emotionally, and physically needy of the earth. Serving, as long as health permits, is a vital part of spiritual formation in old age.

Older Christians have much to teach. They call into question this culture's obsession with consumption, youth, and physical prowess and they model how to live Christianly in this lost world. Older adults have a choice. They can choose to live out the stereotypes of aging as a self-fulfilling prophecy or they can choose to live enriched Christian lives, secure in the One who created and sustains them. They can show younger Christians the importance of "how" over "why." As was the experience of Job, they can learn to stop questioning God's ways, and ask instead "how"—how can life be lived, even within the limitations of old age, in such a way as to please God? And victorious older Christians can teach others how to live with humor. Humor is an expression of faith, as it "bursts through suffering" (McFadden, 1990, p. 138). Trust in God makes laughter possible.

Not only can older adults model how to live, they can teach others how to die. "Numbering our days" (Ps. 90:12) is important as Christians reflect on mortality and determine to live out their days wisely. They face their mortality with hope and confidence and dignity. Tim Stafford tells of his grandfather whose old age was divided into the best and the worst by a stroke. This vibrant, godly man lived his old age with vigor until a stroke left him severely disabled and dependent. Stafford reflects, "If anything, I think of his hard years as the richest. In his suffering, he showed us the stuff he was made of. I would never wish such torment on anybody, but I am grateful I witnessed my grandfather passing through it" (Stafford, 1989). In his diminished physical state, his grandfather demonstrated spiritual greatness. He suffered physical indignity yet entered into eternity with spiritual dignity. He showed his grandson how to die. God has the final victory: "He will swallow up death forever. The Sovereign Lord will wipe away all tears from all faces" (Isa. 25:8). In the New Jerusalem, in the life believers live this one for, God "will wipe every tear from their eyes. There will be no more death or mourning or crying or pain." The old order of sin and death will be gone and everything will be made new! (Rev. 21:4-5)

In community, Christians are spiritually formed from birth

until death. Regardless of age, they are to share their strengths to build each other up in the faith. Together, they celebrate God's truth and goodness, serve, and teach each other how to live as Christians. Older adults live out the paradox of physical death and spiritual life. The hope of the spiritually vital older adult is like no other: "Therefore, we do not lose heart. Though outwardly we are wasting away, yet inwardly we are being renewed day by day. For our light and momentary troubles are achieving for us an eternal glory that far outweighs them all" (2 Cor. 4:16-17).

For Further Reading

Bianchi, E. (1982). *Aging is a spiritual journey.* New York: Crossroad. A summary of the challenges and potentials of midlife and elderhood, including numerous interviews with people at these life stages.

Dychtwald, K. (1990). *Age wave.* New York: Bantam. A secular book, with an eye to the future marketing, social, and lifestyle implications of an aging society. An essential read for those who are willing to do the next step of interpreting these changes for the mission of the church.

Fischer, K. (1985). *Winter grace: Spirituality for the later years.* New York: Paulist. A basic summary of issues of spirituality and aging, this book is written with pastoral warmth and concern, carefully illustrated by the stories of many older people, honest in its dealings with loss and gain in later life, and hopeful in its witness to the resurrection.

Maves, P. (1986). *Faith for the older years.* Minneapolis: Augsburg. A pastoral guide to the issues of aging. Encourages a balanced look at both the losses and opportunities of later life. Gives advice for dealing with the necessary transitions related to aging and focuses on the riches of faith, the call to service, and the hope of faith as one faces death.

Nouwen, H. (1974). *Aging: The fulfillment of life.* New York: Doubleday. Photographs and text combine to bring hope to the process of aging. Encourages the young to invite the elderly into their lives as teachers.

Stafford, T. (1989). *As our years increase: Loving, caring, preparing for life past 65.* New York: Harper. This book is a must reading for pastors, older adults, and the children who will be caregivers for older adults. Stafford presents a biblical framework for understanding aging, and helps explain both the practical (retirement, finances, housing, healthcare) and the spiritual dimensions of aging.

Tournier, P. (1972). *Learn to grow old.* Louisville: Westminster/John Knox. Addresses the practical as well as attitudinal issues of aging, with advice on how to age creatively and with spiritual maturity.

Vogel, L. (1984). *The religious education of older adults.* Birmingham, AL: Religious Education Press. Focuses on the process of learning and reaching in senior adult education. Also advises the Christian educator on the development and implementation of education programs.

TWENTY-TWO

SPIRITUAL FORMATION THROUGH SMALL GROUPS

Peter V. Deison

With the speed of change today, many Christians feel adrift in their spiritual lives. Often the church appears to be floating in dangerous currents without a rudder. Many voices shout for help, yet little seems to be forthcoming. With an increasing desire among many for a stronger faith and firm foundation of spirit, it is time for us all to reexamine spiritual formation.

THE NATURAL SETTING

Many Christian believers today seem to have accepted and even encouraged a thriving misconception—that spiritual formation (growth/nurture) is a personal, individual path only. Such an unwanted conclusion rests in partial truth. God has created us as individuals, unique members of the body with distinct gifts. He also holds us singularly responsible for obedience and disobedience.

North American evangelicalism adds its own flavor to the mix. We serve up a pioneering spirit of individualism which contains admirable qualities. Yet from the opening pages of Scripture, the Creator has always seen us in a broader light. Though we are His individual creatures, He never intended for us to live as a community of independents. God's first commentary following the creation of humans revealed His concern about independence: "It is not good for the man to be alone" (Gen. 2:18). This statement may have a broader scope of meaning than we often give it.

Our own natures tell us that people are not complete as isolated individuals. Humans move naturally toward each other. God created man for fellowship and because of that God gave him a wife, told them to multiply, and thereby formed the first unit of society. Community is part of God's purpose for humanity.

Not only do the Scriptures show that we are created as social beings, they also show that the very nature of the triune God represents community. The biblical concept of God shows that He relates within Himself. The community of Father, Son, and Spirit is admittedly mysterious and incomprehensible; nevertheless, the fact remains that we understand God in this diversity and unity. Theologians call this the ontological Trinity, a distinction unknown in non-Christian thought. The gods of other religions are either singular or mutually independent. The true God of community wants His creation to reflect His image.

The Creation account moves quickly from individual to family, from family to clan, and from clan to nation. Even though God deals directly with individuals throughout the Scripture, they form a collectivity with others such as Israel, the church, or the community of all believers.

> Our religious thinking has for several centuries been so individualistic that it is difficult for us to grasp and appreciate the corporate reality of salvation as the Israelites and the early Christian experienced it. In recent years, we have slowly been regaining some understanding of this communal aspect of salvation and religion. This has happened because of biblical studies which drew our attention to the manner of God's dealings with the people whose experience is recorded in the Bible. (Cooke, 1970, pp. 13–14)

God intends the process of spiritual formation to occur in a community context, so when we speak of spiritual formation through small groups, we really see spiritual formation in the normal context of Scripture—its natural setting is communal. Until a small group develops a true sense of community, spiritual formation will be hindered.

CLARIFYING THE PARTS

Spiritual formation may be defined as the ongoing work of sanctification by the Holy Spirit in the believer's life and with the believer's cooperation. Justification is God's work but spiritual formation calls for our involvement. Even though one can say that God carries out the sanctification process, He does call us to participate and cooperate (Phil. 2:12; Eph. 4:20–5:4).

This process takes place through three primary means. First, we Christians cooperate with the Holy Spirit (Gal. 5:16, 18; Eph. 5:18) who in turn works with us through God's Word (Heb. 4:12; 2 Tim. 3:16-17). Second, as we expose ourselves and respond to God's Word, we grow and are formed spiritually. Third, the Holy Spirit cooperates with us through God's people (Heb. 10:24-25; Gal. 6:10; Eph. 4:15-16) whom He uses to build up one another in faith and life.

Virtually all New Testament commands are plural. God has given them to the body of Christ, the community of saints. We need the community of God just as we do the Word of God and the Spirit of God.

As believers examine their growth and the spiritual formation of their lives, they become increasingly aware of the need for each other. Our prayer and Bible study are deepened and sharpened by interaction with each other as iron sharpens iron.

In addition God has created us with a common thirst for relationships. We all enjoy our moments alone, some more than others; yet as healthy believers we resist loneliness and isolation because God has made us part of a body. Spiritual formation, therefore, requires all three major parts – the Word of Truth, the work of the Spirit, and the warmth of community.

THE NEED FOR COMMUNITY

Our whole society hungers for connectedness as the forces within our country drive us apart. The very system we created for fulfillment has turned against us.

Over twenty years ago Vance Packard wrote an astute commentary on our country. In *A Nation of Strangers,* Packard describes the problem well.

271

Personal isolation is becoming a major social fact of our time. A great many people are disturbed by the feeling that they are rootless or increasingly anonymous, that they are living in a continually changing environment where there is little sense of community. The phrase "home town" may well fade from our language in this century. . . . Great numbers of inhabitants feel unconnected to either people and places, and throughout much of the nation there is a breakdown in community living. . . . We are confronted with a society that is coming apart at the seams. And in the process we appear to be breeding a legacy of coldness in many of the coming generation (Packard, 1972, pp. 1–2).

We have a built-in need for a sense of belonging which increases as our cultural and community values fall apart.

In some cases, society makes its own self-correcting attempts to meet its communal needs. John Naisbitt in his books *MegaTrends* and *MegaTrends 2000* shows the trends of our society are often mere reaction to counter social pressure. The more technological we become, the more dehumanized, and the greater the need for more humane organizational response. Consider the rise of the hospice movement to put a community back in touch with the death of its members rather than isolate the dying in sterile hospitals. Naisbitt calls this counter-reaction high tech versus high touch.

Yet even with these attempts, Western values, morals, and community relationships continue to deteriorate. And the church is not exempt. Social forces pulling us apart pressure believers to isolate and fragment. The proliferation of Christian television and radio programs, tapes, and videos make it easier to remain apart. Increasingly Christians get their spiritual food from the media rather than the community of Christ.

Meanwhile as the megachurch expands, it faces an increasing struggle for intimacy and personal contact to help people grow while protecting individual uniqueness. Many people even seek the anonymity of largeness, in order to stay "unknown" in the crowd.

This all leads to the crucial need for small groups in which true community can occur and spiritual formation thrive. Years ago Swearingen observed:

For a Christian, the term "community" implies the finest quality of fellowship that it is possible for men to achieve. It is the type of fellowship which provides for all of its participants every opportunity to become the kind of persons which God intended each should become. In a true community then, each member is concerned for the creating of conditions under which each individual may develop to the fullest of his capacities. Community in its finest sense involves the delicate but inescapable balance between rights and duties, the privilege of self-fulfillment under God, and the obligation to enable others to achieve the same (Swearingen, 1950, pp. 41).

We have seen that we are created for community—one of the means of spiritual formation—and this group life is desperately needed. But how do small groups contribute to the work of community in developing spiritual formation?

COMMUNITY IN SMALL GROUPS

Small groups have been in and out of popularity in the church for centuries. During the last fifty years they have been studied more closely and we have learned that four essential ingredients mark small groups with a strong sense of community:

(1) a clear purpose;
(2) a commitment to each person involved as well as a commitment of each person to the group;
(3) a strong, loving, serving and accessible leadership, supported with a sense of democratic unity, and
(4) explicitly shared beliefs and values.

Research in sociology has confirmed these elements (Kanter, 1972). Kanter studied the elements of success found in intentional communities in the United States from its beginning. Her study confirmed that these key elements characterized successful communities, with the addition of the clear purpose (1), which I believe is explicit in the leadership element. Sense of community is the glue that holds a small group together. It makes the difference between a group as a collection of individuals or a unity of believers.

For a small group to have *community,* it must develop ways to promote *common unity.* First it must be united around its purpose, one that is collectively clear and often repeated. However, purpose alone is not enough. Many groups have a clear purpose and still fragment.

Group members must also unite around love for each other. This can be a special uniqueness in the Christian community because of Christ's command to love each other as He loved us (John 13:34-35). Christian love is characterized by relational authenticity, men and women who have a deep impact on each other in truth and love. Paul's example is seen in 1 Thessalonians 2:8 where he says, "We loved you so much that we were delighted to share with you not only the gospel of God but our own lives as well, because you had become so dear to us" (1 Thes. 2:8). Commitment to loving relationships within the group's purpose gives depth to community so spiritual formation can take root.

The third essential ingredient is leadership that promotes sharing responsibilities. This gives ownership to the members so the group does not "belong" to the leader. Finally, groups must share beliefs and value the clearly held important commonalties. We grow together around the bond of what we hold dear.

BUILDING COMMUNITY

How does genuine love and relational authenticity occur in groups? It begins with the leader's commitment to community. Group leaders must understand the importance of community as the foundation for spiritual formation. For individuals to openly love one another, be vulnerable to one another, willing to reprove and rebuke one another, encourage one another, deep trust must develop.

Trust develops when people begin to bond. But bonding takes time and the sharing of significant personal information. In order for a small group to develop community, the leader needs to model a process that leads to bonding.

This can take place slowly over a long period of natural events through personal sharing during prayer times and life illustrations used in teaching. Or, it can be speeded up dramatically by purposely introducing exercises that cause people to open and share more of their lives.

Life Maps

One powerful exercise for community building is called a *life map*. This simple process naturally opens the most important door to bonding, the story of a person's life. When we view life in its entirety, individual events of the past (as well as current responses) make greater sense. Understanding is enhanced. I can understand why you think the way you do, because I see your roots, heritage, influence, and experience, both wonderful and tragic. I now have a paradigm larger than my recent history with you.

When one person can clearly identify with another, an internal bonding process begins. When we share our whole lives, we create opportunities for people in the group to have internal "ah-ha" experiences. As life maps are shared, people respond and react to the story. Because we rarely get a chance to share our own personal stories, most of us really pour ourselves into the telling. Since God has made us all so unique, every story becomes an amazing account of His grace and sovereignty.

The key element, though, is the internal connections that are made. In every story, listeners find one or more places where they subconsciously say, "That happened to me"; "I did that too"; or "I can't believe someone else suffered the same thing I did." This cross-connecting which occurs between group members and the one sharing a life map creates the bonding.

Visual tools also assist this crucial process. Persons are given a large piece of butcher paper and asked to draw their lives in any form or style, showing the beginning, the present, and four key factors:

(1) Hereditary influence
(2) Heroes who have impacted them
(3) High times they have enjoyed
(4) Hard times they have suffered and how those times changed them

275

We give each person twenty to forty minutes depending on the size of the group and program schedule. Group members are asked to take notes and to ask appropriate questions. Sharers tell as little or as much of their lives as they desire and answer only those questions with which they feel comfortable.

The visual element deepens the understanding, enhances remembering the story years later, and keeps group members more actively engaged.

The exercise is complete when all group members tell the sharer what they especially enjoyed about the presentation. This gives affirmation to the sharer and ends the time on a positive note, though some sad moments often mark the experience.

The life map can become an end in itself because of its enjoyment, but the leader knows that it is primarily a means to the end of community building. After watching hundreds of such sharings, I consider it the single most important ingredient in helping groups bond. It surfaces needs, problems, and unique abilities. Coupled with the additional ingredients of planned socials and prayer times, the life map leads to even greater bonding with the opportunities of further conversations about unique life events.

Group Leadership

As the group sees the wonderful sovereign work of God and His grace in each person's life, deeper trust occurs because of wider understanding. As trust develops, honesty and appropriate vulnerability can occur. The leader must model this by sharing his or her own life map first. How one models the sharing and vulnerability greatly impacts the depth and genuineness of all subsequent sharing.

Assuming the group follows the leader's example, the next important development of spiritual formation can occur. As members learn to trust each other, they feel freer to share their current struggles and the ministry of spiritual formation begins to blossom. Now the group is not praying about *things*, but about *each other* and doing so spontaneously. The evidence of bonding appears as group members ask about specific needs without the leader's prompting, as members seek out one another outside the group, and as they ask about absent members.

Leaders are again crucial at this point. They enhance the opportunity for formation by seizing open clues of need in the person's life and inviting deeper sharing. They invite group members to respond to what they've heard and the group begins to minister to the sharer as the situation requires — encouragement, teaching, accountability, or reproof. Because of the bonding, more truthfulness and straightforwardness can occur. Now harder questions of dealing with issues of the flesh can be brought up, again because of the trust and confidentiality that has been established.

Real growth and change in life happen because of two key factors — grace and truth. Grace is the foundation of trust, patience, gentleness, and love. It also builds an atmosphere of unconditional acceptance and hope. Truth, on the other hand, is what forces me to examine my life, my sin, my impact on others, and my attitudes. Integrity and character are examined with grace and people can place themselves under accountability in the areas of personal struggles, common to all of us.

Focus of Formation

Now one can examine how much he or she is pursuing Christlikeness and do so in an atmosphere of hope and love. Community sets the atmosphere for spiritual formation and is, in fact, a part of it. Once we establish the atmosphere, specific personal issues can be discussed and new applications of truth can begin. The small group with this kind of community becomes the most obvious place for this to develop as God intended.

Spiritual formation in small groups is where the whole focus of sanctification can happen. It provides a place where God's truth can be discussed, where the Spirit can speak, and God's people can minister to each other. Jesus summed it up for us when He said, "Love the Lord your God with all your heart and with all your soul and with all your mind. This is the first and greatest commandment. And the second is like it: love your neighbor as yourself. All the law and the prophets hang on these two commandments" (Matt. 22:37-38).

Spiritual formation then must have as its focus enhancing the love of God and the love of others. Put another way, if a person passionately pursues Christ in all areas of life and authentically relates to others in seeking to love them, then he or she is

277

fulfilling the goal of spiritual formation, as well as the goal of the Great Commandment. Throughout the New Testament the goal of spiritual growth is clearly defined as loving God and loving others (Rom. 13:9; Gal. 5:6, 14; Eph. 4:16; 1 John 4:17).

Notice that the goal of spiritual formation is not obedient behavior, greater knowledge, ministry results, or even unity. These are results. It is not prayer, spiritual discipline, evangelism, or mutual confession. These are means by which we enhance (but not attain) spiritual formation. Practicing the right "activities" does not guarantee growth in spiritual life. Right activities with wrong motives can feel like the real thing, but in actuality might keep us in complacent rebellion against God. Instead, we want these procedures to put us in a place where God's Spirit, God's Word, and God's people can influence our lives to love Him and others. Small groups centered on the goal of spiritual formation are crucial for the church. Many congregations have discovered that this priority helps all other spiritual activities fall into place.

If we have made the passionate pursuit of Christ our highest aim, we will see the need of His community with a small group of believers. In this safe place with trusted fellow strugglers, we can learn to relate more authentically to each other and love God.

Spiritual formation grows deeper and stronger through the community of a small group. The healthy environment created in such groups allows lives to change and develop. As you seek spiritual growth and formation for your own life and others, do not undervalue the deep hunger for community and use small groups to anchor that process.

Further Readings

Gorman, J. (1993). *Community that is Christian: A handbook on small groups.* Wheaton, IL: Victor. This comprehensive handbook is an interactive manual for transformation of community living. Designed to help implement community in church congregations.

Griffin, E. (1982). *Getting together: A guide for good groups.* Downers Grove, IL: InterVarsity. This book is more frequently recommended in the literature about small groups than any other book. He deals with key areas such as the types of groups and their differences, self-disclosure, conflict, deviance, and biblical examples of leadership styles.

Hestenes, R. (1986). *Building Christian community through small groups.* Pasadena, CA: Fuller Theological Seminary (D.Min. course notebook, available through Fuller Theological Seminary Bookstore). Dr. Hestenes has the most comprehensive manual available. It is filled with copies of ideas, programs, and handouts that are being used from around the country. It contains an extensive seventeen page bibliography and covers communication skills, group life, sharing in small groups, prayer, leadership, developing a church program, and laity programs.

Jones, A. (1985). *Soul making: The desert way of spirituality.* San Francisco. Harper & Row. Alan Jones has a magnetic way of drawing you inward for honest questions about your soul without drawing you down. The three sections deal with taking a look in, entering the emptiness, and the call to joy. He makes one think as few writers do.

Lovelace, R. (1979). *Dynamics of spiritual life: An evangelical theology of renewal.* Downers Grove, IL: InterVarsity. This is by far the most thorough book written on renewal. This book will add depth and breadth to your understanding of spiritual formation. He gives clear thinking to the issues of sin, the flesh, the world, sanctification, prayer, revival, and the history of renewal in American evangelicalism.

Willard, D. (1988). *The spirit of the disciplines: Understanding how God changes lives.* San Francisco: Harper & Row. Willard takes the law out of the disciplines. He has a straightforward way of helping us see and feel the value and joy of the disciplines. He says disciplines are the things we choose to help us do things we would not naturally do on our own. They are means by which we help ourselves achieve what we want in our hearts by God's grace.

TWENTY-THREE

THE FAMILY AS A CONTEXT FOR SPIRITUAL FORMATION
Ronald T. Habermas

The message of *Fiddler on the Roof,* the long-running Broadway hit, epitomizes the fundamental challenge within contemporary Christian homes: what happens when revered traditions encounter modern-day revolutions for change?

In the play, a poor Jewish milkman, Tevye, attempts to marry off his three oldest daughters. But every husband is chosen in spite of this father's wishes. Each successive marriage ceremony strays further and further from Jewish tradition. During the opening monologue, Tevye explains the symbolism of the play's title: "A fiddler on the roof. Sounds crazy, no? But here, in our village of Anatevka, you might say every one of us is a fiddler on the roof, trying to scratch out a pleasant, simple tune without breaking his neck. It isn't easy."

Parents of Christian households easily empathize with the fiddler metaphor. Hostility toward traditional patterns of caregiving swells almost daily, complicating the goal "to scratch out a pleasant, simple" lifestyle. Leaders of such households don't need more opposition. But resistance comes nevertheless. Increasing challenges to totally revamp—or even destroy—foundational practices of Christian faith in the home proliferate like weeds in a newly seeded garden. Value systems topple. Pressures of both single parenting and blended families affect every member of the home, without exception. Mass media infiltrates, resembling the soft pornography of a few years ago. Child abuse skyrockets, along with unsettling statistics on latchkey kids, runaways, and the homeless. Just when we think it can't get worse, it does.

Fiddler paints the countercultural brushstrokes of historic Judaism, pertinent for the backdrop of twenty-first century Christianity. Although its story is set in Czarist Russia 100 years ago, this play's message is as relevant as today's evening news, for Tevye continues his analogy of the fiddler: "You may ask why do we stay up there if it's so dangerous. Well, we stay because Anatevka is our home. And how do we keep our balance? That, I can tell you in one word: tradition!" Then, as the popular opening song ("Tradition") begins, Tevye declares, "We have traditions for everything. How to sleep. How to eat. How to work. How to wear clothes."

Suddenly, the tiniest crack in this bedrock of Judaic traditions appears. Subsequent to his illustrations of how their multiple customs reflect continuous devotion to God, Tevye figuratively backs himself into a corner. He begins the trip to this unsuspecting end with a logical question: "You may ask, 'How did this tradition get started?' " Then he surprises himself by his own answer: "I'll tell . . . I don't know!" Reacting to what he has just said, his own admitted ignorance, Tevye regains his composure. This Jewish milkman, then, partially vindicates himself by concluding, "But it's a tradition. And, because of our traditions, every one of us knows who he is and what God expects him to do." Contemporary Christian parents share this dilemma with Tevye; many, when pressed, claim a certain ignorance of basic faith tenets, yet they somehow retain confidence in those very same beliefs.

THEOLOGICAL AND THEORETICAL CONSIDERATIONS

Various routes have been chartered by those who confront the complex destination of spiritual formation within families. Subtopics of study have ranged from intrapersonal to interpersonal concerns; from perspectives and needs of spouses to that of offspring; and from nuclear to intergenerational to extended family nurture. In light of space restrictions, this study is limited to one primary question: *"How can parents foster spiritual maturity within their child?"*

On the one hand, some people believe that spiritual formation comes exclusively from the *hand of God*. This position claims that all "formulas" for godliness must be avoided. By grace we have been saved; by grace we are sanctified. Attempts to string together a list of "do's" and "don'ts" become reductionistic at best and legalistic at worst.

On the other hand, some people advocate a focus of *human responsibility*. They posit that Scripture supports the fact that certain human knowledge, choices, and behaviors *do* produce maturity, as a part of God's intended plan. For instance, the wise builder is differentiated from the foolish one (Matt. 7:24-27) because he both hears Jesus' words and puts them into practice. In contrast, the foolish builder ignores Jesus' truth. The resulting "house on the rock" (vs. sand) symbolizes spiritual formation via *human response*.

Multiple cautions must be heeded by the caregiver who adheres to either of these two extremes. In particular, consider the caution within the second of these two complementary positions. While valuing the necessary place of human response, parents should avoid two dangers: denying the unique features of the individual child and denying the common features of all children. The former includes denying such factors as the reality of distinctive callings for each person, private dispositions, gifts, perceptions, opportunities, learning styles, and circumstances. (Whether we like it or not, this reality of valuing individual uniqueness also prizes the child's choice to ultimately say "no" to his or her parent's attempt to encourage spiritual maturation.)

In short, spiritual formation is pictured here in terms of art; it is analogous to the direct, customized sculpting of all human beings by their Creator, along with other influences. No single design is ever repeated since each person is unique. The latter aspect of this danger consists of denying human similarities: common needs, shared domains of human composition, universal quests about life's meaning, verified patterns of development, etc.

Godliness is portrayed here in terms of science; growth occurs through divine principles for all believers. *Thus, it is within this tension of human uniqueness and commonness that spiritual formation must be understood.*

When it comes to this refined focus on the meaning of spiritual maturity, no single Old Testament passage is cited more than Deuteronomy 6:1-9. There, parents who love the Lord are commanded to teach God's law to their children when they "sit at home," when they "walk along the road," when they "lie down," and when they "get up." But just as familiarity breeds contempt, it also spawns forgetfulness. Scriptures like this can become so well-known that we ironically neglect their details; we overlook their significant meaning. What does this passage really say?

Looking at this chapter's task from the angle of *relationships* and *realms,* these two broad factors frame spiritual formation, when the perspective of "human response" is employed. *Relationships* address the critical feature of associations with other people, namely our vertical, horizontal, and integrated relationships. *Realms* identify three separate yet connected human domains that impact spiritual maturity. Simply put, *relationships* primarily concentrate on the "who?" and "what?" of maturation, while *realms* typically view the "where?" and "how?" of growth.

Reconsider the aforementioned passage from Deuteronomy 6, especially its opening verses, known as the Shema, "Hear, O Israel: the Lord our God is one. Love the Lord your God with all your heart and with all your soul and with all your strength" (Deut. 6:4-5). A trio of relationships surfaces. First, the godly parents' *vertical relationships* with God are evident. These caregivers have internalized the truth; a pervasive love for God is as obvious as it is mature. This initial point must not be presumed, even in Christian families.

Second, this passage suggests that there are healthy *horizontal relationships* between parent and child. For example, family members are fundamentally described through their lifestyles of common experiences, like sitting together at home, walking together in the community, and so on. Again, as we contemplate the subject of spiritual formation within Christian households, we must never assume that this second relationship is automatically present. Such bonds are created and strengthened only through conscientious plans.

Third, *integrated relationships* exist within this Scripture; the vertical and the horizontal ties are combined. For instance, through formal and informal encounters, mature parents faithfully unite God's Word with their child's real world. Again, this third relationship synthesizes the first two. Reverence for God's message and relevance for the recipients of the message are never set at odds. Christian nurture in the home intentionally weaves changeless truth with changing times. Scripture is not compromised but customized. Boyer's (1988) work represents one of the finest books which successfully blends these three relationships.

To summarize, notice how this threesome of *vertical, horizontal,* and *integrated* relationships appears at the end of Deuteronomy 6: "In the future, when *your son* asks you, 'What is the *meaning* of the stipulations, decrees and laws the Lord *our* God has commanded you?' *tell him:* 'We were slaves of Pharaoh in Egypt, *but the Lord our* God brought us out. . . . The Lord *commanded us to obey* all these decrees and to fear the Lord *our* God, so that we might *always prosper* and be kept alive, as is the case *today*' " (vv. 20-21, 24). All three relationships are nonnegotiable when it comes to promoting spiritual maturity at home.

Three realms of human development also convey the family's task in spiritual formation. Perhaps the best single verse which captures this trio is Acts 2:37. There, following the mighty work of the Holy Spirit through Peter's sermon, a great revival occurred. Luke's precise description of what happened to the crowd pinpoints what must repeatedly happen in modern Christian homes: "when the people *heard* this, they were cut to the *heart* and said to Peter and the other apostles, 'Brothers, what should we *do?*' " Today, we respectively label these three: (1) the cognitive (or intellectual domain); (2) the affective (or emotional and value domain); and (3) the behavioral (or skill domain). All three developmental categories must be equitably combined in order to comprehend the full meaning of effective parenting. Palmer (1983) stresses the balance of these three realms when he broadly redefines the essence of spiritual formation through broad features of education.

Practical Considerations

Several useful dimensions of this theological/theoretical design for parenting are described below. Three particular topics of the spiritual formation task emerge when healthy relationships are fused with human realms of growth.

WHAT PARENTS MUST KNOW

One way to view our mandate as parents is to merge relationships with the *cognitive* realm. We must regularly ask: "What should I *understand* about effective relationships that influence spiritual formation?"

First, effective parents must know *about* God through His Word. Knowledge per se is not our final objective, yet we must believe in something. We must believe in the truth. The cognitive realm provides a useful starting point, specifically as it pertains to our vertical relationship. Among specific examples of knowledge which promote family nurture, several well-known verses stand out, including: (1) Exodus 20:12 — "Honor your father and your mother," the only one of the Ten Commandments with the promise of longer life; (2) Proverbs 31:28 — Here, godly mothers are recognized as those whose "children arise and call her blessed"; (3) Mark 9:37 — Christ's sobering principle is issued that "whoever welcomes one of these little children in my name welcomes me"; (4) Ephesians 6:1 — Perhaps the most popular New Testament passage about youngsters, this verse commands: "Children, obey your parents in the Lord" (cf. Col. 3:20); and (5) 1 Timothy 5:4 — the apostle claims that children should be "caring for their own family and so repaying their parents and grandparents."

But there is obviously more to spiritual formation than just knowing God's Word. Biblical maturity is much more. The cognitive realm also stresses the need to comprehend matters pertaining to human development. That is, we must ask: what makes healthy horizontal relationships? What should we know? Mark 4:33 states: "With many similar parables Jesus spoke the word to them, *as much as they could understand.*" This verse tells us that Christ was handicapped by the limitations of His hearers early in His ministry. They were either unable to understand or unwilling. Christ communicated to the maximum level of their understanding. Nevertheless, their learning was restricted. Jesus was patient with His followers. In order to purposefully adjust His instruction, in accord with their limitations — "as much as they could understand" — Christ had to know what those limits were. And that type of knowledge comes only by a teacher personally knowing his or her individual learners.

Parents today can do no less than Jesus did. We must intimately know the children whom we serve. We must be aware of their similarities and differences (among siblings and others), their motivations, gifts, teachable moments, hardships, and joys. We must use this knowledge about particular individuals to customize God's truth to each child. The most provocative verse lending insight into the unique nature of children is Paul's personal testimony in 1 Corinthians 13:11, "When I was a child, I talked like a child, I thought like a child, I reasoned like a child. When I became a man, I put childish ways behind me." The apostle clearly differentiates between *childlikeness* (i.e., those features appropriate to kids, without labeling them immature) and *childishness* (i.e., characteristics that adults retain from childhood which become inappropriate and immature). As we caregivers also make these distinctions we will ascertain what healthy horizontal relationships require. In short, we parents will let our kids be kids (Habermas, 1993).

In its fullest sense, the cognitive realm must combine both of the categories above. It fashions reverent knowledge about God with relevant knowledge about people. It takes into account shifting traditions while remaining steady in its foundational beliefs. Like Tevye who eventually recognized that change is constant, we parents must acknowledge that certain traditions are regularly amended. But, unlike Tevye, our response should not simply reflect a reactive posture. Nor should we believe that change is inherently evil. A proactive mind-set enables us to create new, fresh patterns of thought which can be truthful as well as contemporary, effectively critiquing tradition.

As a case in point, consider the subject of doubts. Traditionally, this topic has been off limits for evangelicals. It was taboo to discuss. Conservative leaders have tended to equate doubt with disbelief. But such equations are simply untrue. When Christian parents proactively analyze Scripture (i.e., the vertical knowledge), they discover that diverse and legitimate types of doubt exist (Habermas, 1989). Also, when effective parents scrutinize helpful studies in human development (i.e., the horizontal knowledge), they conclude that constructive doubt (or crisis or dissonance) is essential for growth (see Marcia [1967], along with Strommen and Strommen [1985]).

WHAT PARENTS MUST VALUE

Few passages emphasize the potency of the affective realm more than the story of the post-resurrection appearance of Christ to the two disciples on the road to Emmaus (Luke 24:13-35). Although formerly depressed through their own ignorance, these two followers eventually became aware that the risen Lord stood in their presence. Immediately, they experienced "spiritual heartburn." Verse 32 testifies: "They asked each other, 'Were not our hearts burning within us while he talked with us on the road and opened the Scriptures to us?' " These two disciples were so ecstatic, they ran a mini-marathon of seven miles back to Jerusalem, even though it was unsafe for them to do so at night, especially in their exhausted condition.

Translating this testimony into our contemporary scene, we need to wonder how our children would answer this question if they were surveyed: "What does your mom (or dad) really get excited about?" What would they say? Perhaps their answers would identify a parent's favorite hobby, TV show, vocational challenge, or sporting activity. Whatever the response, all answers mirror some form of "heartburn." Would spiritual interests be cited in such surveys?

What must parents *value* in order to produce spiritual formation within the family? First, we must not only know *about* God, we must *know God Himself.* The Apostle John's criticism of the church at Ephesus stands as a legitimate criticism of many Christian homes today: we have forsaken our first love of Christ (Rev. 2:4). Consequently, we must raise several questions regarding our parenting: do we exhibit genuine love for God and His Word? Do we read and study the Scriptures because we are intrinsically motivated out of our compassion for it? Or do we feel extrinsically compelled into such study by others? Do we exhibit the fruit of the Spirit, which expresses affective virtues of character? To repeat, biblical "heartburn" is either illustrated by such persistent expressions of faith-in-life, or it is not.

Besides love for the truth, love for the child is necessary. This fact portrays a second component within an affective realm of spiritual formation. Covey (1989, pp. 188–199) creates an excellent metaphor at this juncture, stating that we need to open "emotional bank accounts" for our family members. This metaphor describes the level of trust built within any relationship: the greater the trust, the richer the deposit. And, the richer the deposit, the safer we feel in that relationship.

Covey suggests a half dozen ways to increase our emotional accounts. First, we must *understand what is important to the other individual* ("one person's mission is another person's minutia"). Parents with young children are constantly reminded of this humbling principle. For example, the mother lecturing her early elementary age son on the importance of respect for authority will be rudely reintroduced to this principle when his first words, subsequent to her lecture, are, "Mommy, why did you comb your hair that way?"

Second, Covey suggests, we must *attend to little acts of kindness and courtesy.* Realize that people are very tender in the deepest recesses of their hearts.

Third, *keep commitments.* Living up to the promises we make strengthens bridges of trust. Conversely, when we break our promise, such bridges fall.

Fourth, emotional deposits are made by *clarifying expectations.* One of the best ways to accomplish this is to have children, in their own words, repeat to parents what they were just asked to do.

Fifth, *show personal integrity.* Integrity, Covey says, is like honesty, but goes beyond it. Honesty is "conforming our words to reality, and integrity is "conforming reality to our words." One specific quality of integrity takes the shape of being loyal and supportive of people even (or especially) in their absence. When family members realize you're not criticizing them behind their backs, "funds" accrue in their "emotional bank accounts."

Sixth, and finally, when a "withdrawal" is made from such accounts (i.e., through a significant faux pas), *sincere apologies* must follow immediately. Everyone makes these mistakes; only mature parents admit them.

In the final analysis, "what must parents value" combines love for the truth and love for the child. Caregivers in the home may demonstrate this affective commitment to spiritual formation by stressing meaningful memorials. This includes valuing well-known, traditional memorials (such as participation in the

Lord's Supper) along with newly created memorials. The critical criterion for fashioning modern-day memorials requires locating contemporary places and events where God's grace is especially evidenced (e.g., celebrating anniversaries of a child's spiritual rebirth, confirmation, or baptism).

Sometimes, certain features of a traditional memorial may take on new meaning through contemporary modifications. For example, a twelve stone monument was established at the Jordan River to remind the Israelites of God's timely intervention in their lives (Josh. 4:1-7). Today, this visual reminder of stones would not be as relevant to Christian families as other symbols, even though the lesson of God's historic intervention does stand the test of time. Therefore, one father suggested the following contemporary modification of tradition, capturing one of the Jordan memorial's valuable instructional aims: to stimulate curiosity among children. During the first two weeks of Advent, he and his wife prominently display the "memorial" of the nativity scene in their home. But they purposefully omit the figurine of Baby Jesus. Like features of the twelve stones ceremony, such an omission prompts their children to raise obvious questions, like, "Why is Jesus missing?" These inquiries, in turn, provide an opportune moment to discuss how the Jews, for centuries, waited for the Messiah to come. This "desire of nations" theme portrays a powerful Christmas lesson for family education; its affective message is timeless, for people continue to search for God.

The *passion* of meaningful memorials, then, is paramount. Consider the mandate to keep the Passover feast in Exodus 12, yet another illustration of biblical memorials. Within its command resides the essence of the affective realm of spiritual formation. Obeying the Passover was never intended to dissolve into mechanical ritual. To the contrary, what sparked the flame of this annual family celebration in the Old Testament was *owned faith* — faith which is voluntarily chosen by an individual without coercion. Participants were never satisfied with the contrasting counterpart of owned faith, *surrogate faith* — faith that centers in someone external from self (e.g., faith we inherit from parents or other leaders). What did our spiritual ancestors do to assure this internalized system of values? A child's simple, yet penetrating, question was consistently raised. Not only were their parents asked, "What does this ceremony mean?" the child added two critical words to that inquiry: "What does this ceremony mean *to you?*" (Ex. 12:26)

Another example of creating new and relevant memorials based on this "owned faith" objective of Exodus 12:26, is raised by Sell (1981, p. 218). He refers to the thankful moment when a family is blessed by a newborn. This celebration of life by all family members constitutes "a sincere and *emotional liturgy* unmatched by any church service" (emphasis added). That is, the affective domain of spiritual formation thoroughly experiences and expresses heartfelt gratitude.

Such natural opportunities to exhibit faith in life prompts Sell to say that Christian families must know how to celebrate Christianly. They should be able to turn such moments of personal reflection and joy into public thanksgiving. In this particular case, one simple exercise might include the challenge for each family member to respond to the obvious question: "What does having a new baby in the house mean to you?" Sell concludes: "And in that sharing of life and awareness and response, we celebrate the gifts and presence of God. In that celebration the Word and the person of God are integrated into our living."

Boyer (1988) offers simple suggestions for meaningful rituals, as well. His "Service for the Night" (pp. 104 and 180–181) assures young children that God will care for them while they sleep. After a song, a brief word of thanks, and a prayer, a night light (used as a symbol) is switched on, as the parent says: "This night light will be on all night; in the same way God will be with you all night."

WHAT PARENTS MUST DO

Several practical parenting strategies have already been provided in this chapter. However, the final section of the behavioral realm concentrates on particular parental actions and skills that are necessary to foster maturity within the child. It singles out specific directives that often go unnoticed. For instance, one challenge of Christian behavior, as it pertains to the caregiver's spiritual formation task, is the need for a functional metaphor, some useful image enabling parents to constantly visualize and to assess what we are to accomplish. How about time travel? A primary task that parents are instructed to "do" is to intentionally pass their faith on to their children by employing a connect-the-dots perspective of time.

This strategy was alluded to earlier from Deuteronomy 6. Parents must honor God's *past* work by recalling His personal acts in history. *Present-day* mandates involving faith must likewise be grounded in God's revelation. *Future* hope emerges through daily obedience to divine historic commands. The comprehensive dimensions of the family's spiritual formation, then, are set within the chronological parameters of the time travel analogy.

But how is this metaphor implemented in today's home? The answer lies in understanding the implicit details of Deuteronomy 6:20-21, 24. Notice, again, what that ideal model of family instruction included: "In the *future,* when *your son asks* you, 'What is the *meaning* of the stipulations, decrees and laws the Lord *our* God commanded *you?*' tell him: 'We were *slaves* of Pharaoh in Egypt, *but the Lord* brought us out. . . . The Lord *commanded us to obey* all these decrees and to fear the Lord *our* God, so that we might *always prosper* and be kept alive, as is the case *today*' " (emphasis mine).

Several detailed behaviors (or issues relating to them) are acknowledged in this passage. They parallel the fifteen characteristics of healthy families that Curran (1985) discovered, including six basic facts. Specifically, spiritual formation appears in children when: (1) a vibrant parent-child relationship exists; (2) the call for daily family instruction is occasionally initiated by the child, revealing his or her curiosity and interest; (3) the reality of the child's natural questioning indicates the relevancy of faith issues in the home; (4) the parent portrays a good model of attractive and provocative faith for the child; (5) the parent is both living by divine laws and able to provide the "meaning" behind those laws; and (6) a common faith between parent and child is evident (the word "our" represents a significant pronoun in Deut. 6).

By way of review, then, Christian nurture advocates the need for vertical, horizontal, and integrated relationships. Parents who ask the question, "But what do we *do?*" must continually assess whether or not these half dozen behaviors (or features like them) are found within their home. To assist in this venture, the six items above are reorganized in the following list of evaluative questions for parents:

- What evidence is there to demonstrate that a close bond exists between my child and me?
- What kinds of subjects do we discuss, especially topics that my child raises?
- What is the instructional environment in our home like, and how does it encourage my child to comfortably and naturally raise questions about faith?
- How could my personal testimony, as a model, be critiqued?
- How does my lifestyle and my ability to answer questions about God's Word stimulate interest in my child regarding topics of Christian concern?
- What examples can be offered to indicate that my child is affirming the faith I profess?

Ideally, as the child gets older, more signs of "owned faith" should become apparent.

Strommen and Strommen (1985, pp. 146–158) summarize their complementary strategy for Christian maturity by noting that spiritual formation occurs three ways: (1) faith is experienced in "the natural flow of home life"; (2) faith is communicated during structured, formal times of education; and (3) faith is shared by *"doing* truth together" (i.e., through live expressions of faith; emphasis added). In a word, Christian education is *relationships.* And effective Christian education means *reconciled relationships.* First, we are reconciled to God in Christ (communion); then to other believers (community), to ourselves (character), and finally to our calling in life (commission) (Habermas and Issler, 1992).

In *Fiddler on the Roof,* the last line of the opening song exclaims: "Without our traditions, our lives would be as shaky . . . as a fiddler on the roof!" Indeed, traditions bring stability. This axiom holds true in a Jewish setting one century ago and in contemporary Christian homes. Unfortunately, some people perceive that traditions are all that believers need. But we require more. If we parents and leaders are to accomplish the nearly overwhelming task of spiritual formation in the home, we'll need much more. By God's grace, we need relevant knowledge, spiritual heartburn, and pertinent skills of caregiving.

For Further Reading

Boyer, E. (1988). *Finding God at home.* San Francisco: Harper & Row. The subtitle of this book, "Family Life As Spiritual Discipline," describes its significant contribution. Boyer compares and contrasts two types of spiritual formation, via analogy: the spirituality of the desert depicts classical ascetic life — withdrawn from the hectic pace of society, solitude, silence, and prayer; the spirituality of the family identifies the pursuit of God within the busyness of life. Daily care for others and the routine of household chores comprise its essence. Perhaps the book's strongest feature is the author's down-to-earth realistic approach. His practical illustrations, life examples, and storytelling abilities are superb (note: This book was originally titled *A Way in the World*).

Campolo, A. (1987). "The youth culture in sociological perspective." In W.S. Benson & M.H. Senter III (Eds.), *The complete book of youth ministry* (pp. 37–47). Chicago: Moody. Four critical social forces and themes emerge in this chapter, taken from a helpful youth textbook. Campolo directs the reader's attention to: the Industrial Revolution and the role of teens; the decline of parental authority; family size and adolescent character; and the effect of television on youth culture.

Covey, S. (1989). *The seven habits of highly effective people.* New York: Simon & Schuster. The author advances a principle-centered approach for solving personal and professional problems. Using holistic and integrated concepts, Covey's seven habits focus on personal vision, personal leadership, interpersonal leadership, personal management, empathetic communication, creative cooperation, and self-renewal.

Curran, D. (1983). *Traits of a healthy family.* San Francisco: Harper & Row. Based on a survey of over 500 professionals who work with families, Curran has identified fifteen characteristics of maturity within the home. Healthy home life, she deduces, is based on quality relationships, including her discoveries that effective families: communicate and listen well; affirm and support their members; teach respect for others; develop trust; exhibit humor and a sense of play; share responsibility; prescriptively teach right from wrong; provide a sense of kinship, with value traditions; display a balance of interpersonal interaction; have a common set of religious beliefs; respect individual autonomy and privacy; value service to others; foster meaningful conversation with its members at mealtime; share leisure experiences; and admit to problems, while seeking help. A complementary fifty-five minute videotape (1987) is also available, along with a study guide (1988).

Habermas, R. (1993). Does Peter Pan corrupt our children? *Christianity Today*, pp. 30–33. Adult caregivers must allow kids to be kids. If children are forced to be miniature adults, it's possible that five other misconceptions about a child's faith and psychological development will be violated: childlikeness will not be inherently valued; healthy and necessary forms of doubt (vs. disbelief) will not be prized; ownership of faith will be neglected; beliefs will be restricted to simplistic slogans; and faith will be perceived as static and never-changing.

————. (1989). "Doubt is not a four-letter word." *Religious Education, 83*(3), 402–410. This article deals with three diverse types of biblical doubt and Christ's consistent response to them. Also, it identifies a handful of development theorists who assess the value of these personal struggles which shape identity. Finally, a contemporary survey concerning the benefits of doubt is summarized, along with ministry implications.

Habermas, R. & K. Issler. (1992). *Teaching for reconciliation*. Grand Rapids: Baker. A foundations-to-practice text, this book establishes a philosophy of Christian education based on the educational views of William Frankena. A series of goals (ultimate, intermediate, and immediate) are combined with the influence of personal perspectives and learning theories, to frame this instructional model. Reconciliation reflects the authors' suggestion for the church's lifelong objective. Age-specific implications for curriculum and the classroom are drawn for children, youth, and adults.

Marcia, J. (1967). Ego identity status: Relationship to change in self-esteem, "general maladjustment," and authoritarianism. *Journal of Personality, 35,* 118–133. Based on Eriksonian theory, Marcia's work employs the two components of crisis and commitment to construct a matrix design for youth identity. Depending upon whether or not an older adolescent has personally encountered either (or both) of these two components, four possible states emerge: (1) the identity-diffused (or identity confused) person—one who has not experienced either crisis or commitment; (2) the foreclosure person—one who has not experienced crisis but who, nonetheless, has made commitments (usually those that have been superimposed by others); (3) the moratorium person—one who is actively struggling with doubts about identity, but has not yet reached any personal conclusions or commitments; and (4) the identity-achieved person—one who has experienced the turbulence of personal crisis and has made personal commitments of resolution concerning identity.

Palmer, P. (1983). *To know as we are known*. San Francisco: Harper San Francisco. This book attacks myths of education. Moreover, it reclaims the biblical meaning of maturity by offering a broader frame of reference. Spiritual formation, for Palmer, is not just a personal endeavor, it is interpersonal; it represents a community of relationships. Therefore, in education, spiritual formation is not just grounded on logic, it centers on love. Furthermore, implicit instruction is as significant as explicit; it's not just "what" is said that matters, "how" it is said also matters.

Postman, N. (1982). *The disappearance of childhood.* New York: Delacorte. A thought-provoking account of how childhood, as it once was known, is virtually absent in our society. Postman addresses the causes—primarily the media, with their opposing value system, which prevents parents from safeguarding their children from "adult" knowledge of violence and sexuality; he identifies the effects—a prominent threat to the healthy development of children; and he suggests a few responsible steps to take, like protecting children from the readily accessible media, especially television.

Sell, C. (1981). *Family ministry.* Grand Rapids: Zondervan. The author clarifies his broad topic, saying that family ministry consists of two processes: Christian education of the home and Christian education in the home. The former refers to all support agencies, especially the church, which serves members of the family (e.g., local youth outreach and fellowship). The latter speaks of all resources within the nuclear family which attend to spiritual formation. Among other issues in this comprehensive work, the author cites arguments that value the first category (i.e., church-centered Christian education), as well as the second category (i.e., family-centered Christian education). He concludes with a variety of helpful programs for family nurture. See especially chapters 16–20.

Strommen, M. & Strommen, A. (1993). *Five cries of parents.* San Francisco: Harper San Francisco. In a thorough research of more than 8,000 young teens and 10,000 parents, the authors discern five overarching concerns of caregivers in the home: the need for understanding both self and adolescent son or daughter; the desire for a close family; the plea for moral behavior; the hope for shared faith; and the call for outside help. The fourth need, the cry for shared faith (chap. 6), is particularly relevant to the subject of spiritual formation within families. Specifically, the discussion on religious doubt (pp. 139–141) offers insight for parents.

THE PIETISTIC TRADITION IN EVANGELICAL SPIRITUALITY: A BIBLIOGRAPHIC ESSAY
Lyle W. Dorsett

In the seventeenth century, a reform impulse known as pietism burst forth among European Christians. Starting first among Lutherans and then spreading to all quarters of Protestant Christendom, this powerful renewal movement eventually penetrated much of the world.

Pietism is alive and thriving in the late twentieth century. Indeed, it is doing for these times what it has done for over three centuries, continually calling Christians to a heartfelt faith manifested in the practical, everyday walk of life.

Pietists, like all orthodox Protestants, have always espoused justification of sinners by grace through faith in the Lord Jesus Christ. They also have held a high view of the Bible, believing it to be God's special revelation of His will for all of His people. But pietists have also advocated things that make them unique among the reformers. First of all, pietists advocate a personal, spiritual new birth manifested in a heartfelt personal relationship with Jesus Christ. This personal relationship must be experienced individually, not just as part of a community of the faithful. This experiential faith, to be valid, should bring assurance of salvation, a new life of piety or holy living, and a zeal for evangelism and missions. Furthermore, the Pietist movement has always been marked by a profound social consciousness that has usually been applied through outreach and care for the poor, especially widows, orphans, prisoners, and those locked in the chains of prostitution and alcohol or drug addiction.

With plenty of history to support them, pietists argue that they do not represent a new trend in Christianity. Instead, they see themselves calling the church back to its first-century origins when the faithful poured everything they had, including their lives, into being disciples of the Lord Jesus Christ. Mere intellectual assent to a body of doctrine and recitation of a creed were never enough for the early Christians. On the contrary, they worshiped the Lord with mind, yes, but also with heart and soul and very life itself.

Just as Martin Luther, John Calvin, and the other reformers called the church back to grace, faith, and the Scriptures, so a host of others followed in the footsteps of Philip Jakob Spener and August Hermann Francke. In the late 1600s, these German Lutherans called their fellow Protestants to turn away from an increasingly cold and calcified orthodoxy and liturgy. As leaders of a movement that called for faith manifested in heart and hands as well as head, these men and their disciples started small groups and schools; they built orphanages and sent out evangelists. The flames that they started spread over time and space, reaching the Moravian Church and Count Zinzendorf, and eventually through him and others all the way to John Wesley and the Methodist movement that burned throughout the United Kingdom in the eighteenth century. These fires of pietism also consumed many Puritans in the United Kingdom, and both they and the Wesleyans carried the message of pietism to North America and the uttermost parts of the earth.

By the nineteenth century, there were strains of pietistic teaching and expression in many Protestant denominations. Where the movement was not welcome—and it frequently met with opposition from inside the colleges and hierarchies of the denominations—it was kept alive by zealous men and women like Catherine and William Booth in England and A.B. Simpson in North America. The Booths left the Methodist Church and started the Salvation Army when they were made unwelcome in increasingly inhospitable English Methodism. And A.B. Simpson quietly slipped away from his North American Presbyterian moorings and formed the Christian and Missionary Alliance.

It can be misleading to label people, inasmuch as some men and women can be identified with only part of what has traditionally been identified as pietism. Also, it is important to understand that some Christians chafe at labels, especially those that are viewed as pejorative or restrictive. Suffice it to say that the seeds of pietism have taken hold in fertile ground for 300 years. The plants have continued to blossom, bear fruit, and reproduce through sermons and mentoring processes but most importantly through the publication and dissemination of devotional literature. It is to some of these pietistic or so-called "deeper life" authors that I now turn.

In the late nineteenth and early twentieth centuries a number of women and men wrote books on various devotional topics that have continued to be extremely useful in spiritual formation. These books have become classics in the fields of devotional and disciple-making literature.

In the next few pages, I will focus on a few key authors and their writings. These works might not completely fit into the pietistic tradition, but they are informed and inspired by it, and they are helpful in pointing growing disciples to the deeper life — the life of vital, heartfelt, personal, experiential Christianity.

E.M. BOUNDS (1835–1913)

Edward McKendree Bounds was born and raised in Missouri. After a brief time as a lawyer, he converted to Christianity and felt constrained to preach the Gospel. He was a chaplain during the Civil War and held pastorates before and after that great conflict. He also served as an editor for the weekly newspaper of the Methodist-Episcopal Church. Bounds is best known for his little book *Power through Prayer*. Originally published in 1907, this book has never been out of print, although it has sometimes appeared under the title *Preacher and Prayer*. Seven other books on prayer by Bounds are still in print: *Purpose in Prayer* (1920); *Prayer and Praying Men* (1921); *The Possibility of Prayer* (1923); *The Reality of Prayer* (1924); *The Essentials of Prayer* (1925); *The Necessity of Prayer* (1929); *The Weapon of Prayer* (1931). A number of Bounds' best devotional writings have only recently been reprinted from the pages of 1890s Methodist newspapers. These are now available in the back of the biography by Lyle W. Dorsett entitled *E.M. Bounds: Man of Prayer* (1991).

SAMUEL LOGAN BRENGLE (1860–1936)

S.L. Brengle gave up a prestigious pulpit to become a cadet in the Salvation Army, but God eventually lifted up this downwardly mobile salvationist enlisted man. He served the organization for forty years, and eventually became its spiritual director. Brengle wrote many books of a devotional nature. Among his best are: *Heart Talks on Holiness* (1900); *The Soul-Winner's Secret* (1903); *When the Holy Ghost Is Come* (1909). A biography of Brengle by C.H. Hall, *Samuel Logan Brengle: Portrait of a Prophet* (1933), is an extremely encouraging and inspirational book.

AMY CARMICHAEL (1867–1951)

No listing of important books on Christian spirituality would be complete without works by Amy Carmichael. One of the most important spiritual writers of the twentieth century, this woman was born in Northern Ireland, converted in early life, and then sent to Japan and finally to India by people active in the Keswick movement. A missionary to orphans most of her adult life, Carmichael wrote dozens of books. Some of her works still in print continue to inspire men and women: *Lotus Buds* (1908); *Mimosa* (1924); *Gold Cord* (1932); *God's Missionary* (1939); *His Thoughts Said . . . His Father Said* (1941); *Edges of His Ways* (1955).

OSWALD CHAMBERS (1874–1917)

Born in Scotland in 1874, Oswald Chambers spent most of his life in Scotland and England. Educated at Edinburgh University at then the Dunoon Gospel Training College near Glasgow, he preached and taught the Bible throughout the United Kingdom and the United States. He and his wife opened a Bible Training School in London. They oversaw the educational institute until Chambers went out to Egypt to serve British soldiers as a Y.M.C.A. chaplain. He died in Egypt in 1917, but his ministry lives on. Soon thereafter, his wife Biddy began publishing her verbatim notes of his lectures. Over two dozen of these books were published in the early years after Chambers' death. The most famous is the best-selling daily devotional work, *My Utmost for His Highest* (1935). Still *Higher for His Highest* (1970) is helpful, but not nearly as good as the earlier book or a volume of recently discovered writings now in print and edited by Glen D. Black, *Devotions for a Deeper Life* (1986).

ROSALIND GOFORTH (1864–1942)

In 1888, Rosalind Goforth and her husband Jonathan left their Canadian home and went to China as missionaries. Although nearly killed by Chinese warriors during the Boxer Uprising in 1900, they faithfully ministered in that vast country until their failing health forced them home in 1934. During the remaining years of her life Rosalind Goforth wrote three books that continue to inspire people to pray and to consider missions for their life's work: *Goforth of China* (1937); *How I Know God Answers Prayers* (1939); *Climbing: Memoirs of a Missionary's Wife* (1940).

ADONIRAM JUDSON GORDON (1836–1895)

A.J. Gordon, a Baptist minister, was born in New Hampshire. College and seminary educated, he pastored churches in Boston throughout his rather brief life. Besides preaching, he established a school to train missionaries and pastors and also wrote six books. Among his works still quite helpful are: *How Christ Came to Church* (1893); *The Holy Spirit in Missions* (1893); and *The Ministry of the Spirit* (1894).

E. STANLEY JONES (1884–1973)

An American who served as a missionary to India from 1907 to 1973, Jones traveled all over the world and preached the Gospel to uncounted thousands. His writings have blessed people for decades. One of his major works still in print is: *Abundant*

Living (1960). *The Song of Ascents: A Spiritual Autobiography* (1968) is out of print but well worth searching for.

ROBERT MURRAY MCCHEYNE (1814–1843)

Only twenty-nine years old when he died, McCheyne nevertheless left a profound mark that can be observed over a century and a half after his death. A pastor in Dundee, Scotland, his sermons still bless us in a paperbound reprint of *Sermons* (1843). By far his most influential and penetrating words are preserved in A.A. Bonar's *Memoir and Remains of Robert Murray McCheyne* (1843). The Banner of Truth in Scotland and the United States keeps both works in print.

CATHERINE MARSHALL (1914–1983)

For over three decades, Catherine Marshall lived in obscurity. Raised in a small southern American city, educated at Agnes Scott College, she married Peter Marshall who became a famous preacher and U.S. Senate chaplain. In the wake of his early and unexpected death in 1949, Catherine was left with no money and their little boy to raise. After much prayer, she decided to pursue her long-time ambition of writing. Beginning with an edited volume of Peter Marshall's sermons, *Mr. Jones, Meet the Master* (1950), she embarked upon a writing career that produced twenty-one books and numerous articles. No woman writer has wielded such enormous influence on the spiritual development of women and men in this century. Her books are all in print. The major works are: *A Man Called Peter* (1951); *To Live Again* (1957); *Beyond Ourselves* (1961); *Christy* (1967); *Something More* (1974); *Adventures in Prayer* (1975); *The Helper* (1978); *Meeting God at Every Turn* (1980).

F.B. MEYER (1874–1929)

Englishman F.B. Meyer was a pastor, teacher, counselor, and friend to numerous people during an unusually fruitful life.

He was renowned for his deeply spiritual teaching. Among the people he tremendously influenced for kingdom usefulness was Oswald Chambers. Meyer, in turn, merely passed on what he had learned from others, especially D.L. Moody who had an indelible influence on this Englishman's preaching and teaching style. Meyer, a deeply spiritual man who labored over his writings and never compromised biblical doctrines, wrote over seventy books, including a dozen major works. Besides his works on books of the Bible such as *The Way into the Holiest* (1893) on Hebrews, *Exodus*, 2 vols. (1911–1913), and *Trial by Fire* (1895) on 1 Peter, his greatest impact has come through *The Call and Challenge of the Unseen* (1928) and *Secrets of Christian Living* (1978).

GEORGE MUELLER (1805-1898)

During his lifetime this German-born minister and missionary moved to England, planted churches, and housed, fed, clothed, educated, and made Christian disciples of thousands of orphans from the streets of Victorian England. Although he never asked for money, God supplied all his needs through prayer. No Christian who reads Mueller's autobiography can fail to be encouraged to trust God more. Indeed, reading *A Life of Trust* (1870) has been a life-changing experience for countless people. This volume has been printed, reprinted, and abridged for nearly 130 years.

ANDREW MURRAY (1828–1917)

Born in South Africa and educated in Scotland and Holland, Murray was ordained in the Dutch Reformed Church. During his rich, long life he traveled the world to encourage Christians to the deeper spiritual life, active as a churchman, educator, and author. He published over 250 books and tracts while he pastored, established missionary schools, and discipled pastors and missionaries. His most significant books include: *With Christ in the School of Prayer* (1885); *Abide in Christ* (1882); and *Absolute Surrender* (1895).

WATCHMAN NEE (1903–1972)

Ni Shu-tsu or Henry Nee was born in Foochow, China. He had an influential life as a preacher, evangelist, and Bible teacher. His ministry continues in those he converted and discipled, and it lives on through his widely read books that have been translated into many languages. Perhaps his most famous book is *The Normal Christian Life* (1957). Also widely read and distributed are *Sit, Walk, Stand* (1957) and *What Shall This Man Do?* (1961).

JESSIE PENN-LEWIS (1861–1927)

One of the key participants in the great Welsh Revival, Jessie Penn-Lewis was never satisfied with just being converted. Indeed, she constantly sought to know God better and receive all that His grace would bestow upon her. She traveled widely, taking her deeper life messages to Keswick, England, Russia, India, and other parts of the world. Writing was an important element in her ministry. She is best known for *War on the Saints* (1913), one of the first major books on spiritual warfare to be published in this century. *Work of the Holy Spirit* (n.d.) and *Life in the Spirit* (n.d.) are two of her important books still in print.

A.B. SIMPSON (1843–1919)

Simpson was born in Canada but spent most of his post-college years in the United States. Educated at Knox College in Toronto, he became a Presbyterian minister and served churches in Toronto, Louisville, and New York City. Unable to get any of his congregations to share his vision to reach the poor and the unevangelized, he resigned his New York church, rented a facility, and ultimately founded the Christian and Missionary Alliance. He did the work of an evangelist, pastored churches, launched urban mission facilities, and promoted world missions. The editor and author of numerous publications, he is still widely read by Christians who seek a richer walk with God.

His most widely acclaimed works include: *When the Comforter Came* (1911); *Christ Life* (1893); *Walking in the Spirit* (n.d.); *Christ in All the Bible* (1885).

AIDEN WILSON TOZER (1897–1963)

Probably no twentieth-century devotional author is read more than A.W. Tozer. He was born in rural Pennsylvania and had little formal schooling. Never able to graduate from high school, Tozer nevertheless read widely and incessantly. Although self-taught, he was one of the best educated clergymen in North America. This Christian and Missionary Alliance minister was extremely humble and only moderately popular during his lifetime. He would be surprised to know that his sermons and magazine columns are now brought out in widely read books. Among his most popular devotional titles are *The Knowledge of the Holy* (1961); *The Root of the Righteous* (1955); *The Pursuit of God* (1948); and *That Incredible Christian* (1964).

Readers interested in reading more on these and other similarly inclined authors should consult Steven Barabas, *So Great Salvation: The History and Message of the Keswick Convention* (n.d.), as well as two books by Warren Wiersbe, *Walking with the Giants* (1976) and *Listening to the Giants* (1980).

CONCLUSION

Among other things, evangelicalism's contribution to Christian spirituality has been the clear conviction that spirituality is not the gradual evolution of the person into God-centeredness. Rather, evangelical spirituality represents a radical departure in that begins with repentance and personal brokenness. But as with any movement, evangelical spirituality has been distorted at times. One distortion has come from those who construe it exclusively as a personal religion of the heart that need not validate itself by behavioral change. Others so emphasize its democratic bent that they fail to be strengthened and encouraged by the practices and stories of the great spiritual writers of the church's past.

However, evangelicalism continues to be a strong movement today and, as its best in times past, has shown itself open to learn from other perspectives on spirituality. Specifically, mainline evangelicalism has been enriched in the last generation by the Charismatic emphasis on the gifts of the Spirit and the Spirit-filled life and the example of Christians who reject the popular warm-heart-versus-social-justice dichotomy and emphasize the need for service and identification with the poor and disenfranchised.

Because of its commitment to always being reformed and always growing in its conformity to Christ's commands, evangelicalism is a movement that is always undergoing self-examination. Today's radically secular culture offers new challenges for spiritual formation. While keeping an emphasis on Scripture, prayer, and repentance today, evangelicals must seek to foster holy living without being legalistic and find ways of being more open to the contemplative side of our faith without minimizing Scripture as our sure guide. Many of us have learned much about formation through the faithful examples of believers in the two thirds world who have demonstrated faithfulness to the Savior at great personal cost. Despite the rich literature and wise advice on this subject, in the end it is those who simply follow the teaching of Jesus and pattern their life after His who will be richly rewarded through the spiritual growth this fosters.

For Further Reading

Brown, D. (1978). *Understanding pietism.* Grand Rapids: Eerdmans. A helpful introduction to the topic.

Erb, P. (Ed.). (1983). *Pietists: Selected writings.* New York: Paulist. A collection of key writing from this movement which is so important to modern evangelicalism.

Foster, R., & Smith, J. (Eds.). *Devotional classics.* San Francisco: HarperSan Francisco. In this volume the authors seek to show how the devotional life of the Christian can be enriched by studying writings from the diverse traditions within broad evangelical spirituality.

McGinn, B., Meyendorff, J., & Raitt, J. (Eds.) (1987). *Christian spirituality: High middle ages and reformation.* New York: Crossroads. A collection of well-written bibliographic essays on spirituality.

Meyendorff J., Dupre, L., & Saliers, D. (Eds.). (1989). *Christian spirituality: Post-reformation and modern.* New York: Crossroads. Another collection of well-written bibliographic essays on spirituality.

Stoeffler, F. (Ed.). (1976). *Continental pietism and early American Christianity.* Grand Rapids: Eerdmans. Traces development of pietism in early America.

_____. (1971). *The rise of evangelical pietism.* Leiden: E.J. Brill. A balanced historical treatment of pietism with rich bibliographic resources.

Toon, P. (1988). *From mind to heart: Christian meditation today.* Grand Rapids: Baker. A practical and historical survey of how meditation has been practiced in the broad evangelical tradition.

Annotated Bibliography of Resources
James C. Wilhoit

Spiritual formation has been the subject of thoughtful writers for twenty centuries. In this bibliography we have identified books that have a proven track record for helping individuals understand the process of discipleship and which, even more importantly, extend a warm invitation to embark on the path of spiritual growth. The following bibliography makes no claims of being exhaustive, but we believe these books will have special relevance to evangelical readers. We refer readers to Magill and McGreal's *Christian Spirituality* and to Foster and Smith's *Devotional Classics* for more comprehensive listings.

While there is no substitute for firsthand knowledge gained through the actual practice of the spiritual life, we must not discount the value of these written guides. Through the centuries men and women have found the spiritual writers to provide needed help, guidance, and inspiration.

GENERAL WORKS ON SPIRITUAL FORMATION

Foster, R.J. (1988). *Celebration of discipline* (Rev. ed.). San Francisco: Harper San Francisco. One of the few comprehensive treatments of the major spiritual disciplines, in addition to being a very readable and practical guide.

————. (1983). *Study guide for celebration of discipline.* New York: Harper & Row. A useful companion to Foster's

Celebration of discipline. It includes helpful reading lists and practical suggestions for beginning the various disciplines.

Foster, R., & Smith, J. (Eds.). (1993). *Devotional classics: Selected readings for individuals and groups.* New York: HarperCollins. A wonderful collection of fifty-two highly edited and abridged readings in the spiritual life. These selections make the great masters accessible to all readers and provide a good place to turn when looking for books in the area of spirituality.

Magill, F., & McGreal, I. (Eds.). (1988). *Christian spirituality: The essential guide to the most influential writings of the Christian tradition.* San Francisco: Harper & Row. A chronologically arranged guide to classics in Christian spirituality. Each classic is devoted a brief chapter, which provides a summary of the book and a brief bibliography.

Nouwen, H. (1975). *Reaching out.* Garden City, NJ: Doubleday. A clearly written brief introduction to what the author sees as the three movements of the spiritual life: reaching out to our innermost self, our fellow human beings, and to God.

Postema, D. (1983). *Space for God.* Grand Rapids: Bible Way. "In this book Don Postema offers us a space to live gratefully in the presence of God. He gives us his personal spiritual journey, his experience in Christian ministry, his wide interest in art and literature, and most of all his own hospitable personality as the space in which we, who read this book, can listen fearlessly to God's own voice" (from the preface by Henri Nouwen).

Richards, L. (1987). *A practical theology of spirituality.* Grand Rapids: Zondervan. A very readable and practical introduction to the whole area of developing a deeper spiritual life. Many suggestions on what to try.

Whitney, D. (1991). *Spiritual disciplines for the Christian life.* Colorado Springs: NavPress. A good introduction to the spiritual disciplines, with a strong emphasis on meditation and Bible study.

Willard, D. (1988). *The spirit of the disciplines.* New York: Harper & Row. Written to explain how God changes lives. The author is at his best when he explains why the yoke of Christ is easy and how true discipleship requires a change that is far deeper than mere behavior.

PRAYER (GENERAL)

Anonymous. (1978). *The way of the pilgrim* (Helen Bacovcin, Trans.). New York: Doubleday. A spiritual classic written by an unknown nineteenth-century Russian peasant who traveled across Russia seeking guidance on "how to pray without ceasing." He finds his answer in repeatedly praying the "Jesus Prayer." Part of its value comes from seeing a man who passionately loves God and humbly serves with love everyone he meets.

Appleton, G. (Ed.). (1985). *The Oxford book of prayer.* New York: Oxford Univ. Press. A well-organized and comprehensive collection of prayer drawn from around the world and across the centuries.

Baillie, J. (1949). *A diary of private prayer.* New York: Scribners. A collection of thoughtful prayers for morning and evening which can easily be personalized.

Bloesch, D. (1988). *The struggle of prayer.* Colorado Springs: Helmers & Howard. An evangelical theology of prayer. The author addresses important issues related to both the practice and theology of prayer. He makes a case for viewing prayer as the heart of spirituality.

Bloom, A. (1970). *Beginning to pray.* New York: Paulist. Covers the basic issues of what prayer is and what it means to pray. Written by a Russian Orthodox archbishop for "people who have never prayed before," it has become a modern spiritual classic. Useful for people at all levels of spiritual development.

Bounds, E.M. (1982). *Power through prayer*. Springdale, PA: Whitaker. A brief classic by a pastor who was personally committed to prayer and whose writings reflect his concern that pastors see prayer as their first calling. This book focuses special attention on the "preacher and prayer."

Bryant, D. (1984). *Concerts of prayer*. Ventura, CA: Regal. A description of a powerful movement of group prayer directed toward world evangelization.

Christenson, E. (1975). *What happens when women pray*. Wheaton, IL: Victor. A guide to developing a praying church which grows out of the author's experience in her church and seminar work on prayer. While based on the stories of her work with women, its principles go beyond the title.

Duewel, W. (1986). *Touch the world through prayer*. Grand Rapids: Francis Asbury/Zondervan. A very practical guide to intercessory prayer.

Foster, R. (1992). *Prayer: Finding the heart's true home*. San Francisco: Harper San Francisco. An inviting explanation of various types of prayer. The subtitle tells much about the author's notion of prayer. A must read for those serious about prayer.

Grou, J. (1982). *How to pray*. Greenwood, SC: Attic. A wonderful work on prayer by an eighteenth-century Jesuit. It is a short and well-written presentation of the essence, use, and effectiveness of prayer. More explicitly biblical than many other writers.

Hunter, W. (1986). *The God who hears*. Downers Grove, IL: InterVarsity. This is a God-centered discussion of prayer. It gives a good presentation of both the essence of prayer and the character of God. Deals with commonly asked questions about prayer's purpose, effectiveness, and necessity.

Hybels, B. (1988). *Too busy not to pray*. Downers Grove, IL: InterVarsity. A practical guide to establishing a prayer life. It emphasizes the need for one's prayer life to include both intercession and listening.

Hallesby, O. (1975). *Prayer* (Clarence J. Carlsen, Trans.). Minneapolis: Augsburg. A simple and attractive treatment of prayer that places emphasis on the character qualities, humility, and simplicity needed for effective prayer. Aimed at the maturing Christian who desires a more effective and meaningful prayer life.

PRAYING SCRIPTURE

Bonhoeffer, D. (1970). *Psalms: The prayer book of the Bible* (James H. Burtness, Trans.). Minneapolis: Augsburg. A small volume on using the Psalms as the basis of one's praying.

Law, P. (Ed.). (1988). *Praying with the New Testament*. London: SPCK. New Testament passages edited and arranged to serve as a guide to individual and corporate prayer. The passages are arranged into chapters which focus on major issues in our lives.

————. (Ed.). (1989). *Praying with the Old Testament*. London: SPCK. Similar to the previous volume, but organized around different topics, and with more emphasis on confession.

Smith, M. (1989). *The word is very near you: A guide to praying with Scripture*. Cambridge, MA: Cowley. A guide to both the theology and practice of Scripture-based prayer. Unfortunately, it adopts a very naturalistic view of Scripture.

LISTENING PRAYER/SOLITUDE

Brother Lawrence. (1977). *The practice of the presence of God* (John J. Delaney, Trans.). Garden City, NY: Doubleday.

The personal account of a man devoted to a single-minded concern for God.

de Caussade, J. (1982). *The sacrament of the present moment.* San Francisco: Harper & Row. This book is taken from a series of letters on the spiritual life. The author warns about the busyness of activistic piety and urges that we develop the virtue of self-abandonment. He avoids the quietism that dominates so much mystical thought.

Huggett, J. (1986). *The joy of listening to God.* Downers Grove, IL: InterVarsity. Practical advice on using prayer to listen and contemplate. The book is based on the author's firsthand experience of learning to wait upon God and enjoy His presence.

Laubach, F. (1946). *Prayer, the most powerful force in the world.* New York: Revell. Laubach's writings reveal a man with love for humanity; he was a pioneer in the modern literacy movement, which grew out of his deep love for Christ. His various books reveal his systematic efforts to cultivate a constant awareness of God.

HEALING PRAYER

Augsburger, D. (1981). *Caring enough to forgive.* Ventura, CA: Regal. A thoughtful treatment of the practical aspects of forgiveness. The book is explicitly biblical and contains many examples from the author's own ministry.

Ensley, E. (1988). *Prayer that heals our emotions.* San Francisco: Harper & Row. An example of a whole genre of books which emphasize the power of visualized prayer to heal and restore. A collection of experiential essays on the power of prayer, most are followed by "prayer experiences" and a "scriptural journey" designed to ensure the healing process.

MacNutt, F. (1985). *The power to heal.* Notre Dame, IN: Ave Maria. Very personal accounts of healing by an influential leader of the Catholic charismatic movement.

Miller, K. (1991). *A hunger for healing.* San Francisco: Harper & Row. A very engaging presentation of the "twelve steps" from a Christian perspective.

Payne, L. (1989). *The healing presence.* Wheaton, IL: Crossway. A practical guide concerning how one can cultivate an awareness of God's presence and receive healing through this relationship.

————. (1991). *Restoring the Christian soul through prayer.* Wheaton, IL: Crossway. A masterful treatment of some spiritual problems which hinder so many. Clear suggestions on how to overcome self-hatred and bitterness are given.

Smedes, L. (1984). *Forgive and forget.* San Francisco: Harper & Row. A key book to understanding forgiveness, Smedes writes with the wisdom of a counselor and the heart of a pastor.

FASTING

Smith, D. (1954). *Fasting: A neglected discipline.* Fort Washington, PA: Christian Literature Crusade. One of the first contemporary book length evangelical treatments of fasting — clear and concise.

Wallis, A. (1968). *God's chosen fast: A spiritual and practical guide to fasting.* Fort Washington, PA: Christian Literature Crusade. A biblically based call to fasting. Offers both useful theory and practical advice.

MEDITATION

Peterson, E. (1989). *Answering God: The psalms as tools for prayer.* New York: Harper & Row. An invitation to turn the Psalms into a prayer book. Filled with both concrete guidance and inspiring insights.

Toon, P. (1988). *From mind to heart: Christian meditation today.* Grand Rapids: Baker. An introduction to meditation. The author does a good job of explaining the essence of Christian meditation. He wisely distinguishes meditation from other spiritual disciplines. Looks at meditation from biblical examples and different theological traditions.

REFERENCES

Allen, R., & Gordon, B. (1982). *Worship: Rediscovering the missing jewel.* Portland: Multnomah.

Anderson, N. (1981). *God's Word for God's world.* London: Hodder and Stoughton.

Anonymous. (1953). Didache. In C.C. Richardson (Ed.), *Early Christian fathers* (pp. 171–179). Philadelphia: Westminster.

Anonymous. (1972a). Letter to the churches of Lyons and Vienna. In H. Musurillo (Ed.), *The acts of the Christian martyrs* (pp. 62–85). Oxford: Clarendon.

————. (1972b). Martyrdom of Polycarp. In H. Musurillo (Ed.), *The acts of the Christian martyrs* (pp. 2–21). Oxford: Clarendon.

————. (1972c). Martyrdom of Perpetua and Felicitas. In H. Musurillo (Ed.), *The acts of the Christian martyrs* (pp. 106–131). Oxford: Clarendon.

Anthony, M. (Ed.). (1992). *Foundations of ministry: An introduction to Christian education for a new generation.* Wheaton, IL: BridgePoint/Victor.

Athanasius (1980). Letter to Marcellinus. In R.C. Gregg (Ed.), *The life of Anthony and the letter to Marcellinus* (pp. 101–129). New York: Paulist.

Augustine (1953). The Teacher. In *Augustine: Earlier writings.* Philadelphia: Westminster.

Baillie, J. (1949). *A diary of private prayer.* New York: Scribners.

Balswick, J., & Balswick, J. (1991). *The family: A Christian perspective on the contemporary home*. Grand Rapids: Baker.

Barna, G. (1990). *The frog in the kettle*. Ventura, CA: Regal.

_____. (1991). *The Barna report: What Americans believe*. Ventura, CA: Regal.

Barna Research Group (1991). *Leadership, 13*(1).

Barna Research Group (1992). To Verify. *Leadership, 13*(1).

Barron, R., Brubaker, J.O., & Clark, R. (1989). *Understanding people* (3rd ed.). Wheaton, IL: Evangelical Training Association.

Baxter, R. (1962). *The saint's everlasting rest*. Westwood, NJ: Revell.

Benson, P.L. & Elkin, C. (1990). *Effective Christian education: A national study of Protestant congregations: A summary report on faith, loyalty, and congregational life*. Minneapolis: Search Institute.

Bergen, F. (Ed.). (1906). *Autobiography of George Mueller*. London: J. Nisbet.

Bianchi, E. (1982). *Aging is a spiritual journey*. New York: Crossroad.

Bloesch, D. (1978). *Essentials of evangelical theology*. San Francisco: Harper & Row.

Bloesch, D. (1991). Lost in the mystical myths. *Christianity Today, 35*(9) 22–24.

Bloom, H. (1992). *The American religion*. New York: Simon & Schuster.

Bonhoeffer, D. (1979). *The cost of discipleship*. New York: Macmillan.

Bouyer, L. (1963). *The spirituality of the New Testament and the fathers.* The History of Christian Spirituality, vol. 1 (M.P. Ryan, Trans.). New York: Desclee.

Boyer, E. (1988). *Finding God at home.* San Francisco: Harper and Row.

Bridge, W. (Ed.). (1989). *The works of the Reverend William Bridge.* Beaver Falls, PA: Soli Deo Gloria.

Bridges, J. (1991). *Transforming grace.* Colorado Springs: NavPress.

Bunyan, J. (1966). *Grace abounding to the chief of sinners and the pilgrim's progess from this world to that which is to come.* New York: Oxford Univ. Press.

Burns, J.P. (Ed.). (1981). *Theological anthropology.* Philadelphia: Fortress.

Cailliet, E. (1943). *The clue to Pascal.* Philadelphia: Westminster.

Calvin, J. (1961). *The epistles of Paul the apostle to the Romans and to the Thessalonians* (R. MacKenzie, Trans.). Grand Rapids: Eerdmans.

Chesterton, G.K. (1987). *St. Francis of Assisi.* Garden City: Doubleday Image.

Chitty, D.J. (1966). *The desert a city.* Oxford: Blackwell.

Clark, R.E., Johnson, L., & Sloat, A.K. (Eds.) (1991). *Christian education: Foundations for the future.* Chicago: Moody.

Clark, R.E., Brubaker, J., & Zuck, R.B. (Eds.) (1986). *Childhood education in the church.* Chicago: Moody.

Cochrane, A. (1962). *The church's confession under Hitler.* Philadelphia: Westminster.

Collinson, P. (1990). *The Elizabethian Puritan movement*. Oxford: Oxford Univ. Press.

Conwell, R. (1976). Acres of diamonds. In R.L. Ferm (Ed.), *Issues in American Protestantism: A documentary history from the Puritans to the present* (pp. 235-242). Gloucester: Peter Smith.

Cooke, B. (1970). *Christian community: Response to reality*. New York: Holt, Rinehart and Winston.

Cotton, J. (1963). Christian calling. In P. Miller, & T.H. Johnson (Eds.), *The Puritans*. New York: Harper.

Covey, S. (1989). *The seven habits of highly effective people*. New York: Simon & Schuster.

Craig, G. (1989). *Human development* (5th ed.). Englewood Cliffs, NJ: Prentice Hall.

Csikszentmihalyi, M., & Larson, R. (1986). *Being adolescent: Conflict and growth in the teenage years*. New York: Basic.

Cullman, O. (1953). *Early Christian worship*. Naperville, IL: Allenson.

Cully, I. (1984). *Education for spiritual growth*. San Francisco: Harper and Row.

Curran, D. (1985). *Traits of a healthy family*. San Francisco: Harper & Row.

Cyprian (1981). Ad donatum. In A. Roberts, & J. Donaldson (Ed.), *The Ante-Nicene fathers* (pp. 275–280). Grand Rapids: Eerdmans.

Davies, H. (1948). *The worship of the English Puritans*. Westminster, U.K.: Dacre.

Dawson, C. (1960). *The historic reality of Christian culture*. New York: Harper and Bros.

DePrine, C. (1982). The corporate worship of God. *Reformation Sentinel, 5*(3).

Dillenberger, J. (Ed.). (1961). *Martin Luther: Selections from his writings.* New York: Doubleday.

Drushal, M. (1991). *On tablets of human hearts.* Grand Rapids: Zondervan.

Dychtwald, K. (1990). *Age wave.* New York: Bantam.

Elkind, D. (1984). *All grown up and no place to go: Teenagers in crisis.* Redding, MA: Addison-Wesley.

Enns, P.P. (1989). *The Moody handbook of theology.* Chicago: Moody.

Erickson, C.D. (1989). *Participating in worship: History, theory, & practice.* Louisville: Westminster/John Knox.

Erikson, E. (1986). *Childhood and society.* New York: Norton.

Extraordinary Synod of Catholic Bishops — 1985. (1985). *Message to the people of God.* Boston: Daughters of St. Paul.

Fahey, C. (1985). Toward an ethic for the Third Age. In L.D. Chiaventone & J.A. Armstrong (Eds.), *Affirmative aging: A resource for ministry* (pp. 12-23) San Francisco: Harper and Row.

Fee, G., & Stuart, D. (1982). *How to read the Bible for all its worth.* Grand Rapids: Academie/Zondervan.

Finn, T.M. (Ed.). (1992). *Early Christian baptism and the catechumenate: Italy, North Africa, and Egypt.* Collegeville, MN: Liturgical.

_____. (Ed.). (1992) Early Christian baptism and the catechumenate: West and east Syria. Collegeville, MN: Liturgical.

Fischer, K. (1985). *Winter grace: Spirituality for the later years.* New York: Paulist.

Flannery, A. (1975). *Vatican Council II: The Conciliar and Post Conciliar Documents.* Grand Rapids: Eerdmans.

Flynn, L.B. (1983). *Worship: Together we celebrate.* Wheaton, IL: Victor.

Fontaine, J. (1986). The practice of Christian life: The birth of the laity. In B. McGinn & J. Meyendorff (Eds.), *Christian spirituality, vol. 1: Origins to the twelfth century* (pp. 453–491). New York: Crossroad.

Forsyth, P.T. (1948). *The justification of God.* London: Independent.

Foster, R.J. (1988). *Celebration of discipline* (rev. ed.). San Francisco: Harper & Row.

Fowler, J.W. (1981). *Stages of faith.* San Francisco: Harper & Row.

———. (1992). Stages of faith: Reflections on a decade of dialogue. *Christian Education Journal, 13*(1).

Fowler, J.W., Nipkow, K.E., & Schweitzer, F. (1991). *Stages of faith and religious development: Implications for church, education & society.* New York: Crossroad.

Funk, W. (1960). *Word origins and their romantic stories.* New York: Bell.

Gangel, K.O., & Hendricks, H.G. (Eds.). (1988). *Christian educator's handbook on teaching.* Wheaton, IL: Victor.

Garland, D.E. (1992). The Lord's Prayer in the Gospel of Matthew. *Review and Expositor, 89,* 215–228.

George, B. (1989). *Classic Christianity.* Eugene, OR: Harvest House.

George, W., & George, K. (1961). *The Protestant mind of the English reformation, 1570–1640*. Princeton: Princeton Univ. Press.

Gesell, A. (1940). *The first five years of life: The preschool years*. New York: Harper & Brothers.

Gilkey, L. (1964). *How the church can minister to the world without losing itself*. New York: Harper & Row.

González, J.L. (1990). *Mañana: Christian theology from a Hispanic perspective*. Nashville: Abingdon.

Gorman, J. (1990). Christian Formation. *Christian Education Journal, 10*(2), 65–73.

Habermas, R. (1989). Doubt is not a four-letter word. *Religious Education, 84*(3), 402–410.

————. (1993). Does Peter Pan corrupt our children? *Christianity Today, 37*(3), pp. 30–33.

Habermas, R., & Issler, K. (1992). *Teaching for reconciliation*. Grand Rapids: Baker.

Hanko, R. (1983). The church and her creeds. *Standard Bearer, 59*(10), 236-238.

Hart, L.A. (1983). Three cheers for smaller failures? *Phi Delta Kappan, 64*(5), 303–308.

Hauerwas, S., & Westerhoff, J. (Eds.) (1992). *Schooling Christians: "Holy experiments" in American education*. Grand Rapids: Eerdmans.

Hill, C. (1964). *Society and Puritanism in Pre-Revolutionary England*. New York: Schocken.

Hippolytus (1992). Apostolic tradition. In G. Dix (Ed.), *The treatise on the apostolic tradition of St. Hippolytus of Rome* (pp. 1-72). London: Alban.

Howard, T. (1977). Contra Spontaneity. *HIS, 37*(5), pp. 16-21.

Hughes, R.K. (1991). *Disciplines of a godly man.* Wheaton, IL: Crossway.

Hunt, T.W., & Walker, C. (1988). *Disciple's prayer life: Walking in fellowship with God.* Nashville: The Sunday School Board of the Southern Baptist Convention.

Hustad, D.P. (1987). Let's not just praise the Lord. *Christianity Today, 31* (16), pp. 28-31.

Huxhold, H.N. (1982). What is the place of pastoral prayer in the context of worship? *Encounter, 43*, pp. 395-400.

Ignatius (1953). To the Romans. In C.C. Richardson (Ed.), *Early Christian fathers* (pp. 102–106). Philadelphia: Westminster.

Irenaeus (1985). Adversus haereses. In A. Roberts & J. Donaldson (Eds.), *The Ante-Nicene fathers* (pp. 315–567). Grand Rapids: Eerdmans.

Jenson, R.W. (1988). *America's theologian: A recommendation of Jonathan Edwards.* New York: Oxford Univ. Press.

Johnson, S. (1989). *Christian spiritual formation in the church and classroom.* Nashville: Abingdon.

John Paul II (1986). *Lord and Giver of life: Encyclical letter on the Holy Spirit in the life of the church and the world.* Washington, DC: United States Catholic Conference.

Kanter, R. (1972). *Commitment and community: Communes and utopias in sociological perspective.* Cambridge: Harvard Univ. Press.

Kaufmann, U. (1966). *The pilgrim's progress and traditions in Puritan meditation.* New Haven: Yale Univ. Press.

Kavanagh, A. (1990). Catechesis: Formation in stages. In M.W. Merriman (Ed.), *The baptismal mystery and the catechumenate* (pp. 36–52). New York: Church Hymnal.

Kreeft, P. (1988). *Fundamentals of the faith.* San Francisco: Ignatius.

Larkin, E. (1981). *Silent presence.* Denville, NJ: Dimension.

Laux, J. (1989). *Church history.* Rockford, IL: TAN.

Lavos, D. (1990). Searching for abundant life. *United Church News, 6*(9), 4.

Lea, L. (1987). *Could you not tarry one hour?* Altamonte Springs, FL: Creation House.

Lee, P. (1987). *Against the Protestant Gnostics.* New York: Oxford Univ. Press.

Lewis, C.S. (1960). *The four loves.* New York: Harcourt, Brace.

———. (1963). *Letters to Malcolm: Chiefly on prayer.* New York: Harcourt, Brace.

———. (1970a). Dogma and the universe. In W. Hooper (Ed.), *God in the dock* (pp. 38–47). Grand Rapids: Eerdmans.

———. (1970b). On the transmission of Christianity. In W. Hooper (Ed.), *God in the dock* (pp. 114–119). Grand Rapids: Eerdmans.

Lewis, P. (1977). *The genius of Puritanism.* Haywards Heath U.K.: Carey.

Lovelace, R. (1988). *Evangelicalism: A tradition of spiritual renewal.* Paper presented at To Serve the Present Age: Consultation on Evangelicals and American Public Life. Philadelphia, PA.

Luther, M. (1953). *A commentary on St. Paul's epistle to the Galatians* (Philip Watson, Trans.). London: James Clarke.

MacArthur, J. (1983). *The ultimate priority.* Chicago: Moody.

Mackay, J. (1969). *Christian reality and appearance.* Richmond, VA: John Knox.

Marcia, J. (1967). Ego identity status: Relationship to change in self-esteem, "general maladjustment," and authoritarianism. *Journal of Personality, 35,* 118–133.

Martin, F. (1990). *The Life-changer.* Ann Arbor, MI: Servant.

Martin, R.P. (1983). New Testament hymns: Background and development. *The Expositor Times, 94,* pp. 132-136

Maves, P. (1986). *Faith for the older years.* Minneapolis: Augsburg.

Maximus the Confesser (1985). Mystagogy. In G.C. Berthold (Ed.), *Selected writings* (pp. 181–214). New York: Paulist.

McDaniel, J.B. (1990). *Earth, sky, gods & mortals: Developing an ecological spirituality.* Mystic, CN: Twenty-Third Pubs.

McDonnell, K., & Montague, G. (1991). *Fanning the flame: What does baptism in the Holy Spirit have to do with Christian initiation?* Collegeville, MN: Liturgical.

McFadden, S. (1990). Authentic humor as an expression of spiritual maturity. *Journal of Religious Gerontology* 7 (1-2), pp. 131-142.

McGee, J. (1976). *The godly man in Stuart England: Anglicans, Puritans, and the two tables.* New Haven: Yale Univ. Press.

McGrath, A. (1988). *Reformation thought: An introduction.* New York: Blackwell.

McGuire, M.B. (1990). Religion and the body: Rematerializing the human body in the social sciences of religion. *Journal for the Scientific Study of Religion, 29,* 293–296.

Merton, T. (1970). *The wisdom of the desert.* New York: New Directions.

Meyendorff, J. (1986). Liturgy and spirituality, Part 1: Eastern liturgical theology. In B. McGinn & J. Meyendorff (Eds.), *Christian spirituality, vol. 1: Origins to the twelfth century* (pp. 350–363). New York: Crossroad.

Miller, P., & Johnson, T.H. (Eds.). (1963). *The Puritans* (rev. ed.). New York: Harper.

Morgan, E. (1966). *The Puritan family: Religion and domestic relations in seventeenth-century New England.* New York: Harper & Row.

Niebuhr, R. (1937). *The kingdom of God in America.* New York: Harper & Row.

Norris, R. (1990). The result of the loss of baptismal discipline. In M.W. Merriman (Eds.), *The baptismal mystery and the catechumenate* (pp. 20–35). New York: Church Hymnal.

Ouspensky, L. (1986). Icon and art. In B. McGinn & J. Meyendorff (Eds.), *Christian spirituality, vol. 1: Origins to the twelfth century* (pp. 382–393). New York: Crossroad.

Packard, V. (1972). *A nation of strangers.* New York: David McKay.

Palmer, P.J. (1983). *To know as we are known: A spirituality of education.* San Francisco: HarperSanFrancisco.

Parker, W. (1968). *Milton: A biography.* Oxford: Clarendon.

Payne, L. (1989). *The healing presence.* Wheaton, IL: Crossway.

Pazmiño, R.W. (1988). *Foundational issues in Christian education: An introduction in evangelical perspective.* Grand Rapids: Baker.

———. (1992). *Principles and practices of Christian education: An evangelical perspective.* Grand Rapids: Baker.

Peck, M.S. (1978). *The road less traveled.* New York: Simon & Schuster.

Pentecost, J.D. (1966). *Pattern for maturity.* Chicago: Moody.

Pettit, N. (Ed.). (1985). *The life of David Brainerd.* In *The works of Jonathan Edwards.* New Haven, CT: Yale Univ. Press.

Postman, N. (1982). *The disappearance of childhood.* New York: Delacorte.

Rambo, D.L. (1992). *Presidential Report to the Christian and Missionary Alliance.*

Richarson, R. (1972). *Puritanism in north-west England: A regional study of Chester to 1642.* Manchester, U.K.: Manchester Univ. Press.

Ryken, L. (1991). *Wordly saints: The Puritans as they really were.* Grand Rapids: Zondervan.

Ryrie, C.C. (1986). Basic theology. Wheaton, IL: Victor.

———. (1989). So great salvation. Wheaton, IL: Victor.

Sawicki, M. (1988). *The Gospel in history; Portrait of a teaching church: The origins of Christian education.* New York: Paulist.

Schaeffer, F.A. (1972). *True spirituality.* Wheaton, IL: Tyndale.

Schneiders, S. (1986). Scripture and spirituality. In B. McGinn

& J. Meyendorff (Eds.), *Christian spirituality, vol. 1: Origins to the twelfth century* (pp. 1–20). New York: Crossroad.

Schreck, A. (1987). *The compact history of the Catholic Church.* Ann Arbor, MI: Servant.

_____. (1990). *The Catholic challenge.* Ann Arbor, MI: Servant.

_____. (1993, May/June). Keys to dynamic church life. *Faith and Renewal, 17*(6), 3–8.

Sell, C. (1981). *Family ministry.* Grand Rapids: Zondervan.

Senn, F.C. (1983). *Christian worship and its cultural setting.* Philadelphia: Fortress.

Shepherd, M. (1952). *The worship of the church.* Greenwich, CN: Seabury.

Spangler, D. (1976). *Revelation: The birth of a new age.* Middletown, WI: Lorian.

Spangler, D., & Thompson, W.I. (1991). *Reimagination of the world.* Santa Fe, NM: Bear & Company.

Sproul, R.C. (1977). *Knowing Scripture.* Downers Grove, IL: InterVarsity.

Stafford, T. (1989). *As our years increase: loving, caring, preparing for life past 65.* New York: Harper & Row.

_____. (1993). The therapeutic revolution. *Christianity Today, 37*(6), pp. 24–32.

Stone, L. (1977). *The family, sex and marriage in England, 1550–1688.* New York: Harper & Row.

Strommen, M.P. (1988). *Five cries of youth* (rev. ed.). San Francisco: Harper San Francisco.

Strommen, M.P., & Strommen, A.I. (1993). *Five cries of parents.* San Francisco: Harper San Francisco.

Swearingen, T.T. (1950). *The community and Christian education.* St. Louis: Bethany.

Swift, J. (1957). On the poor man's contentment. *Prose works of Jonathan Swift* (vol. 9, pp. 190-198). Oxford: Blackwell.

Sykes, N. (1934). *Church and state in England in the XVIII century.* Cambridge: Cambridge Univ. Press.

Taylor, J. (1992). *Holy living and holy dying.* New York: Paulist.

Tishler, C.L. (1981). Adolescent suicide attempts: Some significant factors. *Suicide-and-life-threatening-behavior, 11*(2), pp. 86-92.

Underhill, E. (1936). *Worship.* New York: Harper & Row.

Walzer, M. (1982). *The revolution of the saints: A study in the origins of radical politics.* Cambridge: Harvard Univ. Press.

Watkins, O. (1972). *The Puritan experience: Studies in spiritual autobiography.* London: Routledge.

Webber, R. (1982). *Worship old and new.* Grand Rapids: Zondervan.

————. (1985). *Worship is a verb.* Waco, TX: Word.

————. (1986). *Celebrating our faith.* San Francisco: Harper & Row.

Weitzmann, K. (Ed.). (1980). *Age of spirituality: A symposium.* New York: Metropolitan Museum of Art.

Wesley, J. (1955). The new birth. In E. Sugden (Ed.), *Standard sermons* (vol. 2, pp. 226–243). London: Epworth.

Westerhoff, J. (1992). *Schooling Christians.* Grand Rapids: Eerdmans.

Westerhoff, J. (1992). Fashioning Christians in our day. *Faculty Dialogue (17).*

White, D.M. (1983). *The search for God.* New York: Macmillan.

White, J.F. (1980). *Introduction to Christian worship.* Nashville: Abingdon.

————. (1990). Where the Reformation was wrong on worship. *The Christian Century, 99,* pp. 1074-1077.

————. (1993). *A brief history of Christian worship.* Nashville: Abingdon.

Whitney, D. (1991). *Spiritual disciplines for the Christian life.* Colorado Springs: NavPress.

Willard, D. (1991). *The spirit of the disciplines.* New York: Harper & Row.

Williford, C. (1990). Christian formation in the home. In R.E. Clark, L. Johnson, & A.K. Sloat (Eds.), *Christian education: Foundations for the future.* Chicago: Moody.

Wimberly, E. (1990). Spiritual formation in theological education and psychological assessment. In R.A. Hunt, E. Hinkle, & H.N. Maloney (Eds.), *Clergy Assessment and Career Development.* Nashville: Abingdon.

Winter, R., & Hawthorne, S.C. (Eds.). (1981). *Perspectives on the world Christian movement.* Pasadena, CA: William Carey Library.

Wong, P., & Watt, L.M. (1991). What types of reminiscence are associated with successful aging? *Psychology and Aging, 6*(2), pp. 272-279.

World Council of Churches, Programme on Theological Education. (1987). *Spiritual formation in theological education: An invitation to participate.* Geneva, Switzerland: World Council of Churches.

Youth Resources (1990, May). *Youthworker Update,* p. 3.

SUBJECT INDEX

A
Adolescents *247–57*
Asceticism *33–34, 66, 159*

B
Baptism *23, 24–27, 134, 222, 289*
Body *38, 69, 114, 143, 207, 215, 225–33, 261, 264*

C
Children *26, 53–54, 139, 146, 189–90, 234–46, 280–95*

D
Didache *28*
Disciple *16, 19, 27, 100, 102, 118, 122, 190–91, 203–4, 206, 209, 233, 256, 298*
Discipleship *11–16, 27 144, 147–50, 200, 206–7, 228*
Disciplines, the spiritual *16, 18, 23, 32, 43, 66, 70–71, 104, 111, 116, 159, 170, 172, 229–30, 250, 260, 278, 293*

F
Faith *19, 21, 68, 77, 83, 91, 112, 229, 249*
  basis of life *143, 161, 223*
  faith development *40–41, 235–39, 260*
  growth *195*
  imitation *200, 205*
  justification *38, 40, 42, 60, 66, 146, 255*
  liturgy as expression *23–24, 119, 130, 138*
  monasticism *33–34*
  syncretistic *22, 68, 91–92*
  underdeveloped & mature *12–13, 161*
Fasting *16, 111, 139, 159, 175, 230*

G
Gnosticism *22, 70–71*

H
Healing *60, 107, 213–16*

SCRIPTURE INDEX

CONTRIBUTORS

Rev. Lynn Bauman is director of the Elwood Farm Retreat in Telephone, Texas; interim rector of Holy Cross Episcopal Church in Paris, Texas; and a professor at the University of Dallas.

Dr. Craig Blaising is Professor of Systematic Theology at the Southern Baptist Theological Seminary.

Dr. Donald G. Bloesch is Professor of Theology Emeritus at Dubuque Theological Seminary.

Dr. Beth Brown is Associate Professor of Educational Ministries and Administration at Denver Seminary.

Dr. Robert Clark, retired Professor of Christian Education at Moody Bible Institute, is Christian Education Pastor at Southwest Baptist Church in Denver, Colorado.

Dr. Larry Crabb is founder and director of the Institute for Biblical Counseling and Professor of Biblical Counseling at Colorado Christian University in Morrison, Colorado.

Dr. Peter V. Deison is an adjunct professor at Dallas Theological Seminary and Associate Pastor at Park Cities Presbyterian Church.

Dr. John Dettoni is President of Chrysalis Ministries, an international educational ministry for church leadership development, based in San Clemente, California. He was formerly Associate Professor of Christian Formation and Discipleship at Fuller Theological Seminary.

Dr. Lyle Dorsett is Professor of Educational Ministries and Evangelism at Wheaton College.

Dr. Kenneth O. Gangel is Executive Director of the Toccoa Falls College Graduate Studies Division.

Dr. Ronald Habermas is McGee Professor of Biblical Studies at John Brown University in Siloam Springs, Arkansas.

Dr. T.W. Hunt is Prayer Specialist with the Baptist Sunday School Board in Nashville, Tennessee.

Dr. Robert Lightner is Professor of Systematic Theology at Dallas Theological Seminary.

Dr. D. Bruce Lockerbie, president of PAIDEIA (Stony Brook, New York), a consulting agency for institutions of higher education and the public interest, is well-known as an educator, lecturer, author, and consultant.

Dr. Robert P. Meye is Dean Emeritus and Professor Emeritus of New Testament Interpretation at Fuller Theological Seminary.

Leanne Payne is director of Pastoral Care Ministries, Wheaton, Illinois.

Dr. Robert W. Pazmiño is Professor of Religious Education at Andover Newton Theological School.

Dr. Timothy R. Phillips is Professor of Historical and Systematic Theology at Wheaton College.

Dr. John Piper is Senior Pastor at Bethlehem Baptist Church, Minneapolis, Minnesota.

Dr. Leland Ryken is Professor of English and Department Chair at Wheaton College.

Dr. Alan Schreck is chairman of the theology department at the Franciscan University at Steubenville (Ohio).

Rev. James Bryan Smith is instructor of practical theology and chaplain at Friends University, Wichita, Kansas.

Rev. Donald Whitney is Assistant Professor of Spiritual Formation at Midwestern Baptist Theological Seminary.

Dr. James C. Wilhoit is Professor of Christian Education at Wheaton College.

Dr. Dallas Willard is Professor of Philosophy at the University of California.

Kenneth O. Gangel (Ph.D., University of Missouri), after a distinguished career at Dallas Theological Seminary, is now executive director of the Toccoa Falls College Graduate Studies Division. A noted expert on Christian education and a prolific author, his many books include *Feeding and Leading*.

James C. Wilhoit (Ph.D., Northwestern University) is professor of Christian education at Wheaton College. His published works include a number of scholarly articles and books, including *Christian Education and the Search for Meaning*.